Understanding the Public Health Implications of Prisoner Reentry in California

State-of-the-State Report

T0302961

Lois M. Davis, Malcolm V. Williams, Kathryn Pitkin Derose,
Paul Steinberg, Nancy Nicosia, Adrian Overton, Lisa Miyashiro,
Susan Turner, Terry Fain, Eugene Williams III

Prepared for The California Endowment

RAND

HEALTH and
INFRASTRUCTURE, SAFETY, AND ENVIRONMENT

This work was prepared for The California Endowment and produced within the RAND Health Promotion and Disease Prevention Program and the RAND Infrastructure, Safety, and Environment Safety and Justice Program.

Understanding the public health implications of prisoner reentry in California : state-of-the-state report / Lois M. Davis ... [et al.].
p. ; cm.
Includes bibliographical references and index.
ISBN 978-0-8330-5914-7 (pbk. : alk. paper)
I. Davis, Lois M. II. Rand Corporation.
[DNLM: 1. Health Services Needs and Demand—California. 2. Prisoners—California. 3. Community Health Services—California. 4. Medical Indigency—California. 5. Medically Uninsured—California. 6. Socioeconomic Factors—California. WA 300 AC2]

LCclassification not assigned
365'.6087409794—dc23

2011044929

Published 2011 by the RAND Corporation
1776 Main Street, P.O. Box 2138, Santa Monica, CA 90407-2138
1200 South Hayes Street, Arlington, VA 22202-5050
4570 Fifth Avenue, Suite 600, Pittsburgh, PA 15213-2665
RAND URL: http://www.rand.org/
To order RAND documents or to obtain additional information, contact
Distribution Services: Telephone: (310) 451-7002;
Fax: (310) 451-6915; Email: order@rand.org

Preface

We began this study to assess the health care needs of the prisoner reentry population in California in 2008, at the beginning of what has now become the most significant national recession since the Great Depression. When we finished the initial set of analyses on the capacity of the health care safety net in 2009, we were already witnessing the impact of the recession on that safety net. Now, the advent of California's new Public Safety Realignment Plan in 2011, the continuing impact of the economic crisis in terms of even deeper cuts to the health care safety net, and the prospects of health care reform provide a changing landscape in which to assess the impact of prisoner reentry in California—one that places California clearly at a crossroads.

In this state-of-the-state report, RAND researchers summarize the state of prisoner reentry in California and the public health challenges that California faces in addressing the health care and rehabilitative needs of those returning from prison back to local communities. The authors present a set of recommendations for improving California's planning and services to better meet the needs of the reentry population in the changing landscape that has emerged.

In particular, RAND examines the public health issues surrounding prisoner reentry in California, the type of health care needs ex-offenders bring with them, which communities are disproportionately affected, and the health care system capacity of the communities to which ex-offenders return. The research team also examined in depth the experiences of returning prisoners in seeking care and the role that health plays in their efforts to reintegrate into the community and rejoin their families; and factors that have facilitated or hindered ex-prisoners' ability to obtain health care and providers' efforts to serve them. In addition, the research team sought to explore the impact that incarceration has on families, including what challenges they face and the need for programs and services.

These results will be of interest to state and local policymakers; state and local departments of corrections, public health, mental health and alcohol and drug treatment; health care and safety-net providers; mental health and alcohol and drug treatment providers; and community leaders, advocacy organizations, and community organizations that provide services to the reentry population. These results will also be of interest to The California Endowment and other foundations that are committed to ensuring the availability of services and improving collaboration between key stakeholders at the state and local levels to successfully address the public health challenges of prisoner reentry.

This work was funded by The California Endowment and conducted in the Safety and Justice Program within RAND Infrastructure, Safety, and Environment (ISE) and Health Promotion and Disease Prevention Program (HPDP) within RAND Health.

The mission of ISE is to improve the development, operation, use, and protection of society's essential physical assets and natural resources and to enhance the related social assets of safety and security of individuals in transit and in their workplaces and communities. Safety and Justice Program research addresses all aspects of public safety and the criminal justice system—including violence, policing, corrections, courts and criminal law, substance abuse, occupational safety, and public integrity. Information about the Safety and Justice Program is available online (http://www.rand.org/ise/safety). Inquiries about research projects should be sent to the following address:

Greg Ridgeway, Director
Safety and Justice Program, ISE
RAND Corporation
1776 Main Street
Santa Monica, CA 90407-2138
310-393-0411, x7734
sjdirector@rand.org

RAND HPDP is a division of RAND Health and addresses issues related to measuring healthy and unhealthy behaviors, examining the distribution of health behaviors across population subgroups, identifying what causes or influences such behaviors, and designing and evaluating interventions to improve health behaviors. Information about RAND Health and its research and publications can be found at http://www.rand.org/health/.

More information about RAND is available at http://www.rand.org.

Questions or comments about this report should be sent to the project leader, Lois M. Davis (Lois_Davis@rand.org).

Contents

Preface ... iii
Figures ... xiii
Tables ... xv
Summary ... xvii
Acknowledgments ... xxxvii
Abbreviations ... xxxix

CHAPTER ONE
Introduction ... 1
Background ... 2
Health Care Needs of Returning Prisoners Are High ... 2
The Size and Composition of California's Prison Population Are Changing ... 4
Recent Policy Changes Will Influence How California Approaches Meeting the Health Care Needs of the Reentry Population ... 5
Study Objective and Scope ... 9
Study Limitations ... 11
Organization of This Report ... 12

CHAPTER TWO
What Do We Know About Prisoners' Health Care Needs and the Capacity of the Safety Net to Meet the Needs of the Reentry Population? ... 13
Introduction ... 13
What Are the Health Care Needs of the Reentry Population? ... 14
Where Do Prisoners Go Upon Release from Prison? ... 19

Concentration and Distribution of Parolees Within California........... 19
What Are the Demographic Characteristics of Parolees and of the Socioeconomic Areas in Which They Locate?........................... 26
Results of Analysis of Demographic Characteristics of California Parolees... 27
Results of Analysis of Demographic and Socioeconomic Characteristics of Areas in Which Parolees Locate.................... 29
What Does the Health Care Safety Net Look Like for Parolees in Four Focus Counties?.. 31
Conceptual Framework... 31
Analysis of Geographic Distribution of Health Care Facilities in Los Angeles County... 34
Analysis of Accessibility of Reentry Population to Health Care Safety-Net Facilities in Four Counties................................. 40
Discussion... 45

CHAPTER THREE
Understanding the Challenges of Reentry: Ex-Prisoner Focus Group Results... 49
Introduction.. 49
Approach... 49
Key Findings from the Focus Groups.................................... 53
How Ex-Prisoners Think About Their Health Care Needs................ 53
Views About Access to Substance Abuse Treatment Programs in Prison... 56
Views About Access to and Quality of Health Care in Prison............ 59
Experiences in Having Care Transitioned to Community Providers..... 63
Interest in Preventive Care.. 64
Prerelease Planning.. 64
Parole and Community Team (PACT) Meetings.......................... 66
Where the Focus Group Participants Sought Care and Other Services on Release... 68
Views About Cultural Competence...................................... 71
The Importance of Family.. 73
The Experience of Being Released...................................... 75
Discussion.. 77

CHAPTER FOUR
Understanding the Challenges of Dealing with Released Prisoners: Provider Interview Results 85
Introduction 85
Literature on Ex-Prisoners' Access to Insurance and Health Care Reform 86
Ex-Prisoners' Access to Health Insurance 87
Safety-Net Health Care Resources in California 88
Potential Impact of Health Care Reform in Improving Ex-Prisoners' Access to Health Care 92
Provider Interviews: Approach 96
Provider Interviews: Results 97
From the Provider's Perspective, the Reentry Population Has a Wide Range of Treatment Needs 97
Lack of Medications and Medical Records Can Affect Continuity of Care 99
Individuals May Be Reluctant to Seek Help from Parole 101
Low Levels of Health Insurance and Lack of Finances Limit Treatment Options 102
Challenge of Linking Individuals to Mental Health Treatment 104
Communication Problems on Both the Individual and Provider Sides 105
Difficulties in Navigating Health Care and Social Services Systems 106
Uncertainty Among Safety-Net Providers About How to Access Reentry Population 107
Impact of Budget Cuts on Providers 108
Providers' Recommendations for Improving Access to Services for the Reentry Population 110
Discussion 111

CHAPTER FIVE
The Impact of Incarceration on Families: Key Findings 117
Introduction 117
Literature on the Impact of Incarceration on Children and Families 118

Impact of Individual-Level Effects of Parental Incarceration............ 118
The Impact of Child Welfare Laws and Other Legislation 121
What Is Known About Programs to Help Children and Incarcerated Parents 123
Family Caregiver Focus Group: Approach................................... 125
Family Caregivers Focus Group: Results 128
The Challenges Incarcerated Parents Face Upon Release 128
The Suddenness of Being Thrust into a Caregiver Role 129
The Degree to Which the Children Want to Have Contact with Their Parents.. 130
Children's Support Needs 133
Caregivers' Support Needs 136
Discussion.. 138

CHAPTER SIX
Conclusions and Recommendations 143
California at a Crossroads.. 143
An Historic Opportunity to Improve Access to Health Care for the Reentry Population 147
What Can California Do to Prepare? 151
Develop Informed Estimates About the Percentage of the Medicaid Expansion Population That the Reentry/Criminal Justice Population Will Represent 152
Develop Medicaid Enrollment Strategies................................. 152
Leverage the Experience of Other States That Have Previously Expanded Coverage to Childless Adults Under Medicaid.......... 153
Develop Health Homes for the Reentry/Criminal Justice Population 154
Develop Care/Case Management Systems That Can Account for Special Populations' Needs, Including the Reentry/Criminal Justice Population.. 156
Assess Workforce-Development Strategies for Alcohol, Drug, and Mental Health Treatment 157
Consider Developing Electronic Medical Records........................ 158
Consider Expanding Prerelease Planning Efforts 159

Undertake a Comprehensive Assessment of California's New Public Safety Realignment Plan to Inform Future Policy Refinements.......... 161
What Can Counties and Providers Do to Prepare?.......... 162
Develop County-Level Estimates to Inform Planning for Rehabilitative Services and for Increased Demand for Mental Health and Alcohol Care and Drug Treatment.......... 163
Convene All Relevant Stakeholders for Planning and Coordination of Services.......... 164
Assess Local Capacity to Meet New Demands for Health Care.......... 165
Develop "Welcome Home" Guidebooks Tailored to Individual Counties, Particularly for Counties and Communities with High Rates of Return.......... 166
Train Providers on Cultural Competence.......... 167
Consider the Role of Patient Navigators.......... 168
Address the Needs of Families and Those That Care for Children of Incarcerated Parents.......... 169
Final Thoughts.......... 170

APPENDIXES
A. Methodology.......... 173
B. Protocols.......... 181

References.......... 197

Figures

2.1. Relative Concentrations of Parolees in California, by County ... 20
2.2. Relative Concentrations of Parolees in Alameda County ... 22
2.3. Relative Concentrations of Parolees in Kern County ... 23
2.4. Relative Concentrations of Parolees in Los Angeles County ... 24
2.5. Relative Concentrations of Parolees in San Diego County ... 26
2.6. Summary of Statewide Socioeconomic Clusters of Census Tracts ... 30
2.7. Conceptual Framework for Evaluating the Health Care Safety Net for the Reentry Population ... 33
2.8. Health Care Safety Net in Los Angeles County Relative to Parolee Concentrations ... 36
2.9. Mental Health Care Safety Net in Los Angeles County ... 38
2.10. Substance Abuse Treatment Safety Net in Los Angeles County ... 39

Tables

S.1. Preparing to Meet the Health Care and Rehabilitative Needs of California's Reentry Population: Summary of Recommendations xxxii
2.1. Prevalence of Infectious Diseases Among Male Prison Inmates in the United States and California, by Race/Ethnicity for California Inmates 16
2.2. Prevalence of Drug Abuse/Dependence and Mental Illness Among Male Prison Inmates in the United States and California, by Race Ethnicity for California Inmates 17
2.3. Demographic Characteristics and Term Served of California Parolees, Overall and for Four Counties 28
2.4. Socioeconomic Characteristics of the Seven Cluster Categories 29
2.5. Summary of Accessibility Results for Hospitals and Clinics, by County 42
2.6. Summary of Accessibility Results for Hospitals and Clinics, by County and Race/Ethnicity 43
2.7. Summary of Accessibility Results for Mental Health and Alcohol and Drug Treatment Providers, by County 44
2.8. Summary of Mental Health and Alcohol and Drug Treatment Accessibility Results by County and Race/Ethnicity 45
5.1. Characteristics of the Families 127

Summary

Introduction

As an increasing number of prisoners are released from prisons and return to local communities, there are key questions about (1) what health care needs they have and (2) what role health plays in affecting their success at integrating back into communities. In terms of the first issue, prior research has found that the prison population is disproportionately sicker, on average, than the U.S. population in general, with substantially higher burdens of infectious diseases (such as HIV/AIDS, tuberculosis, and hepatitis B and C), serious mental illness, and comorbidities, or co-occurring disorders (National Commission on Correctional Health Care, 2002).

In terms of the second question, about the impact of ex-prisoners' health care needs on reentry, research shows that individuals with physical and mental health problems reported poorer employment outcomes than those without such problems (Mallik and Visher, 2008). Also, ex-prisoners returning to communities face a number of obstacles to accessing care, as low insurance rates among this population limit their ability to access health care services and provide case managers with few options for linking them to services. Further, many providers lack experience in treating this population.

Such concerns are especially acute in California, where the number of individuals released from California prisons has increased nearly threefold over the past 20 years. Most of the state's prisoners ultimately will return to California communities, bringing with them a host of health and social needs that must be addressed. Yet the public is largely unaware of the health needs of released prisoners, and the challenges they present to their communities are not being addressed explicitly, despite the fact that reentry directly affects almost every California community.

Further, the current debate about California's 2011 Public Safety Realignment Plan has focused on public safety concerns in counties rather than on how counties will meet the rehabilitative and health care needs of individuals who will be housed and supervised at the local level. At the same time, implementation of the 2010 Patient Protection and Affordable Care Act (ACA) (Pub. Law 111-148) will eliminate a critical barrier to accessing care for many ex-prisoners. The ACA will expand Medicaid eligibility to include all non-Medicare-eligible citizens and legal residents[1] under age 65 with incomes up to 133 percent[2] of the federal poverty level, opening up the possibility for many ex-prisoners and other individuals involved with the criminal justice system to become eligible for Medicaid (or Medi-Cal in California) and to have drug treatment services, prevention services, and wellness programs—services important to the reentry population—more fully covered. Thus, California is at a critical juncture: It faces numerous challenges, but recent changes in policy also present important opportunities to improve the state's ability to meet the needs of individuals returning from state prison.

It is critical to address the public health challenges of returning ex-prisoners to assist communities in meeting the reentry needs of this population. We also need to better understand the impact of incarceration on their families and children of incarcerated parents, their risk factors, and what options exist to change the trajectories of their lives.

This state-of-the-state report examines the specific health needs of California's reentry population, the public health challenges of reentry in California, and the policy options for improving access to safety-net resources for this population.

To achieve this overall goal, the study first examined the health care needs of the reentry population by analyzing data from the Bureau

---

[1] That is, legal residents who have been in the country five years or longer.

[2] Taking into account the 5 percent waiver under the ACA, this would translate to incomes up to 138 percent of the federal poverty level.

of Justice Statistics (BJS) Survey of Inmates in State and Federal Correctional Facilities; conducted a geographic analysis to identify where parolees are concentrated in California (all 58 counties) and which counties and communities are disproportionately affected by prisoner reentry; and examined the types of health care services available in four counties—Alameda, Los Angeles, San Diego, and Kern—and developed measures to assess the capacity of the safety net in these counties to meet the health care needs of the reentry population.

The study then "bored down more deeply" in Alameda, Los Angeles, and San Diego counties, using focus groups with former prisoners and their family members and key-actor interviews with relevant service providers and community groups to understand the experiences of returning prisoners in seeking care and the role that health plays in their efforts to reintegrate back into the community and rejoin their families, what models of service provision are being used by local communities for this population, and what factors have facilitated or hindered ex-prisoners' and providers' efforts. In addition, we sought to understand the impact that incarceration has had on families, including what challenges they face and the need for programs and services.

Assessing Prisoner Health Care Needs and the Capacity of the Health Care Safety Net

Health Care Needs Are High, but Mental Health and Drug Treatment Needs Are Even Higher

Our analysis of self-reported data from the BJS survey of California inmates provides a rich understanding of the range of physical health, mental health, and substance abuse problems that this population brings upon their return to local communities. We found that returning prisoners self-report a high burden of chronic diseases, such as asthma, diabetes, and hypertension, as well as infectious diseases, such as hepatitis and tuberculosis—conditions that require regular access to health care for effective management.

In addition, the burden of mental illness and drug abuse or dependence is especially high in this population. About two-thirds of California inmates reported having a drug abuse or dependence problem, but only 22 percent of those inmates reported receiving treatment since admission to prison. More than half of California inmates reported a recent mental health problem, with about half of those reporting receiving treatment in prison. These results underscore the importance of access to mental health and alcohol and drug treatment services and of continuity of care for this population. But the likelihood of ex-prisoners receiving adequate health care once they are released is poor given the high rates of uninsurance among this population and other barriers to accessing care.

Certain Counties and Communities Are Disproportionately Affected by Reentry

A number of trends complicate the successful reentry of parolees into communities. Our analysis of the geographic distribution and concentration of parolees across California and in the four focus counties showed that reentry disproportionately impacts 11 counties statewide and that, within counties, parolees tend to cluster in certain communities and neighborhoods. Such clustering has implications for linking to and providing health care services to this population and for considering how to effectively target reentry resources. As illustrated by Los Angeles County, which has a combination of both urban and more sparsely populated areas, there is a need to tailor outreach and service delivery strategies to areas where the reentry population is more concentrated versus areas where it tends to be more dispersed.

Our analyses also showed that African-American and Latino parolees, in particular, tend to return to disadvantaged neighborhoods and communities, defined by high poverty rates, high unemployment rates, and low educational attainment. This suggests that reentry will be especially challenging for these groups.

Access to Health Care Safety-Net Resources Varies Substantially

An important contribution of this study is formally defining what the health care safety net is for the reentry population and developing measures to assess the capacity of the safety net to meet this population's health care needs. Taking into account differences in capacity, the underlying demand for safety-net services, and travel distance, our measures of accessibility (i.e., of potential versus realized access) showed that parolees' access to health care safety-net facilities varies by facility type, by geographic area, and by race/ethnicity. As policymakers consider how to improve access to health care services for the reentry population in California, they will need to take into account this variation in counties' safety nets.

In all the counties, community clinics appear to play an important role in filling gaps in primary care coverage vis-à-vis the reentry population. For mental health care and drug and alcohol treatment, separate networks provide services to the reentry population and serve as the initial safety net for them. These include, for example, the parole outpatient clinics (POCs), the Parolee Services Network (PSN), state-funded community-based alcohol and drug treatment programs, and Proposition 36 (the Substance Abuse and Crime Prevention Act), which diverts nonviolent drug offenders to treatment instead of incarceration. But these networks have limited capacity and, as discussed below, have been impacted by budget cuts, suggesting that much of the reentry population must rely instead on county mental health and alcohol and drug treatment services.

Budget Cuts Have Impacted the Health Care Safety Net the Reentry Population Relies On

Because of budget cuts, the California Department of Corrections and Rehabilitation (CDCR) has reduced funding for rehabilitative services, including alcohol and drug treatment programs, by 40 percent. The treatment capacity of in-prison substance abuse programs (SAPs) went from a capacity of 10,119 treatment slots in June 2008 to only 2,350 slots in January 2010 (CDCR, Division of Addiction and Recovery Services, *Annual Report*, 2009; CDCR, "Adult Programs Key Performance Indicators January 2010–December 2010," 2010).

Budget cuts have also impacted treatment networks out in the community. For example, the PSN, which provides community-based alcohol and drug treatment and recovery services to parolees in 17 counties statewide, has had its funding reduced. Community-based treatment programs have experienced cutbacks in state funding resulting in reductions in local treatment capacity. Finally, although Proposition 36 remains in effect, it is no longer being funded. Beginning in October 2011, Proposition 36 will become instead a fee-based, participant self-pay counseling program.

Given these changes, individuals leaving state prison are returning to California's communities having received less and less rehabilitative programming. This means that the reentry population will have greater unmet needs and will have to be even more self-determined than previously.

Understanding the Perspectives of Ex-Prisoners and Providers About Health Care Challenges

Ex-Prisoner Perspectives

Health Needs Were Ranked Lower Than Other Basic Needs. Focus group participants tended to view their physical health care needs as distinct from their mental health care and substance abuse treatment needs. For example, focus group participants typically ranked health needs lower than economic considerations, such as housing and employment, which were described as the most important challenges they faced. Yet participants also identified "getting sober" and finding regular care and support for mental health issues as critical.

Many discussed their struggles with substance abuse problems, and, in a number of instances, these problems were the underlying factor that resulted in their incarceration. Substance abuse problems often continued after release, resulting in violations of their parole or new crimes that led to their being returned to prison. A number of focus group participants reported having problems accessing substance abuse treatment programs in prisons, noting the limited availability of programming slots.

Other commonly mentioned health concerns included oral health problems, diabetes, hypertension, cancer, prostrate problems, and infectious diseases, such as hepatitis, tuberculosis, and sexually transmitted diseases. Also, a number of participants discussed feeling depressed at times during their period of incarceration and after release.

Factors mentioned by focus group participants as limiting their access to health care while in prison included long waiting times to be seen by a physician or nurse, correctional staff serving as informal gatekeepers and influencing what type of care prisoners might receive, and a general indifference by the system.

As a result, focus group participants felt that it was up to them to do what they could to stay healthy. They expressed an interest in preventive health care and informally shared information among themselves about what one could do to stay healthy and about what type of screening exams were important. There were some misperceptions about what preventive care was needed and when, which added to the viewpoint that the correctional health care system was indifferent to their needs.

Few Received Prerelease Planning or Help in Transitioning Their Care to Community Providers. Most focus group participants had not participated in prerelease planning classes, and some felt that what little they had received was inadequate. Instead, they tended to rely on word of mouth, on a mentor in prison, or on family members, or they were self-motivated to find out where they could go to seek services. Participants who needed substance abuse treatment or help with housing or employment tended to rely on other offenders with prior experience in seeking out such care in the community.

Transitioning of care to community providers was problematic in several instances. For example, participants with diabetes or cancer reported little or no continuity of care. Many focus group participants lacked health insurance and had little prior contact with a community's health care system, making it difficult for them to understand basic steps, such as knowing where to go to get care or their medications refilled.

PACT Meetings Are One Way to Link Individuals to Health Care Services, but the Meetings Vary in the Information Available. Individuals released on parole are required within a specified period of time to attend a Parole and Community Team (PACT) meeting at which a variety of providers (e.g., housing, employment, drug treatment) are available to briefly discuss what services they offer. Focus group participants varied in their knowledge about the PACT meetings. The types of providers present at these meetings also can vary from meeting to meeting, making it an inefficient way for parolees to learn about what services may be available to them.

The type of information focus group participants desired to know was how to apply for Medi-Cal insurance and for General Relief, where to go to get free health care, and where to seek treatment for specific problems. In addition, they were interested in information related to housing, transportation, and employment.

The focus group participants suggested that one way to improve access to information is to have community health care providers routinely participate in the PACT meetings. More importantly, they said that having this information available prior to release from prison, including packets specifically tailored to each individual county, would be particularly helpful.

Family Is Important for Motivating Individuals to Change and in Helping with the Reentry Process. A number of focus group participants honed in on the central role that family plays in providing them motivation to seek rehabilitative services while incarcerated and in assisting them with their transition back to the community. For example, individuals mentioned being motivated to participate in substance abuse treatment programs while incarcerated and continuing to do so upon release, with the goal of reuniting with their family and children. Upon release, family also helped them meet basic needs, such as food, housing, clothing, or help in finding jobs. At the same time, in some instances, family reunification also could be a significant stressor.

Ex-Prisoners' Stressed the Importance of Culturally Competent Care and Getting Information on Health Services and Health Insurance Enrollment Prerelease. Some of the focus group participants felt that having access to support services that were provided in a culturally competent manner was important. A primary concern was having someone who understood their experience of incarceration, who would treat them with respect, and who could help them access services. Also, they felt it was important to have health care providers and staff who are empathetic to their circumstances and needs. They tended to prefer interacting with staff who had been formerly incarcerated themselves or who had substantial experience in working with the reentry population.

Participants also felt that having information available prior to release from prison on where to seek health care services and how to apply for Medi-Cal or get their benefits reinstated was important. They also suggested that packets specifically tailored to each individual county would be the best way to get this information to them.

Provider Perspectives

The Reentry Population Has Substantial Treatment Needs. From the providers' perspective, the reentry population has substantial mental health and substance abuse treatment needs, as well as significant health problems, including diabetes, hypertension, renal disease, and infectious diseases, such as HIV/AIDS and hepatitis C. As several providers noted, this is a population with a large amount of unmet need; illnesses such as uncontrolled diabetes, asthma, and hypertension that are typically the result of neglect or lack of access to care.

Also, this is a population with a range of other non-health-related needs, such as those related to transportation, employment, housing, and family reunification. Given this complex set of needs and the prevalence of untreated health conditions, parolees tend to be more resource-intensive to treat. Also, health care providers face the challenge of how to link these individuals with a range of other services. And when making treatment decisions for individuals who may be homeless, providers must take into account, for example, whether the individual has a place to keep his or her medications.

Inadequate Discharge Planning Raises Concerns About Continuity of Care. From the perspective of providers, a particular concern is continuity of care for those being released with serious medical conditions or mental health or substance abuse treatment needs. Lack of adequate medications upon release is problematic because it often can take time for an individual to access care in the community. As a result, individuals are at risk of self-medicating, and problems with timely access to care can negatively impact continuity of care.

Some providers had tried to coordinate with prison facilities in their region to establish bridging services for those about to be released and who likely would need health care from their network of clinics or health centers. However, they were unsuccessful in doing so.

Lack of medical records was also seen as problematic, because providers are faced with treating individuals without any information about their past health status and care. For individuals with infectious diseases, such as HIV/AIDS or hepatitis—important public health concerns—providers felt it was critical to know what kind of care and education a patient had received while incarcerated. This was also true for those with chronic health and mental health conditions.

Financial and Communication Barriers Limit Access to Care. The providers identified a number of factors that make it difficult for recently released prisoners to access care, including lack of health insurance or funding. These factors also hinder the ability of providers and nonprofit community organizations to link individuals to needed services. Other factors include communication barriers, lack of understanding of the complexities of accessing safety-net health care services, long waiting times for appointments, and the impact of budget cuts, which limit treatment options. Combined, these barriers make it difficult for recently released prisoners to successfully navigate the health care system. They also make it challenging for health care providers and community programs to assist individuals in placing them into treatment and in referring them to services.

For example, the lack of health insurance means that although inpatient treatment programs may be available for those with mental illness, the cost is often prohibitive. Even counseling clinics that provide services on a sliding fee scale may be too expensive for these individuals, who simply lack the ability to pay. As a result, one mental health counselor tended to rely on crisis homes, which are, at best, only as a stopgap measure. In addition, long wait times to see a psychiatrist at county mental health clinics mean that some individuals are at risk of running out of medications or of self-medicating.

Individuals Are Reluctant to Seek Help from Parole. Parole outpatient clinics are one way that individuals with mental health problems can be seen by a psychiatrist and prescribed medications. However, providers commented that there are important disincentives for an individual to seek help from these clinics or for a parolee to ask his or her parole officer for help in accessing services. Providers said that individuals reported that they felt the parole officer may view them as troublemakers or as individuals who need to be watched closely if they report needing help accessing drug treatment or mental health services.

Communication Issues and Difficulties Navigating the Health Care System Are Key Concerns. Providers commented that adaptive behaviors that may have worked in an incarcerated setting, such as intimidating others and not trusting them, are seen as maladaptive and even threatening in a health care setting. Individuals released from prison may misinterpret delays in appointments or long waiting times as a sign of disrespect or rejection. In addition, individuals often have difficulties navigating the health care system, and the different silos in the health care and social services systems can complicate the referral process for those with a complex set of needs. Therefore, having patient navigators who are empathetic and understand the experience of incarceration was seen as essential in helping the formerly incarcerated to link to services.

Providers Are Uncertain About How to Access the Reentry Population. The providers interviewed had the sense that they are increasingly serving the reentry population but lack the data to quantify this assessment. In general, they do not know whether an individual was formerly incarcerated unless that individual self-identifies or there is another mechanism for disclosure. Nonprofit community organizations that serve the reentry population are important referral mechanisms for community health care providers.

Budget Cuts Have Impacted Providers. Providers interviewed reported on the various effects of state, county, or city budget cuts. These included having to eliminate programs, such as HIV or dental programs, or cut back on services, such as mental health programs. A provider from a community assessment center noted that it needed to reassess whether to focus only on conducting assessments or to continue to also provide other services, such as drug treatment and mental health care. State-level cuts in community-based treatment programs meant the elimination of one provider's sober living facility. Importantly, budget cuts also have impacted alcohol and drug treatment program models, including decreasing the length of stay in residential treatment programs.

Providers' Suggested Ways to Improve Access to Health Care Services. As for suggestions on how to improve access to care and better facilitate the transition of their care to community health care providers, our interviewees indicated that there is an important need for bridging services to help transition ex-prisoners' care to community providers and to address such issues as ensuring an adequate supply of medications, obtaining the medical records or developing a detailed history that can accompany the individual, and having individuals begin the process of reinstating benefits prior to release for health insurance and other services.

A related set of recommendations centered around the critical need for patient navigators who can help individuals understand the health care system, help communicate and serve as patient advocates, and help individuals access a range of services.

Prisoner Family Perspectives

As of 2000, an estimated 856,000 California children—approximately 1 in 9—have a parent involved in the adult criminal justice system (Simmons, 2000). When a parent is incarcerated, the children of that parent also are deeply affected. Not only do such children lose a parent, they must also cope with altered systems of care—such as having to live with grandparents or even having to go into foster care. Parental incarceration can have a range of negative effects on children, including feelings of shame, social stigma, loss of financial support, weakened ties to the parent, poor school performance, increased delinquency, and increased risk of abuse or neglect.

Our discussion with a small group of seven caregivers enabled us to explore these issues. Most of them were grandmothers who provided us with initial insights about the experiences of caregivers providing this type of kinship care to children with incarcerated parents. They discussed the challenges of raising young children and teenagers, of coping with behavioral problems among these children, and of trying to keep their families together (but not knowing where to turn to for help). Although our discussion was exploratory in nature and not indicative of the full range of experiences of caregivers, the themes and issues that the discussion participants raised were conistent with the research literature.

For caregivers who were middle-aged and older, the experience of being thrust into a caregiver role later in life was emotionally and physically trying. Most of the caregivers were motivated to try and keep the family together in that they did not want these children to go into the foster care system.

The support needs for children mentioned by the caregivers included assistance with school and tutoring services; mentoring opportunities; role models; and programs aimed specifically at children with incarcerated parents that enable them to feel less isolated. They emphasized the importance of having positive male role models for teenage boys, in particular. They also felt it was important to provide the children, especially teenagers, with a realistic understanding of what the juvenile justice system is like so that they understand the negative consequences of getting involved in crime.

The caregivers we spoke to said that the children they cared for had mixed feelings about seeing their parent when they returned from prison. The challenges that a newly released incarcerated parent faces in terms of meeting basic needs, such as employment and housing, also had a direct effect on their children, who experienced them firsthand. A common experience was the child going back to live with the parent, but eventually returning to the grandparent because of the unstable living situation they found themselves in.

Lastly, the support needs of caregivers included better information on what community resources and social services are available to them, assistance in obtaining help for children with learning disabilities, mentoring and family support programs, and a critical need for respite care.

Conclusions and Recommendations

We began this study to assess the health care needs of the prisoner reentry population in California in 2008, at the beginning of what has now become the most significant national recession since the Great Depression. When we finished the initial set of analyses on the capacity of the health care safety net to meet the needs of this population in 2009, we were already witnessing the impact of the recession on the safety net. Now, California's 2011 Public Safety Realignment Plan, the continuing impact of the economic crisis in terms of even deeper cuts to the health care safety net, and prospects of health care reform provide a changing landscape in which to assess the impact of prisoner reentry in California—one that places California clearly at a crossroads.

The results of our analyses over the past four years show the following:

- The capacity of the health care safety net varies across California communities by county, type of services, and race/ethnicity and, since our first report, has become even more constrained while demand has grown.
- California's new Public Safety Realignment Plan represents an almost tectonic shift in the state's criminal justice system that will have a number of implications for thinking about how to meet the health care and rehabilitative needs of the reentry population.
- Public safety realignment presents some challenges, such as the fact that traditional mechanisms for linking ex-prisoners to health care and social services—e.g., parole officers, PACT meetings—will change dramatically for individuals placed on county-level postrelease community supervision and for low-level offenders who will serve their time in county jail.
- Realignment also presents an important opportunity to address the public health issues associated with reentry, not only to reduce the size of the state's prison population and reduce the state's high parole revocation rates, but also to focus attention on the need to improve prerelease planning, build better mechanisms to transition care from correctional health to safety-net providers, and create local partnerships among probation, law enforcement, county agencies, and community- and faith-based organizations to better address the needs of those individuals returning back to communities.
- Health care reform provides important opportunities as well as challenges to expand insurance coverage through Medicaid for the reentry/criminal justice population, to improve access to drug treatment, and to better manage their care.

Given these findings, in Table S.1 we summarize our recommendations for how California can meet the public health challenges of reentry and to put into place mechanisms to be prepared for the new opportunities realignment and health care reform represent. These recommendations are based on a combination of our review of the literature and analyses of the BJS inmate survey, parolee data, data on the health care safety net in four counties, provider interviews, and focus group discussions with formerly incarcerated individuals and family members.

The recommendations in Table S.1 can be acted on at both the state level—by departments and agencies that have a role to play in preparing California for health care reform and public safety realignment—and the county level—by county probation, law enforcement, jail systems, county and community health care safety-net providers, and community organizations and leaders. More detail on these recommendations is provided in Chapter Six.

Final Thoughts

The changes described here that California is experiencing are also occurring in other states, as they, too, grapple with how to reduce corrections costs and the size of their prison populations. Ultimately, most individuals who are incarcerated will eventually return home to local communities. We began our study with the premise that the reentry population eventually will become part of the uninsured and medically indigent populations in counties. This is even more the case today.

Importantly, our analyses were conducted prior to the October 1, 2011, implementation of California's new Public Safety Realignment Plan. Therefore, our results of the geographic distribution and concentration of parolees and the capacity of the health care safety net reflect conditions prior to the implementation of this new policy. Nevertheless, we believe that these findings will provide the state and counties with an important context for understanding and examining the impact of realignment moving forward.

Table S.1
Preparing to Meet the Health Care and Rehabilitative Needs of California's Reentry Population: Summary of Recommendations

Recommendation	Description
What Can California Do to Prepare?	
Develop informed estimates about the percentage of the Medicaid expansion population that the reentry and criminal justice population will represent.	There is a need for more informed estimates of the size of the reentry/criminal justice population that will be eligible for Medicaid and of the likely impact of different enrollment strategies. These estimates should also take into account citizenship status and what percent of the reentry/criminal justice population will be eligible for subsidies as part of California's Health Benefit Exchange.
Develop Medicaid enrollment strategies.	The participation of the reentry/criminal justice population in Medicaid will largely depend on how much states' departments of corrections and county probabtion and jails facilitate enrollment in Medicaid, as well as other stakeholders. California may want to consider developing strategies to enroll or reinstate Medicaid benefits for the reentry/criminal justice population.
Leverage the experience of other states that have previously expanded coverage to childless adults under Medicaid.	Research on other states that expanded Medicaid coverage provides a rich source of information on issues and analyses California may want to undertake (e.g., effectiveness of different outreach efforts and enrollment practices on participation rates) to understand the impact of insurance expansion for the reentry/criminal justice population.
Develop health homes for the reentry/criminal justice population.	The Medicaid expansion population (including the reentry/criminal justice component) is expected to include individuals with multiple comorbidities and high rates of mental illness and substance abuse, suggesting that health homes will be an important way to manage their complex care needs.
Develop care/case management systems that can account for special populations' needs, including the reentry/criminal justice population.	California may want to consider applying for planning grants to support the development of tailored care/case management programs that will include coordination with social services and community organizations that serve special populations, including the reentry/criminal justice population.

Table S.1—Continued

Recommendation	Description
Assess workforce-development strategies for alcohol, drug, and mental health treatment.	Given that existing publicly funded treatment provider networks may become overwhelmed in the face of Medicaid expansion occurs and public safety realignment, California may want to consider establishing a health task force to identify workforce-development strategies that will help build treatment provider capacity in general, and specifically to meet the expected increase in demand for services by the reentry/criminal justice population.
Consider developing electronic medical records.	Electronic medical records are one tool by which to improve the transition of care from prison to safety-net providers; as such, California may wish to consider developing a pilot study to assess the feasibility of developing such records for the reentry/criminal justice population.
Consider expanding prerelease planning efforts.	CDCR's prerelease planning for prisoners with medical or mental health conditions is based on acuity and need; CDCR and counties may want to consider expanding prerelease planning to include those with chronic medical and mental health and substance abuse problems in general.
Undertake a comprehensive assessment of the impact of California's new Public Safety Realignment Plan to inform future policy refinements.	California's 2011 Public Safety Realignment Plan represents a profound change to the state's criminal justice system. The legislature may wish to consider allocating funding to undertake a comprehensive assessment of the impact of realignment and require counties to track a standard set of metrics to enable cross-county comparisons and facilitate an assessment of the plan's overall impact.
What Can Counties and Providers Do to Prepare?	
Develop county-level estimates to inform planning for rehabilitative services and for increased demand for mental health and alcohol and drug treatment.	Given the growing need for mental health and alcohol and drug treatment services, county departments of mental health and alcohol and drug treatment and safety-net providers will need more-informed estimates of the number of individuals that will make up the reentry/criminal justice population at the local level and of their expected demand for services.
Convene all relevant stakeholders for planning and coordination of services.	As counties refine their plans for implementing the Public Safety Realignment Plan and health care reform, they may want to consider broadening the group of stakeholders to include community- and faith-based organizations that have long been involved in serving the reentry/criminal justice population.

Table S.1—Continued

Recommendation	Description
Assess local capacity to meet new demands for health care.	Given the important role of local public health departments and agencies, counties might wish to draw on them in assessing local capacity for care, especially for those communities disproportionately affected by reentry and realignment, and in developing strategies for addressing service gaps for the reentry/criminal justice population.
Develop "welcome home" guidebooks tailored to individual counties, particularly for counties and communities with high rates of return.	Counties can use public safety realignment as a chance to improve and update these guidebooks to include problem-solving strategies—highlighting services that address immediate needs (e.g., housing, transportation, health care) and providing detailed information about local resources, especially about organizations committed to serving this population. They should be written in a culturally competent manner, take into account literacy levels, and be provided in Spanish and other languages as needed.
Train providers on cultural competence.	Counties may want to implement provider training to improve their cultural competence, especially in primary care/public health clinics and in other settings where the primary care and specialty care needs of the reentry/criminal justice population will be addressed. Also, counties could work with community-based and faith-based organizations to ensure this training includes the perspective of the formerly incarcerated.
Consider the role of patient navigators.	Being able to navigate the maze of needed services is critical. Staff who are experienced in working with this population or who have been formerly incarcerated themselves are particularly well suited to fulfill this role. Counties might want to undertake a demonstration project to explore the use of patient navigators, particularly in counties with large reentry populations.
Address the needs of families and those that care for children of incarcerated parents.	Given the importance of families to the successful reintegration of individuals returning from prison and the challenges the families face, there is a need for programs to address the needs of children of incarcerated children, the needs of caregivers (e.g., respite care), and the family reunification process. Also, to inform planning decisions, counties also need better estimates on the number of children with incarcerated parents.

In light of California's new Public Safety Realignment Plan and federal health care reform, California faces both substantial challenges and unprecedented opportunities to address the needs of this population by improving rehabilitative services at the local level and by improving access to health care for the reentry population (and other components of the criminal justice population) through Medicaid and other coverage expansions. Both will require the state and counties to establish new partnerships with the range of stakeholders that serve this population.

Lastly, private philanthropy can also play an important role in helping to address the uncertainty created by this unique confluence of public safety realignment at the state level and health care reform at the federal level. Such a role for California and national foundations includes supporting (1) local demonstration projects and collaboration among relevant stakeholders; (2) Medicaid enrollment strategies; (3) pilot projects to test innovative ideas; (4) efforts to increase the capacity of local communities and organizations to provide reentry services; and (5) ongoing evaluations and research on the impact of realignment and health care reform on the reentry population.

Acknowledgments

This work was funded by The California Endowment. We are particularly grateful for the guidance and feedback provided throughout this study by our project officer, Steve Eldred.

We received input from a number of reentry stakeholders throughout California—too numerous to mention here—but we gratefully acknowledge their time and valuable insights. We especially wish to thank those individuals who participated in the focus group discussions and willingly shared their experiences and thoughtful perspective on the support needs of those returning home and of families and children. We also are appreciative of the time and valuable insights given by the providers who participated in this study.

We wish to thank the California Department of Corrections and Rehabilitation for making available for this study parolee data that was analyzed to understand the distribution of the reentry population within California.

In addition, we would like to thank the focus group facilitators who drew on their own experiences in working with the reentry population: Elizabeth Marlowe, Ph.D., Pastor William T. Grajeda, Reverend Eugene Williams III, and Clovis M. Honoré. In addition, we would like to recognize the assistance of many organizations in helping to recruit focus group participants or hosting us for the focus group discussions and provider interviews. These organizations provide important social services, support, and health care to ex-prisoners, their families, and other hard-to-reach populations in their communities. They include Healthy Oakland and The Gamble Institute in Alameda County; Los Angeles Metropolitan Churches and the Community Assessment Service Center, South Los Angeles, in Los Angeles County; and the Second Chance Program, the United African American Ministerial Action Council, and Social Advocates for Youth in San Diego County.

We are appreciative of the insights provided by our technical reviewers—Jeff Mellow of the John Jay College of Criminal Justice and Audrey Burnam of RAND—for helping to ensure the quality of this research report. We also wish to thank Christine Eibner of RAND for her insights on health care reform and review of selected sections of the report. At RAND, we greatly benefited from the editing and publications production support provided by James Torr and Stacie McKee. We appreciated their responsiveness and flexibility in editing and producing this final report.

Finally, while we appreciate the improvements provided by all who reviewed and commented on this document, we emphasize that the findings and recommendations, as well as any errors, are those of the authors alone.

Abbreviations

ACA	Patient Protection and Affordable Care Act
ADT	alcohol and drug treatment
BJS	Bureau of Justice Statistics
CASC	community assessment service center
CDCR	California Department of Corrections and Rehabilitation
CHC/MACC	comprehensive health services/multiservice ambulatory care clinic
DHS	Disproportionate Share Hospital
FIPS	Federal Information Processing Standard
FPL	federal poverty level
FTE	full-time equivalent
HCCC	Hampden County Correctional Center
HRSA	Health Resources and Service Administration
MHSA	Mental Health Services Act
MISP	Medically Indigent Service Program
NCCHC	National Commission for Correctional Health Care
Nnh	Nearest Neighborhood Hierarchical
PACT	Parole and Community Team
POC	parole outpatient clinic

PPP	public/private partnership
PRCS	postrelease community supervision
PSA	Prostate-Specific Antigen
PSN	Parolee Services Network
SACPA	Substance Abuse and Crime Prevention Act
SAP	substance abuse treatment program
SPECTRM	Sensitizing Providers to the Effects of Correctional Incarceration on Treatment and Risk Management
STD	sexually transmitted disease

CHAPTER ONE

Introduction

In California, much is changing in terms of the current landscape within which the state and counties will be considering options for how to better meet the health care and rehabilitative needs of the reentry population. When we began this project to assess the public health implications of prisoner reentry in California, the country was in the initial stages of what has now become the most significant national recession since the Great Depression. When we completed our initial set of analyses on the capacity of the health care safety net in 2009, we were already witnessing the impact of the recession on that safety net. Now, the advent of California's new Public Safety Realignment Plan in 2011, the continuing impact of the economic crisis—in terms of even deeper cuts to the health care safety net—and prospects of health care reform provide a changing landscape in which to assess the challenges associated with prisoner reentry in California and opportunities to meet those challenges—one that places California clearly at a crossroads.

In this chapter, we first summarize what is known about the health care needs of returning prisoners and the implications for California, and then discuss the changing size and composition of the prison population. We next discuss recent policy changes that will dramatically affect how California will approach meeting the needs of the reentry population. We move on to provide an overview of the study's objectives and scope, the study's limitations, and a road map for the remaining chapters.

Background

Health Care Needs of Returning Prisoners Are High

As an increasing number of prisoners are released from prisons and return to local communities, there are key questions about what health care needs they have and what role health plays in affecting their success at reintegrating back into communities. A retrospective cohort study by Binswanger et al. (2007) highlighted how those released from prison have substantial health risks and higher mortality rates than the general population. The most important finding was that inmates released from prison had a high risk of death, particularly during the first two weeks following release, with the leading causes of death being drug overdose, cardiovascular disease, homicide, and suicide.

In its 2002 landmark study *The Health Status of Soon-to-Be-Released Inmates: A Report to Congress*, the National Commission for Correctional Health Care (NCCHC) commissioned a series of papers to summarize what was known about the health status of prisoners and their treatment needs upon release from prison and to examine the implications for the correctional treatment and community health care systems. The NCCHC study represents one of the most comprehensive sources of information on the health status of inmates.

The NCCHC study found that the prison population is disproportionately sicker, on average, than the U.S. population in general, with substantially higher burdens of infectious diseases (such as HIV/AIDS, tuberculosis, and hepatitis B and C), serious mental illness, and comorbidities, or co-occurring disorders (NCCHC, 2002).[1]

Mallik-Kane and Visher (2008) provide important insights about how health care impacts the reentry process. They conducted a survey of Ohio and Texas state prisoners during 2004 and 2005, asking prisoners what their health status was, what treatment they had received, and how health had impacted the reentry process. They also conducted interviews with these individuals shortly before release and at several points following their release. Most returning prisoners (68 percent of

---

[1] The NCCHC did not estimate the prevalence of substance abuse and dependence among state prisoners.

men and 58 percent of women) were without health insurance 8–10 months after release from prison. Yet they were also heavy users of health care services, including emergency room visits and hospitalizations. Mallik and Visher note that "although returning prisoners received these health services, their rates of treatment for specific health conditions deteriorated, suggesting that they received episodic care for acute problems but that continuous treatment of specific health conditions suffered."

In addition, individuals with physical and mental health problems reported poorer employment outcomes than those without such problems (Mallik and Visher, 2008). Mentally ill men and women and substance-abusing women were more likely to be homeless upon release from prison. Individuals with substance abuse problems reported more criminal behavior and were more likely to earn money through illegal activities. Having any type of health condition was associated with engaging in criminal activity or having a higher likelihood of being reincarcerated. One out of five individuals interviewed by these researchers was reincarcerated within a year of his or her release.

Individuals returning to communities upon release from prison face a number of obstacles to accessing care. Low insurance rates among this population limit their ability to access health care services and provide case managers with few options for linking them to services. The linkages between prison health care and community health care may be limited, thus making continuity of care problematic, particularly for those with chronic health conditions or mental health or substance abuse problems (Mallik and Visher, 2008). Reliance on county health care services and medically indigent providers may mean long waiting times to access care. Further, many providers lack experience in treating this population. Low levels of health care safety-net resources in the communities to which ex-prisoners typically return also limit access to services (Freudenberg, 2004). Other obstacles to accessing care include language barriers and low literacy rates (Greenberg, Dunleavy, and Kutner, 2007).

What do such insights mean for California? Most of the state's prisoners ultimately will return to California communities, bringing with them a variety of health and social needs that have public health implications. Yet the public is largely unaware of the health needs of this population, and the challenges they present to their communities are not being addressed explicitly, despite the fact that reentry directly affects almost every California community. Further, the current debate about California's new 2011 Public Safety Realignment Plan, discussed below, has focused primarily on public safety concerns rather than on how well counties will be able to meet the rehabilitative and health care needs of individuals who will serve their sentence and be supervised at the local level.

Although detailed data on the health status of the reentry population in California are not available, the nationwide Survey of Inmates in State and Federal Correctional Facilities conducted by the Bureau of Justice Statistics (BJS, no date-b) represents the best available data on California prison inmates. Data from this survey can serve as a useful proxy for understanding the health care needs of those individuals who will be returning from prison to local communities.

The Size and Composition of California's Prison Population Are Changing

California's prison population and the numbers of individuals who will be returning to local communities have significantly increased over time. The growth in California's prison population from 1987 and 2005 alone has been three times faster than that of the general adult population. Between 1987 and 2007, California's state prison population grew from about 67,000 inmates to 171,000 inmates (CDCR, *Historical Trends, 1987–2007*, 2008).[2] In the past five years, the size of the state prison population has stabilized (Hayes, 2011). As of July 2010, it had even decreased to about 163,000 (CDCR, *Fall 2011 Adult Population Projections*, 2011).

Over the past 20 years, the number of individuals released from California prisons to local communities has increased nearly threefold. Between 1987 and 2007, the number of felon releases to parole increased

---

[2] These numbers represent the size of the correctional institution population. That is, the number of adult offenders incarcerated in California's state prisons, conservation camps, community correctional centers, or Department of Mental Health hospitals during these time periods.

from 50,512 to 137,590 (CDCR, *Historical Trends, 198–2007*, 2008). This means that, over this time period, an increasing number of individuals have returned to California's communities, bringing with them a range of health care needs.

In California, African-Americans are disproportionately represented in the prison population: Although African-Americans make up 6.2 percent of the state population, they represent 29 percent of the state prison population (CDCR, *California Prisoners and Parolees 2009*, 2010; U.S. Census Bureau, 2010). Latinos represent 39.3 percent of the state prison population, which is comparable to their representation in the state population, according to the 2010 census. As we discuss in Chapter Two, African-American and Latino parolees further are more likely than white parolees to return to disadvantaged communities and neighborhoods characterized by high poverty and unemployment rates, suggesting that reentry will be particularly challenging for these two groups.

In addition, California's prison population is aging. In 1990, 20 percent of prisoners were under age 25; by 2010, only 13 percent were under age 25. During this time period, the share of prisoners age 50 and older grew from 4 percent to 17 percent (Hayes, 2011). Because of this transition, the burden of chronic diseases, such as diabetes and hypertension—typically associated with older people—among the prison population is likely to grow.

As discussed below, the size and composition of the prison population are not static, and recent policy changes will lead to a very different picture for California.

Recent Policy Changes Will Influence How California Approaches Meeting the Health Care Needs of the Reentry Population

In 2005, California's prison medical system was put under a court-appointed federal receiver whose charge was to bring the level of medical care in California prisons up to a standard that no longer violates the U.S. Constitution (California Prison Health Care Services, 2010). The receivership was the result of a 2001 federal class-action lawsuit that argued that the state of medical care in California state prisons violated the Eighth Amendment of the U.S. Constitution. Despite

California's early attempts to reform the system, the court removed control of prison medical care from the state and appointed a federal receiver to oversee the reform process. The receiver is responsible for the medical care provided in California's state prisons and all medical personnel (e.g., physicians, nurses, and other medical staff) who work for the California Department of Corrections and Rehabilitation (CDCR) Division of Correctional Health Care Services (California Correctional Health Care Services, 2011). However, the receiver's mandate does not include mental health, dental health, substance abuse and treatment, or juvenile health in the state's prison systems.[3]

On May 23, 2011, the U.S. Supreme Court ordered California to reduce the number of inmates in the state's prisons to 137.5 percent design capacity by May 24, 2013, which requires a reduction of about 33,000 inmates. The Court held that medical and mental health care for inmates still falls below a constitutional standard of care and that the only way to meet these constitutional requirements was by further reductions in the size of the prison population (CDCR, "Three-Judge Panel and California Inmate Population Reduction," 2011).

California's new Public Safety Realignment Plan, signed into law in April 2011, will enable the state to close the revolving door of low-level inmates cycling in and out of prison and will also help reduce the size of the prison population. This new plan changes how the state handles low-level offenders, who are defined as individuals sentenced for non-serious, non-violent, non-sex offenses. Beginning October 1, 2011, counties will assume new responsibilities for such offenders: Low-level offenders will serve their sentences in county jails instead of state prisons, and low-level offenders released from state prison will be placed on county-level postrelease community supervision (PRCS). In addition, individuals who violate their terms of parole (except for those previously sentenced to a term of life) will now serve their revocation time in county jail instead of prison. CDCR will retain responsibility for parole supervision for offenders released on parole prior to October 1, 2011, and for violent and serious offenders, high-risk sex offenders,

---

[3] Mental health and dental care (and the rights of disabled inmates) are the subject of separate federal class-action law suits.

mentally disordered offenders, and inmates paroled from a sentence of life, including three-strikes offenders (CDCR, "2011 Public Safety Realignment," 2011).

Funding for realignment will come from a dedicated portion of state sales tax revenue and vehicle license fees (CDCR, "2011 Public Safety Realignment," 2011). This will provide revenue to counties for local public safety programs and establish the Local Revenue Fund 2011 for counties to receive the revenues and appropriate funding for 2011 public safety realignment. Initial funding for counties to implement the realignment plan is $400 million in 2011 and is expected to increase to more than $850 million in 2012 and more than $1 billion in 2013–2014 (CDCR, "2011 Public Safety Realignment," 2011).

These changes in California's corrections policies and legislation will significantly impact the growth of the state's prison population. Under California's new Public Safety Realignment Plan, the number of incarcerated individuals in California prisons is projected to decline from a high of about 173,000 in 2007 to 124,017 by 2017 (CDCR, *Fall 2011 Adult Population Projections*, 2011).

This means that counties will now be responsible for meeting the rehabilitative and health care needs of those offenders who will serve their sentence and be supervised at the county level. Yet some might argue that counties have had little experience in managing this population and providing rehabilitative services to them.

Lastly, another major change in policy that will have implications for the reentry population is that a critical barrier to accessing care will be eliminated for many ex-prisoners as part of federal health care reform. Under the Patient Protection and Affordable Care Act (ACA) (Pub. Law 111-148), Medicaid eligibility will be expanded to include all non-Medicare-eligible citizens and legal residents[4] under age 65 with incomes up to 133 percent[5] of the federal poverty level (FPL). Also, the

---

[4] That is, legal residents who have been in the country five years or longer.

[5] The ACA specifies that childless adults are eligible for Medicaid with modified adjusted gross income (AGI) at or below 133 percent of the FPL. However, the ACA also adds a 5 percentage-point deduction from the FPL, which effectively makes the Medicaid eligibility threshold 138 percent of the FPL (State Health Access Data Assistance Center, 2011).

ACA will provide subsidies to purchase insurance for individuals below 400 percent of the FPL without coverage from their employers, and the law will penalize employers for not offering coverage.

The net effect of the ACA is that there will be more options available to low-income populations, either through an employer, the exchanges, or Medicaid. Importantly, these changes open up the possibility for many ex-prisoners and other individuals involved with the criminal justice system to become eligible for Medicaid (California's Medicaid program is referred to as Medi-Cal) thus, removing a key barrier to access to care. Further, Medicaid will be expanded to more fully cover drug treatment, prevention services, and wellness programs—services important to the reentry population. At the same time, there are also some challenges. Expanded Medicaid eligibility could lead to increased demand for health care safety-net services that are already stretched thin, thus possibly impacting access to care given limited capacity at the county level. In addition, Disproportionate Share Hospital (DSH) payments are being cut, which means that fewer resources will be available for individuals who remain uninsured.[6] Noncitizens will not necessarily qualify for Medicaid. Finally, under the ACA, individuals can be penalized for not having health insurance, which likely will include a portion of the reentry population.[7] Combined, these changes and restrictions suggest that facilitating Medicaid enrollment for eligible ex-prisoners and soon-to-be-released prisoners will be important.

Thus, California is at a critical juncture: It faces numerous challenges, but recent changes in policy also present important opportunities to improve the state's ability to meet the needs of individuals returning from state prison. As part of public safety realignment and health care reform, it is critical to address the public health challenges associated with reentry to assist communities in meeting the health care and rehabilitative needs of this population. We also need to better

---

[6] DSH adjustment payments provide additional help to those hospitals that serve a significantly disproportionate number of low-income patients. States receive an annual DSH allotment to cover the costs of DSH hospitals that provide care to low-income patients that are not paid by other payers, such as Medicare, Medicaid, or other health insurance (U.S. Department of Health and Human Services, no date).

[7] Although penalties are waived for the lowest-income groups (non–tax filers).

understand the impact of incarceration on their families and children of incarcerated parents, their risk factors, and what options exist to change the trajectories of their lives.

Study Objective and Scope

The overall goal of this study is to examine the public health challenges of prisoner reentry in California and to identify policy options for improving access to health care services and other resources for this population. In this study—a "state-of-the-state" report—we asked the following questions:

- What are the health care needs of individuals who will be returning from prison to local communities?
- Which counties and communities are particularly impacted by reentry?
- What is the capacity of the health care safety net to meet the needs of this population?
- What are the experiences of returning prisoners in seeking health care, and what role does health play in their efforts to reintegrate back into the community?
- What challenges do community health care providers face in serving this population?
- What effects does parental incarceration have on families and children?
- What options do California and counties have to improve services to this population?

To answer these questions, we conducted a number of analyses. First, we analyzed self-reported data from a survey of California inmates to understand what their health care needs are, using them as a proxy to provide insights about the types of health needs individuals returning from prison will bring.[8] Second, we conducted a geographic analysis to identify gaps in parolees' health care access by comparing where parolees are concentrated in California to the capacity of the health care safety net in four counties—Alameda, Los Angeles, San Diego, and Kern—that represent a large share of the reentry population. An innovation of this study was that we explicitly defined what the health care safety net was for the reentry population and developed measures to assess the capacity of the safety net to meet the needs of this population.

Third, we conducted focus groups with formerly incarcerated individuals in three of the four focus counties—Alameda, Los Angeles, and San Diego—to understand the experiences of returning prisoners in seeking care and the role that health plays in their efforts to reintegrate back into the community. Fourth, we interviewed community providers to learn about the challenges they experience in providing services to this population. Lastly, we conducted a focus group with individuals who care for children of incarcerated parents to gain some initial insights about the impact that parental incarceration has on families and particularly children.

Finally, we synthesized the results of these various analyses to discuss their implications for California and make recommendations for how the state and counties can better prepare to meet the needs of this population. Our recommendations are based on a combination of our review of the literature and analyses of the inmate survey, parolee data, data on the health care safety net in four counties, provider interviews, and focus group discussions with the formerly incarcerated and family members.

We focused our analyses on the health care needs and experiences of men returning from prison. Although we recognize that women represent a growing segment of the prison population, 9 out of 10 inmates are men. Because women prisoners' socioeconomic, health, and other concerns differ in important ways from their male counterparts, we decided that it was not feasible within the scope of this study to com-

[8] We defined *health care needs* to mean both physical health care needs and mental health care and substance abuse treatment needs.

prehensively address the public health issues and needs of women returning from prison to local communities.

Study Limitations

As with all studies, there are some study limitations that the reader should keep in mind. To understand the health care needs of the parolee population in California, we relied on self-reported survey data on inmates in California's prisons that served as a proxy for examining the needs of the reentry population.

Importantly, our analyses were conducted prior to the October 1, 2011, implementation of California's new Public Safety Realignment Plan. Therefore, our results of the geographic distribution and concentration of parolees and the capacity of the health care safety net reflect conditions prior to the implementation of this new policy. Nevertheless, we believe that these findings will provide the state and counties with an important context for understanding and examining the impact of realignment moving forward.

Also, in assessing parolees' access to health care resources through the geographic analyses, we focused on *potential access* to health care (e.g., having health care resources in a community and the capacity of those resources) and, specifically, to health care safety-net resources; within the scope of this study, we did not measure *realized access* to health care (e.g., actual use of health care) nor whether individuals returning from prison have better treatment and criminal justice outcomes as a result.

The focus group discussions and provider interviews represent the perspective only of individuals who were formerly incarcerated in state prison and of community health care providers. They do not include the perspective of state agencies (i.e., CDCR), the federal receiver appointed to oversee California's prison reform, or county agencies (sheriff, police, county probation, courts). In addition, we recognize that the focus group discussions and provider interviews are based on small samples, and this, along with the purposive sampling approach, may limit the generalizability of these results. To address this, we compared these findings with those of other research studies that have similarly looked at the health experiences of individuals returning from prison, of providers that serve this population, and of families of the incarcerated.

Organization of This Report

We organized the remainder of this report as follows. Chapter Two summarizes the results of our analyses of the health care needs of California's prison population, the geographic distribution of parolees and which counties and communities disproportionately are impacted by reentry, and the capacity of the health care safety net to meet the needs of this population in four focus counties that represent a large share of the reentry population.

Chapters Three through Five present the results of our qualitative research in Alameda, Los Angeles, and San Diego counties. In Chapter Three, we discuss the key findings from focus groups with ex-prisoners, exploring how health affects the process of reentry and barriers to accessing care. In Chapter Four, we discuss the findings from our examination of the challenges providers face in trying to reach this population and provide services to them. In Chapter Five, we discuss how incarceration and reentry affects families, particularly children.

In Chapter Six, we provide our overall summary of the state of prisoner reentry in California and discuss our recommendations about how the state as a whole and the counties within it can improve access to health services for this population.

CHAPTER TWO

What Do We Know About Prisoners' Health Care Needs and the Capacity of the Safety Net to Meet the Needs of the Reentry Population?

Introduction

As noted in Chapter One, over the past 20 years, the number of individuals released from California prisons has increased nearly threefold, and most of the state's prisoners ultimately will return to California communities, bringing with them a variety of health and social needs that must be addressed. This raises key public health challenges, especially because ex-prisoners are returning to communities whose safety nets have already been severely strained. To address these challenges, policymakers need to better understand the health care needs of those returning from prison to communities and the capacity of the health care safety net in those communities to handle them.

In this chapter, we summarize the results of analyses aimed at helping to improve that understanding for policymakers. Specifically, we examined the health care needs of the reentry population, conducted a geographic analysis to identify where parolees are concentrated in California and which California communities are disproportionately impacted by prisoner reentry, and examined the types of health care safety-net services—hospitals, clinics, mental health clinics, and substance abuse treatment providers—available in these communities and the capacity of the health care safety net to meet the needs of the reentry population.

We found the following:

1. The reentry population's health care needs are high, and its mental health care and substance abuse treatment needs are even higher.
2. Certain counties and communities will be particularly affected by reentry.
3. Access to safety-net resources varies by facility type, by geographic area (across counties and within county), and by race/ethnicity.

These findings are discussed in more detail in this chapter and form the context for the results that are presented in the subsequent chapters. Appendix A summarizes the methods used for these analyses. Davis et al. (2009) provides a full reporting of the results and the methods used.

What Are the Health Care Needs of the Reentry Population?

To examine the health care needs of the reentry population, we conducted a state-level analysis using data for California from a national survey of state prison inmates—specifically, self-reported data from the BJS's 2004 Survey of Inmates in State and Federal Correctional Facilities. All the results presented here are based only on responses among males incarcerated in state prisons.[1] Although, ideally, we would like to have detailed information on the health care needs of ex-prisoners, such data do not exist, and primary data collection would be very expensive. However, the BJS Survey of Inmates provides a rich source of information on the self-reported health care needs of the prison population and serves as a useful proxy for understanding the needs of the reentry population. The summary below is based on the results of our analysis of this survey.

---

[1] We excluded federal prisoners from our study.

Our analyses of parolees' socioeconomic characteristics and of the BJS inmate survey tell us a number of things about the men returning from prison in California. First, California prisoners are relatively young, with the average age being 36. In terms of race/ethnicity, 29 percent of California state prisoners are African-American, 37 percent are Latino, and 34 percent are white or of other race/ethnicity. California has a large foreign-born population, and 16 percent of inmates are foreign-born. Not surprisingly, foreign-born status is higher among Latino inmates in California (33 percent). California's state prisoners also have substantially lower educational attainment than the general California population. Eighty-five percent of California adults have a high school diploma, compared with 60 percent of state prisoners. Although the BJS survey did not ask about literacy, it is well known that 50 to 75 percent of inmates are functionally illiterate—rates that are three times that of the general population (Greenberg, Dunleavy, and Kutner, 2007). This low educational attainment and low literacy are likely to negatively affect prisoners' employment opportunities, as well as their health and health care access, postrelease.

At the time of the BJS survey, half of California inmates had minor children, and approximately 21 percent of California inmates (or 41 percent of those who reported minor children at the time of the interview) were living with their children at the time of their latest arrest. The imprisonment of parents disrupts parent-child relationships, alters the networks of familial support, and places new burdens on governmental services, such as schools, foster care, adoption agencies, and youth-serving organizations (Travis, McBride, and Solomon, 2005).

With respect to *physical health conditions*, our analysis of survey data showed that California prison inmates self-report a high burden of chronic diseases, such as asthma and hypertension, and infectious diseases (see Table 2.1), such as hepatitis and tuberculosis, which require regular use of health care for effective management. Although not shown in Table 2.1, nearly 14 percent of California prison inmates reported lifetime health problems with asthma, 18 percent with hypertension, and nearly 5 percent with diabetes.

Compared with state prisoners nationally (Table 2.1), California inmates were more likely to report tuberculosis (13 percent versus

Table 2.1
Prevalence of Infectious Diseases Among Male Prison Inmates in the United States and California, by Race/Ethnicity for California Inmates (%)

	United States	California	California: Race/Ethnicity			
	All	All	White	African-American	Latino	Other
Lifetime Health Problems						
Hepatitis	9	***13***	20	***9***	***11***	***8***
STD	11	***9***	8	13	7	***2***
Tuberculosis	10	***13***	9	11	***17***	***25***
HIV	2	1	<0.5	2	1	0
Current Health Problems						
Hepatitis	5	***7***	13	***3***	***7***	***3***
STD	1	<0.5	<0.5	<0.5	<0.5	0

SOURCE: BJS 2004 inmate survey.

NOTES: Sample includes male inmates incarcerated in state prisons only. Statistical significance denoted by bold italic font—California versus U.S.; race/ethnicity comparisons are African-American, Latino, and other versus white. Numbers have been rounded.

10 percent) and hepatitis (13 percent versus 9 percent), but less likely to report sexually transmitted diseases (STDs) (9 percent versus 11 percent). In terms of race/ethnicity, nearly 20 percent of white inmates reported lifetime health problems with hepatitis, compared with only 9 percent of African-American inmates and 11 percent of Latino inmates. More Latino inmates (17 percent) reported lifetime health problems with tuberculosis than African-American or white inmates.

The substance abuse treatment and mental health care needs of prisoners are even more pronounced than their physical health care needs. About three-quarters of California inmates reported regular drug use, with marijuana/hashish, stimulants such as methamphetamine, and cocaine/crack being the mostly commonly reported drugs

Table 2.2
Prevalence of Drug Abuse/Dependence and Mental Illness Among Male Prison Inmates in the United States and California, by Race Ethnicity for California Inmates (%)

	United States	California	California: Race/Ethnicity			
	All	All	White	African-American	Latino	Other
Drug Abuse/Dependence						
Drug abuse/dependence	53	***58***	67	***49***	60	37
Drug abuse	52	***56***	66	47	59	37
Drug dependence	35	***44***	55	35	44	21
Lifetime Prevalence of Mental Illness						
Depression	18	19	24	22	***12***	15
Mania	9	10	15	11	***6***	5
Posttraumatic stress disorder	5	6	9	8	***2***	3
Schizophrenia	4	6	8	10	***3***	3
Anxiety	6	8	11	10	***5***	5

SOURCE: Bureau of Justice Statistics 2004 inmate survey.

NOTES: Sample includes male inmates incarcerated in state prisons only. Statistical significance denoted by bold italic font—California versus United States. Race/ethnicity comparisons are African-American, Latino, and other versus white. Numbers have been rounded.

used. Fifty-eight percent of California inmates met the diagnostic criteria for drug abuse/dependence (Table 2.2).[2] Yet among Califor-

[2] We used the methodology developed by the BJS (Mumola and Karberg, 2006) for the 2004 Survey of Inmates in State and Federal Correctional Facilities (see BJS, no date-a) to assess the prevalence of symptoms of drug abuse and dependence among inmates. The BJS survey included questions designed to measure the prevalence of drug abuse or dependence as defined in the DSM-IV. Abuse symptoms included repeated drug use in hazardous situations or recurrent occupational, educational, legal, or social problems related to drug use. Inmates reporting any of these symptoms in the 12 months prior to their admission to prison met the abuse criteria. Dependence criteria covered a range of symptoms, including behavioral, cognitive, and physiological problems. Inmates reporting three or more symptoms in the 12 months before their admission to prison met the dependence criteria (Mumola and Karberg, 2006).

nia inmates with drug abuse or dependence, only 39 percent reported receiving treatment since admission to prison for substance abuse problems (not shown in Table 2.2), which is lower than that reported by state prisoners nationally.

Overall, about 1 out 5 California prisoners reported having been diagnosed with a mental health disorder during their lifetime. In terms of lifetime prevalence of mental illness, 19 percent reported being diagnosed with depression, between 8 and 9 percent reported being diagnosed with anxiety or mania, and 6 percent reported being diagnosed with schizophrenia or posttraumatic stress disorder (Table 2.2). In addition, more than half of California inmates reported being diagnosed with a recent mental health problem and of these inmates, about half reported receiving treatment for the disorder while in prison (not shown in Table 2.2). While this is the same rate as in the U.S. prison population, it still suggests that mental health care may not be reaching all those in need. Given the high prevalence of mental illness and drug abuse and dependence problems in the prison population, ex-prisoners' need for services upon returning to communities is particularly high and underscores the importance of ensuring continuity of care for these conditions.

The above summary provides us with a rich picture of the physical health care, mental health care, and substance abuse treatment needs of California inmates and serves as a useful proxy for understanding the reentry population's needs. However, it is important to remember that these numbers are based on self-reported data, so they have to be taken as rough estimates. From previous research, we know that there likely will be some underreporting in some areas, such as mental health, substance abuse, and infectious diseases, and that it will vary by race or ethnicity. That said, these findings suggest that ex-offenders returning to California communities will bring with them a host of physical and mental health care and substance abuse treatment needs. However, as discussed in Chapter Four, the literature indicates that ex-prisoners face a number of barriers with respect to accessing health care services given high uninsured rates among this population and other identified barriers.

Where Do Prisoners Go Upon Release from Prison?

We also analyzed the geographic distribution and concentration of parolees in California, as well as the overall characteristics of parolees and the communities to which they return.[3] To do so, we used geocoded data for parolees released from California state prison in 2005–2006 and cluster analysis to examine the geographic distribution of parolees and to identify concentrations of parolees across and within counties. We first took a statewide view, identifying those counties with the greatest concentration of parolees in the state. We then provided an in-depth examination at four counties in the state—Los Angeles, Alameda, Kern, and San Diego. We selected these counties because they are home to a significant share of the parolee population and because we wanted to achieve a balance between northern, central, and southern California, as well as include both urban and rural counties in our comparisons. Appendix A provides a summary of the methods used for this analysis.

Concentration and Distribution of Parolees Within California

Figure 2.1 shows the cluster of parolees in California. The clusters are shown as yellow ellipses with the black dots representing the count of parolees, where each dot represents one parolee. The blue shading indicates statewide parolee rates per 1,000, with dark blue indicating those areas with higher parolee rates of return and lighter blue indicating those areas with lower rates of return.

The figure shows that 11 counties have the highest parolee rates, concentrated around the Bay Area and in the southern part of the state. By far, the highest rates of parolee returns are in southern California, especially, Los Angeles, Orange, San Bernardino, Riverside, and San Diego counties. Looking within counties on the map, we find that most of the clusters are in urban areas, for example, near San Francisco–Oakland, the city of Los Angeles, and the city of San Diego.

3 Focusing on parolees captured the majority of individuals released from prison. We exclude from our sample those individuals unconditionally released from prison. In a typical year, approximately 97 percent of individuals released from California's prisons are parolees; only 3 percent are released unconditionally, having served their entire sentence.

Figure 2.1
Relative Concentrations of Parolees in California, by County

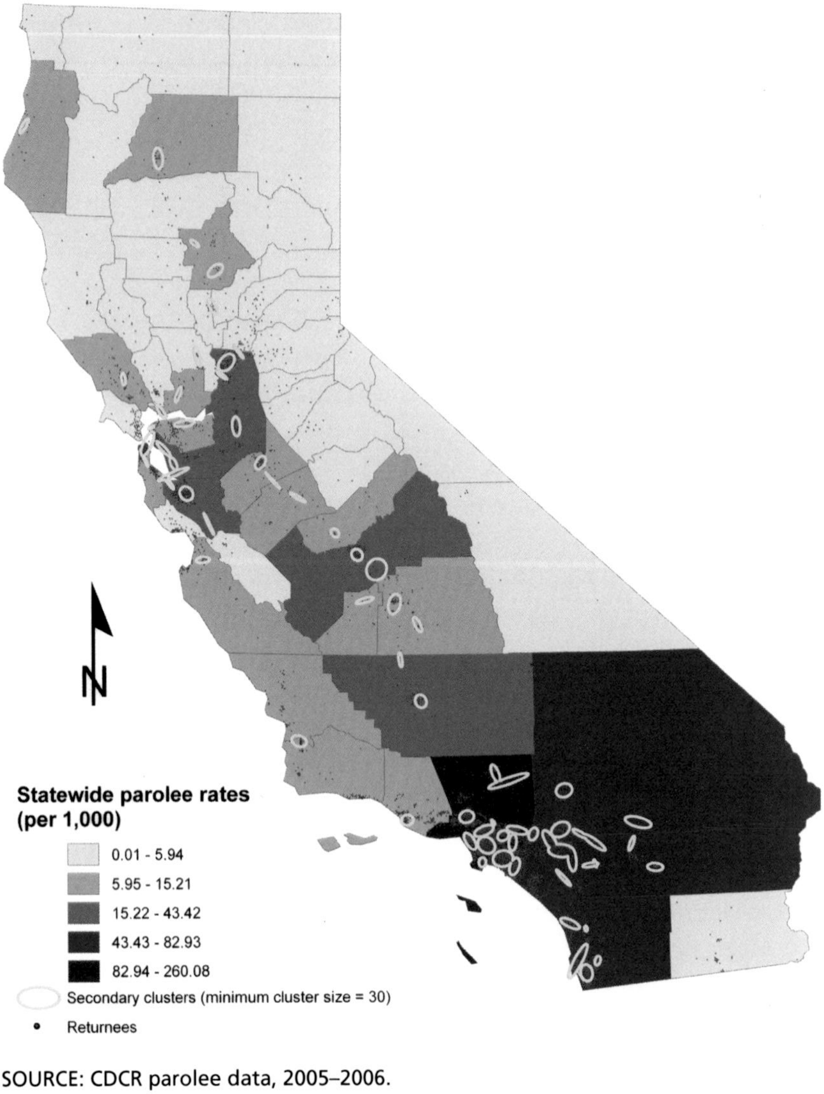

SOURCE: CDCR parolee data, 2005–2006.
RAND *MG1165-2.1*

Given that the amount of concentration varies across urban and rural counties, a different strategy will be needed to provide services to parolees located in these different types of counties.

Concentration and Distribution of Parolees Within the Four Selected Counties. Given the uneven distribution of parolees across California, we next analyzed the cluster of parolees in the four focus counties—Alameda, Kern, Los Angeles, and San Diego.

In doing this, we shaded the maps based on the concentration of parolees, using rate of return for each census tract, which allowed us to identify which areas or neighborhoods in a county are more burdened by returning prisoners. This background was overlaid with the clusters of parolees identified using the cluster analytic methodology described in Appendix A. The borders shown on each of the maps in Figures 2.2–2.5 identify the county supervisorial districts within each county, to help maximize their use for policymakers, health providers, and community organizations.

Alameda County. Alameda County is located in northern California, east of San Francisco, and has a population of 1,510,271 and a density of 2,047.5 people per square mile. The county's major cities—Oakland (population 397,067), Berkeley (population 101,555), San Leandro (population 78,030), Hayward (population 140,606)—make up about 47.5 percent of the total population (U.S. Census Bureau 2011a). Twenty-two percent of the county's population is Hispanic or Latino, 12.6 percent is African-American, and 26.1 percent of the population is Asian.

Figure 2.2 shows the cluster of parolees in Alameda County overlaid on the census tract parolee rates of return per 1,000 parolees. In Alameda County, we identified five distinct clusters of parolees, concentrated primarily around Oakland and the northern section of the county. These five clusters—located near south Oakland, Emeryville, Hayward, north Oakland, and San Leandro—account for almost 45 percent of the parolee population returning to Alameda County, suggesting that these areas are likely to be more impacted by reentry and face a higher demand for health care services by the reentry population than other areas in the county.

Figure 2.2
Relative Concentrations of Parolees in Alameda County

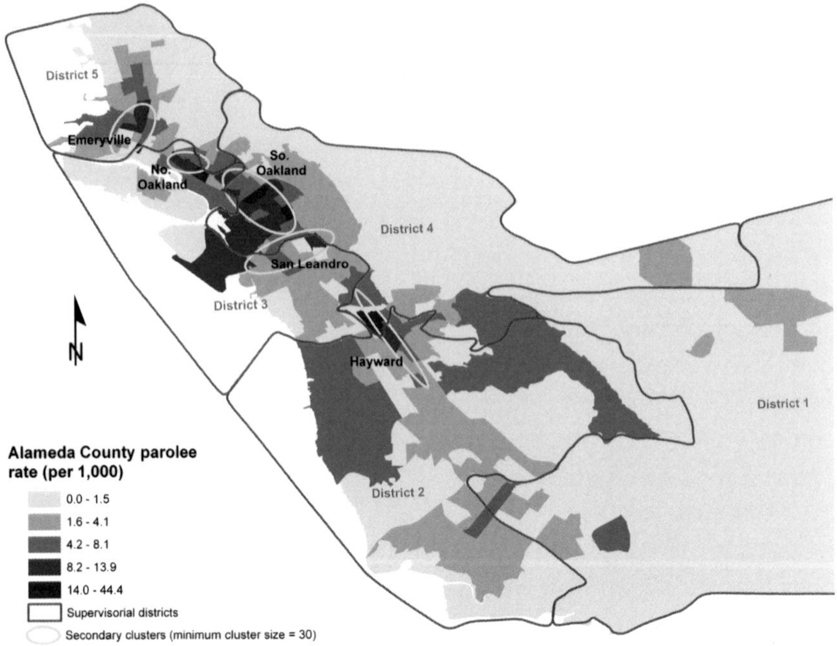

SOURCE: CDCR parolee data, 2005–2006.
RAND *MG1165-2.2*

Kern County. Kern County is located in central California, north of Los Angeles County, and has a population of 839,631 and a density of 103.1 people per square mile. The major city is Bakersfield (population 308,392), which represents about 37 percent of the county's total population (U.S. Census Bureau, 2011c). The rest of the county is rural and heavily agricultural. Nearly half of the county's population is Hispanic or Latino, 5.8 percent is African-American, and 4.2 percent is Asian.

Figure 2.3 shows that in Kern County there are four distinct clusters of parolees—two of the clusters show concentrations primarily around the urban area of Bakersfield, and two others are located in the northern and northeastern sections of the county (County Supervisorial District 1). These four clusters account for almost 58 percent of the

Figure 2.3
Relative Concentrations of Parolees in Kern County

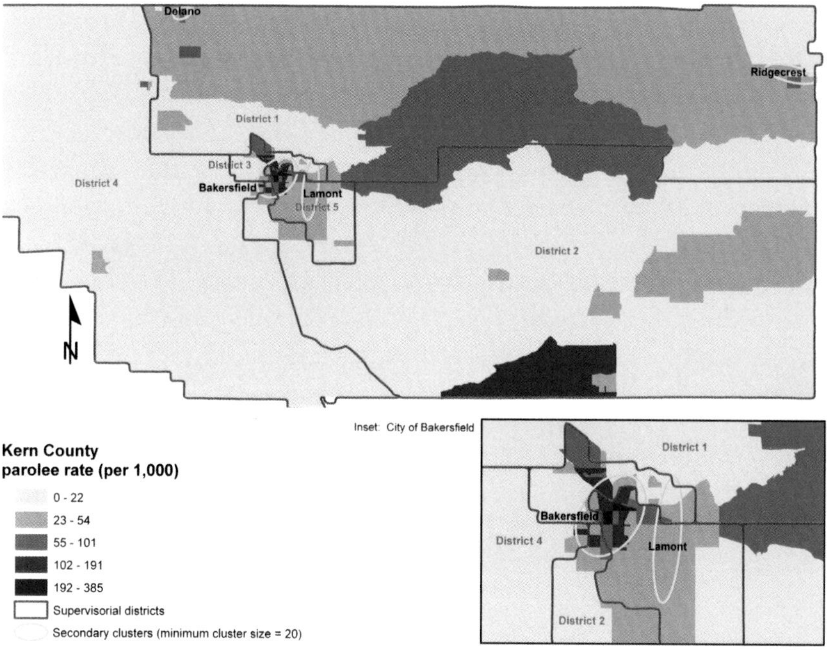

SOURCE: CDCR parolee data, 2005–2006.
RAND *MG1165-2.3*

parolee population returning to Kern County, with Bakersfield alone accounting for nearly 50 percent of the parolees. Thus, the Bakersfield area in particular bears the burden with respect to meeting the health care needs of the reentry population in Kern County.

Los Angeles County. Los Angeles County is located in southern California, north of Orange and San Diego counties, and has a population of 9,818,605 and a density of 2,417.9 people per square mile. The county covers a broad geographic area (4,060.87 square miles) made up of densely urban areas and more sparsely populated areas. Some of the major cities in the southern half—the more urban areas of the county—include the City of Los Angeles (population 3,849,378), Long Beach (population 472,494), Compton (population 95,701), Gardena (population 91,756), Pasadena (population 144,133, and Inglewood (population 114,914). In the northern and more rural part of the county, there are Lancaster (population 140,804) and Palmdale (138,790). The City of Los Angeles alone accounts for 39 percent of the county's total population (U.S. Census Bureau, 2011d). Forty-eight percent of the county's population is Hispanic or Latino, 8.7 percent is African-American, and 13.7 percent is Asian.

Figure 2.4 shows that there are many more clusters in Los Angeles County than in the other counties—23 distinct clusters of parolees covering a large geographic area—suggesting that providing services to the reentry population requires a targeted approach in the different county supervisorial districts. Two clusters are located in the northern part of the county around Lancaster and Palmdale and in the southern section of District 5 around Pasadena. The San Fernando Valley

Figure 2.4
Relative Concentrations of Parolees in Los Angeles County

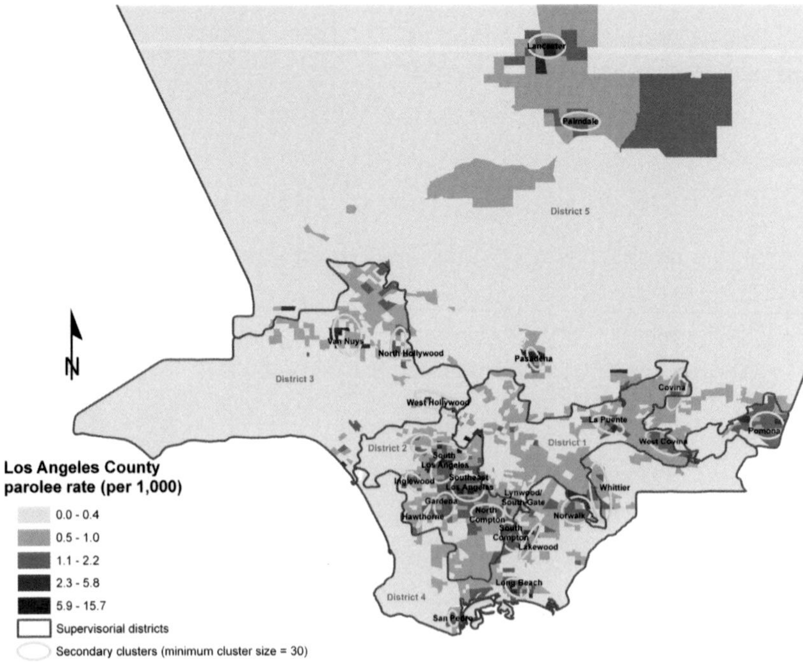

SOURCE: CDCR parolee data, 2005–2006.
RAND *MG1165-2.4*

has three distinct clusters of parolees. The southern half of the county is where the majority of parolees clusters are concentrated, primarily around South and Southeast Los Angeles, Inglewood, Compton, and Long Beach (County Supervisorial Districts 2 and 4) and in the eastern section of the county around Covina, West Covina, and Pomona (County Supervisorial District 1).

Unlike in the other counties, Los Angeles County has 23 distinct clusters of parolees covering a large geographic area but accounting for only 35 percent of the total number of parolees that returned to this county in 2005–2006. This dispersion suggests that providing health care and other services to the reentry population will require a targeted approach that takes into account the different urban and rural areas of this county.

San Diego County. San Diego County is located in southern California, south of Los Angeles and Orange counties, and has a population of 3,095,313 and a density of 737 people per square mile. The county's major cities—San Diego (population 1,256,951), Oceanside (population 165,803), Escondido (population 133,510), Chula Vista (population 212,756), and El Cajon (population 91,756)—make up about 60 percent of the county's total population (U.S. Census Bureau, 2011e). Thirty-two percent of the county's population is Hispanic or Latino, 5.1 percent is African-American, and 10.9 percent is Asian.

Figure 2.5 shows that in San Diego County, there are eight distinct clusters of parolees. Three clusters are located in the northern part of the county around Oceanside, Vista, and Escondido (County Supervisorial District 5 and the northernmost section of County Supervisorial District 3). The remaining clusters are concentrated around Downtown and Southeast San Diego and moving eastward toward Spring Valley and El Cajon (County Supervisorial Districts 4 and 2). In addition, there is a cluster of parolees around Chula Vista (County Supervisorial District 1).

The eight clusters account for nearly half the parolee population returning to San Diego County, with the largest clusters being in the areas of Downtown San Diego and Southeast San Diego. Thus, communities that make up these eight clusters will be especially affected by the health care needs of the reentry population in San Diego County.

Figure 2.5
Relative Concentrations of Parolees in San Diego County

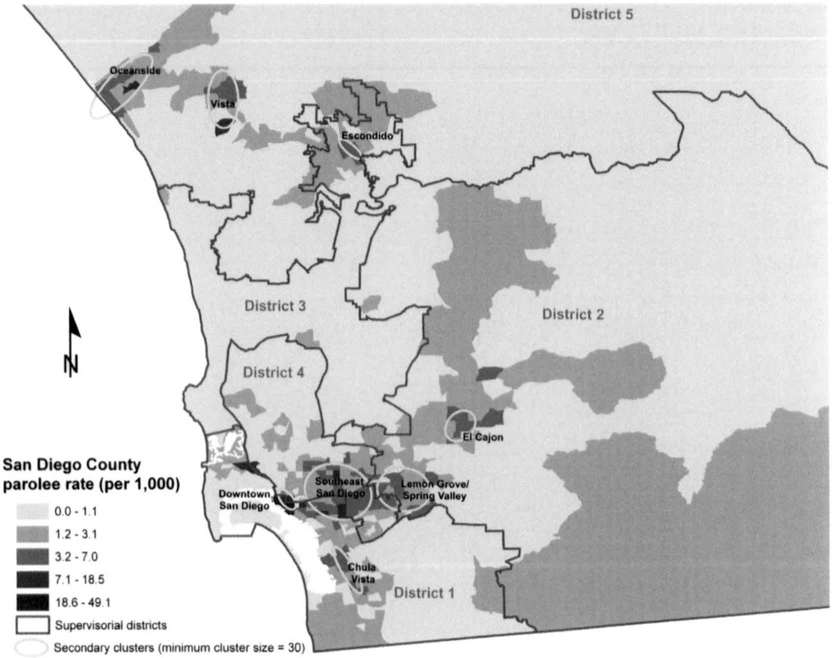

SOURCE: CDCR parolee data, 2005–2006.
RAND *MG1165-2.5*

What Are the Demographic Characteristics of Parolees and of the Socioeconomic Areas in Which They Locate?

To summarize the characteristics of parolees overall and of the four focus counties in particular, we used parolee data from CDCR. Also, we were interested in understanding the demographic and socioeconomic characteristics of the neighborhoods and communities to which parolees tend to return. To do so, we used census data to determine the characteristics (e.g., race/ethnicity of the population, educational attainment, poverty rate, and degree of linguistic isolation of households) of the different census tracts within California and then used cluster analysis to aggregate the census tracts into seven clusters with similar characteristics. We then summarized the percentage of parolees that return to each of the seven cluster areas. We present the results of these analyses below.

Results of Analysis of Demographic Characteristics of California Parolees

Table 2.3 summarizes the demographic characteristics of parolees returning in calendar years 2005–2006, overall and for each of the four focus counties. Overall, nearly 9 out of every 10 parolees were male. Latinos/Hispanics represent about 36 percent of the total California population. Kern and Los Angeles counties' shares of the Latino/Hispanic population in 2007 were 46 percent and 47 percent, respectively; Alameda and San Diego counties' shares of the Latino/Hispanic population were 21 percent and 30 percent, respectively. African-Americans represent about 6.7 percent of the total California population. Alameda and Los Angeles counties have larger shares of the African-American population (13.7 percent and 9.5 percent, respectively); San Diego and Kern counties have 5.5 percent and 6.4 percent, respectively (U.S. Census Bureau, 2011b).

The four counties in our study account for nearly one-third of the parolees released in 2005–2006. Los Angeles County received one out of every five parolees in California, while San Diego received 6 percent and Kern and Alameda each received 3 percent. The racial/ethnic composition of the parolee population varied by county. Overall, 38 percent of parolees were Latino/Hispanic. However, Los Angeles and Kern counties have a larger share of Latino/Hispanic parolees relative to Alameda and San Diego counties. This is consistent with the overall demographics of these counties. Although African-Americans make up only a quarter of the parolee population statewide, they represent three-fifths of parolees in Alameda County and 36 percent of the parolees in Los Angeles County.

With respect to the characteristics of the prison term served, nearly a quarter of parolees in this two-year period were violent offenders, a third were property offenders, and another third were incarcerated for drug-related offenses. There are few differences in the proportion of these offender categories across the four counties, except for Kern County, which appears to have a higher proportion of drug-

Table 2.3
Demographic Characteristics and Term Served of California Parolees, Overall and for Four Counties

Variable	California Parolees (n = 176,618; 100%)	Los Angeles County Parolees (n = 35,710; 20%)	Alameda County Parolees (n = 4,689; 3%)	San Diego County Parolees (n = 9,782; 6%)	Kern County Parolees (n = 5,936: 3%)
Demographic characteristics					
Gender: % male	89	88	90	88	88
Median age	34	34	34	36	33
Ethnicity/race					
% Latino/ Hispanic	38	42	17	29	38
% black	26	36	62	27	19
% white	32	19	17	38	42
% other	4	3	5	6	2
Characteristics of term served					
% violent offenders	23	21	22	21	18
% property offenders	33	35	36	35	27
% drug-related offenders	32	32	33	35	43
Mean # of prior offenses	2	2	2	2	1
Mean # of serious priors	<0.5	<0.5	<0.5	<0.5	<0.5
Mean # of violent priors	<0.5	<0.5	<0.5	<0.5	<0.5
Mean # of offenses	1	1	1	1	2

SOURCE: CDCR parolee data, 2005–2006.

NOTES: The numbers represent the total number of parolees released in fiscal years 2005 and 2006 that comprise the data provided to us by the CDCR. Numbers have been rounded.

related offenders of the total 5,936 parolees returning to this county. The average number of prior offenses was 2.

Results of Analysis of Demographic and Socioeconomic Characteristics of Areas in Which Parolees Locate

To summarize the characteristics of the neighborhoods and communities that parolees tend to return to, we grouped the census tracts into seven categories or clusters that summarize the key demographic and socioeconomic characteristics of these clusters. Table 2.4 summarizes the socioeconomic characteristics of the seven clusters identified. Figure 2.6 shows visually where these clusters are located within California.

Table 2.4
Socioeconomic Characteristics of the Seven Cluster Categories

	Race/Ethnicity (%)				Socioeconomic Characteristics (%)			
Cluster #	White	Black	Latino/ Hispanic	Asian	Linguistically Isolated Households[a]	No High School Diploma[b]	Unemployment Rate[c]	Household Poverty Rate[d]
1	39	6	18	33	11	15	3	8
2	32	5	54	6	15	33	5	11
3	64	3	25	4	33	22	5	12
4	72	4	13	7	5	10	3	6
5	16	13	64	5	33	50	7	25
6	25	9	38	24	35	34	5	18
7	77	2	13	4	18	12	3	8

[a] The Census Bureau defined linguistically isolated households as ones in which no one 14 years old and over speaks only English or speaks a non-English language and speaks English "very well."

[b] No high school diploma is measured as the percentage of adults 25 years or older without a high school diploma.

[c] Unemployment rate is calculated for those 16 years or older and are in the labor force.

[d] Household poverty rate is the percentage of households below the FPL.

NOTE: Numbers have been rounded.

Figure 2.6
Summary of Statewide Socioeconomic Clusters of Census Tracts

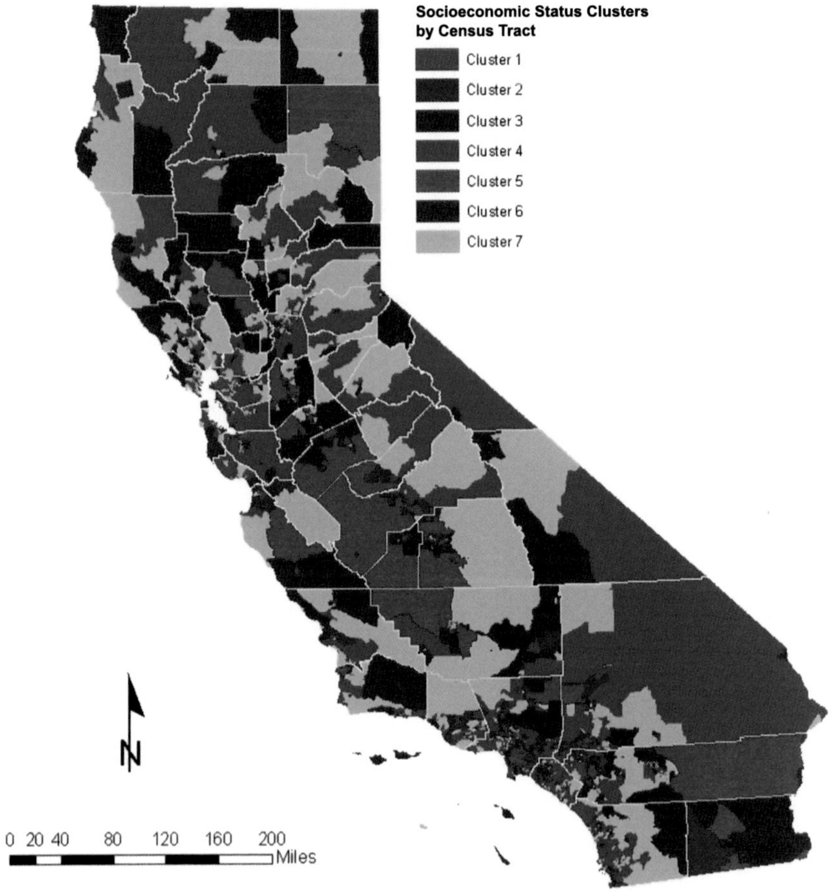

RAND *MG1165-2.6*

Our analyses showed that African-American and Latino parolees, in particular, tend to return to disadvantaged neighborhoods or communities, as defined by high poverty rates, high unemployment rates, and low educational attainment. For example, the three most common clusters to which parolees returned are Clusters 4, 5, and 6. Overall, 43 percent of parolees returned to Cluster 5 areas (shown in red in the map in Figure 2.6 and highlighted in Table 2.4). About half of African-American and Latino parolees returned to Cluster 5 areas, whereas only a little more than a quarter of white parolees returned to Cluster 5 areas. Cluster 5 areas are those of greatest disadvantage, as measured by high poverty rates, high unemployment rates, and low educational attainment. In Cluster 5 areas, the median household poverty rate is 25 percent, the median unemployment rate is 7 percent, and the percentage of adults age 25 years or older without a high school diploma is 50 percent. In terms of Cluster 5's ethnic composition, 64 percent of the population is Hispanic or Latino and 13 percent is African-American or black.

In comparison, white parolees were least likely to return to disadvantaged neighborhoods or communities. Overall, 15 percent of parolees returned to Cluster 4 areas (shown in blue in the map and highlighted in Table 2.4). More white parolees (23 percent) than African-American parolees (11 percent) and Latino parolees (10 percent) returned to Cluster 4 areas. Cluster 4 areas fare better on all socioeconomic indicators (see Table 2.4). The population of Cluster 4 areas tended to be predominantly white (72 percent).

What Does the Health Care Safety Net Look Like for Parolees in Four Focus Counties?

To examine the four counties' health care safety nets and their ability to meet the health care needs of the reentry population, we first must define what constitutes the safety net for the reentry population. We present our conceptual framework, which is the basis for identifying the different components of the health care, mental health, and substance abuse treatment safety nets for parolees. We then summarize our findings about the characteristics of health care safety nets in the four focus counties and the potential access of the reentry population to health care safety-net services in each of these counties.

Conceptual Framework

To conceptualize the health care safety net for the reentry population, we drew on two prior frameworks, both of which extend the Andersen behavioral model of access to care. The Andersen model (Andersen, 1968; Andersen and Newman, 1973) emphasizes the importance of predisposing factors (demographics, social structure, health beliefs), enabling factors (personal, family, and community resources), and illness-level or need factors. The first extension, by Davidson et al. (2004), builds on the Andersen framework to examine the effects of safety-net and other community-level factors on access to care and outcomes, particularly for low-income populations. The second extension, by Gelberg, Andersen, and Leake (2000), includes factors in the predisposing, enabling, and need categories that are particularly important to consider when studying access for vulnerable populations, such as the homeless. We modified these frameworks to include predisposing and enabling factors and community characteristics important to the reentry population and access outcomes at the individual level (see Figure 2.7).

Our conceptual framework shows three needs under individual characteristics: predisposing needs, health care needs, and enabling needs. Under "predisposing needs," we include those that commonly affect individuals' access to and use of health services, such as demographics (age, gender, race/ethnicity), social factors (education, employment), and health beliefs (those about disease and health services), as well as factors that are particularly relevant to the reentry population, such as incarceration history, prison health care experiences, and length of time in the community. Under "health care needs," we include those health conditions that disproportionately affect the reentry population (infectious diseases, such as HIV, TB, hepatitis B and C; mental illness; substance abuse; and chronic health conditions, such as hypertension and diabetes). Under "enabling needs," we include personal/family resources, such as income, health insurance, and social support. Community characteristics draw on the Davidson et al. (2004) framework and elaborate on the safety-net characteristics and other community-level factors that affect the availability and accessibility of health services for the reentry population.

Importantly, we defined the safety net for the reentry population as health resources that aim to provide services to the uninsured or medically indigent adults. California's safety net includes county facilities (hospitals, clinics, and public health centers), free and com-

Figure 2.7
Conceptual Framework for Evaluating the Health Care Safety Net for the Reentry Population

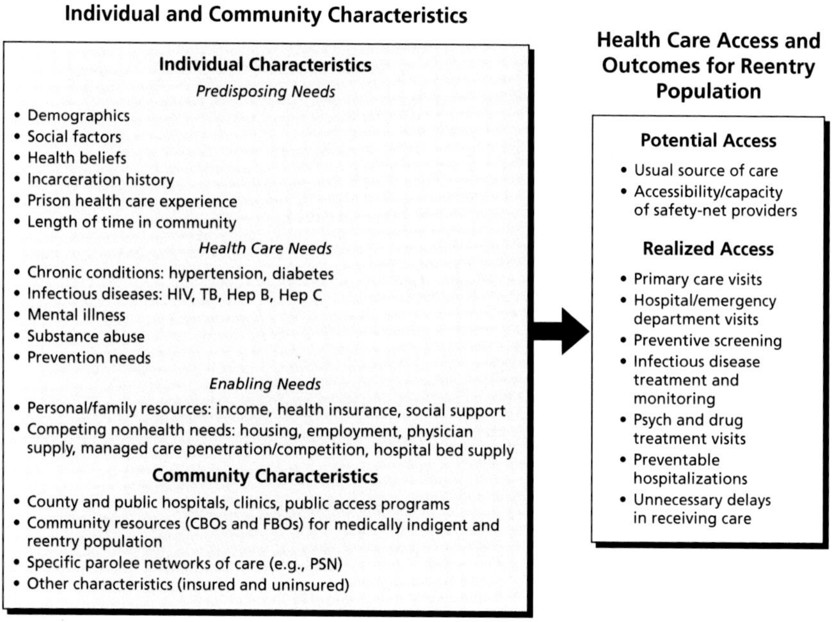

NOTE: CBO = community-based organization. FBO = faith-based organization. PSN = Parolee Services Network.
RAND *MG1165-2.7*

munity clinics, some private hospitals, physicians who see large numbers of uninsured patients, and some health plans that have designated innovative coverage plans for the uninsured (Tuttle and Wulsin, 2008). County health care resources can include government and public hospitals, county primary care clinics, public health centers, and county mental health and substance abuse treatment providers. In addition, counties may contract with private nonprofit and for-profit clinics and hospitals to provide services to the safety-net population. Finally, in the area of mental health and substance abuse treatment, there are specific and small networks targeted to the parolee population. For example, in certain counties, the Parolee Services Network (PSN) provides substance abuse services funded by the state that target a relatively small number of parolees.

For the most part, parolees must share these limited safety-net resources with other vulnerable populations, such as the uninsured, Medicaid recipients, the homeless, and undocumented immigrants. Thus, the safety-net population is an important community characteristic to measure because of competition for scarce resources (Pauly and Pagan, 2007).

Together, individual and community characteristics ultimately affect the health care access of the reentry population, including (1) *potential* access (usual source of care, accessibility/capacity of safety-net providers) and (2) *realized* access, or health service utilization (doctor and clinic visits and preventive screening, plus areas of utilization that are particularly relevant for the reentry population, such as emergency department visits and mental health and drug treatment services), and access outcomes, such as preventable hospitalizations or unnecessary delays in receiving care.

In this study, we defined the potential safety net for parolees in terms of health care, mental health care, and substance abuse treatment services and described how it varies across the four counties. In addition, we focused specifically on parolees' potential access to safety-net services, taking into account the capacity of safety-net providers and the potential demands placed on these facilities from other sources. Our analyses focused on potential access versus measuring realized access per se (in terms of whether parolees take advantage of this access or whether they have better outcomes as a result which is outside the scope of this study).

Analysis of Geographic Distribution of Health Care Facilities in Los Angeles County

We examined the geographic distribution of health care facilities in each of the four counties using GIS to map the distribution of facilities relative to the concentration of parolees in each county. We present the results for Los Angeles County to illustrate the geographic variation in the location of safety-net facilities vis-à-vis the concentration of parolees. We conducted similar analyses for the other three counties as well, although they are not reported here. The detailed maps and results for all four counties can be found in Davis et al. 2009. See Appendix A for a summary of the methodology.

Los Angeles County. In presenting the results for Los Angeles County, we used a different map than the one shown earlier in Figure 2.4, which covered the entire county; here, we focus on the southern half of the county, where the majority of parolees are located.

Health Care Safety Net. For the health care safety net of Los Angeles County, we focused on both primary care clinics and general acute care hospitals. In terms of the primary care clinics, we included those contracted to provide care to the Medically Indigent Services Program (MISP clinics), county primary care and comprehensive health services/multiservice ambulatory care clinics (CHC/MACC), and public/private partnership (PPP) community clinics contracted by the county to provide services to the medically indigent population. The map in Figure 2.8 shows the parolee concentrations and then overlays the hospitals and clinics to which they go. The map also shows the county supervisorial district boundaries.

The map shows that in certain county supervisorial districts with high concentrations of parolees (shown in the darkest shade of blue) there are relatively sparse hospital and clinic resources. The most striking gaps in coverage are in County Supervisorial District 2, which covers the area called South Los Angeles and includes the cities of Inglewood, Hawthorne, Gardena, Compton, Lawndale, and Carson. County Supervisorial District 2 includes Martin Luther King/Charles R. Drew Medical Hospital, which currently functions as a multiservice ambulatory care center. The district also includes Harbor/University of California, Los Angeles (UCLA), Medical Center in Torrance, which is one of the few hospitals in the county designated to serve the medically indigent.

In terms of the primary care clinics, those that serve the medically indigent (shown as red dots on the map) tend to be located in areas with some of the highest concentration of parolees (shown as darker shades of blue on the map). Yet in some areas, particularly County Supervisorial District 2, the distribution of primary care clinics is relatively sparse.

Figure 2.8
Health Care Safety Net in Los Angeles County Relative to Parolee Concentrations

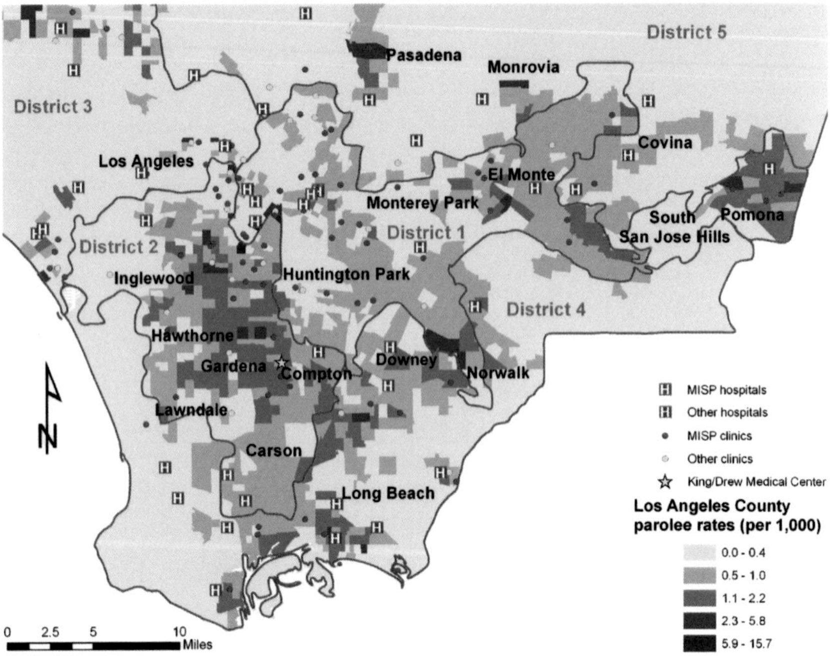

RAND *MG1165-2.8*

Mental Health Care and Substance Abuse Treatment Safety Nets. For the mental health care safety net of Los Angeles County, we mapped the location of mental health providers listed in the Substance Abuse and Mental Health Services Administration (SAMSHA) database and the distribution of mental health providers receiving funding under California's Mental Health Services Act (MHSA) (Figure 2.9).[4] We also mapped the location of the 16 parole offices in Los Angeles County. Most of these offices have associated with them parole outpatient clinics (POCs), which provide limited mental health services to the parolee population, including medication management and some individual or group therapy. There are 12 POCs in Los Angeles County.

[4] The MHSA was passed in November 2004 and is also known as Proposition 63.

The POCs (shown as yellow stars in the map) tend to be located near large concentration of parolees; however, they are relatively few in number, suggesting that many parolees who are eligible for treatment from these clinics must travel long distances to access these basic mental health services.

The community mental health providers (shown as yellow circles) tend to be located more broadly and in a number of areas where there are relatively large concentrations of parolees, although there are some gaps in coverage in County Supervisorial District 2 (South Los Angeles) and County Supervisorial District 3 (San Fernando Valley).

We also mapped the distribution of the mental health clinics that are MHSA providers (show as red circles on the map in Figure 2.9) to illustrate how these clinics generally seem to be near large concentrations of parolees and so could help ensure adequate geographic coverage of mental health services for the reentry population. However, parolees are exempt from receiving services funded under the MHSA.

For the substance abuse safety net, we focused on the alcohol and drug treatment providers in the county listed in the SAMSHA database as well as those designated as Proposition 36 contract providers.[5] The Proposition 36 providers are shown as red dots in Figure 2.10, and the other treatment providers are shown as yellow dots (labeled substance abuse providers). In addition, we indicate on the map which facilities represent community assessment service centers (CASCs), shown as yellow stars,[6] which are responsible for assessing treatment needs and triaging individuals to Proposition 36 services.

---

[5] Parolees are eligible to participate in the Substance Abuse and Crime Prevention Act (also known as Proposition 36), which was passed in 2001. The act increased state funding for drug treatment and allowed eligible nonviolent drug offenders to be diverted to drug treatment instead of receiving a traditional sentence. If individuals commit a violation while on parole that meets the criterion for Proposition 36, they are technically eligible to participate in this program in lieu of incarceration (Gardiner, 2008). Proposition 36 allows for dismissal of charges upon successful completion of treatment. In FY 2005–2006, 1,684 parolees participated in Proposition 36 programs in Los Angeles County (Davis et al., 2009).

[6] CASCs provide screening, comprehensive assessment, and referral services for individuals seeking assistance for their alcohol and other drug problems.

Figure 2.9
Mental Health Care Safety Net in Los Angeles County

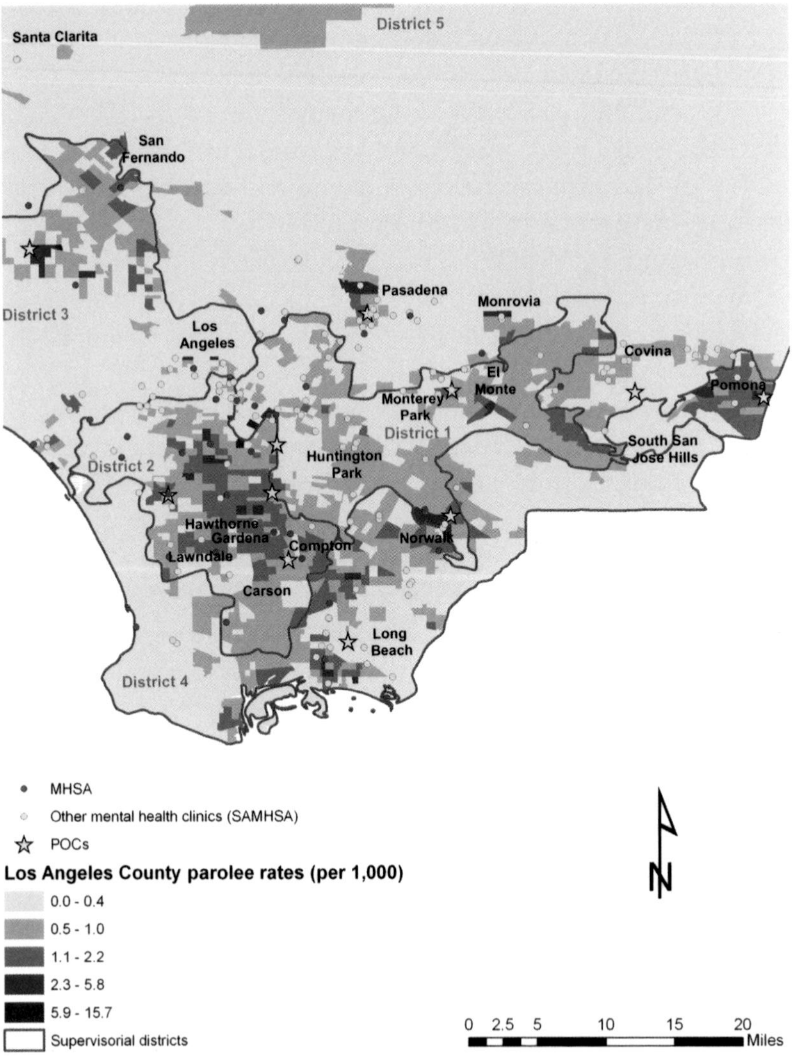

RAND *MG1165-2.9*

Overall, as shown in Figure 2.10, the distribution of Proposition 36 and other treatment providers seems to be generally near the majority of the concentrations of parolees. However, we see sparser coverage in County Supervisorial District 2 (South Bay/Carson) and County Supervisorial District 4 (North Long Beach/Huntington Park). Although the CASCs focus primarily on the Proposition 36 population, these assessment centers appear to be located relatively near concentrations of parolees throughout the county and so potentially could play an important role in linking them to treatment services.[7]

As noted earlier, for substance abuse treatment there are smaller networks specific to the parolee population. We did not show the eight

Figure 2.10
Substance Abuse Treatment Safety Net in Los Angeles County

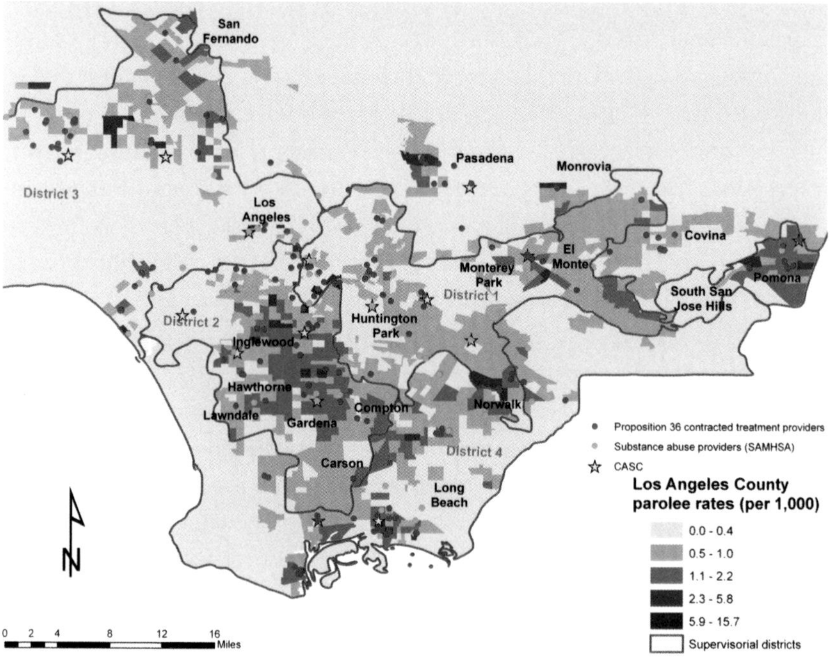

RAND *MG1165-2.10*

---

[7] There are a total of 19 CASCs in Los Angeles County.

PSN substance abuse treatment providers in Los Angeles County on the map, for several reasons. The funding for these providers was recently reduced as part of correctional budget cuts for rehabilitative services. Further, the PSN providers have generally limited treatment capacity (e.g., in fiscal year 2004 they represented approximately 36 residential beds, 72 nonresidential slots, and 12 Sober Living Environment beds). The limited number and capacity of these facilities suggests that most parolees in need of alcohol and drug treatment services instead must rely primarily on Proposition 36 and other substance abuse treatment resources in the county.

Analysis of Accessibility of Reentry Population to Health Care Safety-Net Facilities in Four Counties

Analyzing the geographic distribution of facilities represents an important step in understanding the relationship between the concentration of parolees within counties and proximity to different safety-net facilities; however, it provides a somewhat limited perspective in that it does not take into account the capacity of safety-net facilities, the underlying demand for services, nor the distance ex-prisoners would have to travel to access health care services. To provide a richer understanding of the interaction between the health care needs of ex-prisoners and the safety nets in the individual counties, we generated quantitative measures of accessibility, which represent measures of potential access. The term *accessibility* refers to the relative ease by which locations of activities, such as work, shopping, and seeking health care, can be reached from a given location (BTS, 1997). Because we did not have access to data on realized or actual access to care and utilization of health care services by parolees in California, we settled for a measure of accessibility from a single point in an area—in this case, census tracts.

Our accessibility measures provide useful summaries of the availability of health care safety-net resources in each of the four counties and allow us to examine how that availability varies by type of facility and by race/ethnicity. Our measures take into consideration the following factors: (1) the supply of safety-net facilities and how they are geographically distributed, (2) potential demands placed on the safety net by those who may not have the ability to pay for services, (3) the capacity of safety-net facilities, and (4) the distance ex-prisoners would have to travel to access care at a given facility. We adopted Allard's (2004) notion of potential demand as being the total population living in households with incomes below the FPL. In addition, we used total full-time equivalents (FTEs) as our measure of capacity for these facilities (when available). To measure travel distance, we used ten-minute drive time to each facility location. To improve our estimate of the approximate location of the majority of the resident population, we used a population-weighted geographic center point, or centroid.

To summarize our analytic results, we classified the resulting accessibility scores for each census tract into four quartiles, ranging from lowest levels of accessibility to highest levels of accessibility. Results presented below focus on the findings for the two lowest-quartile categories. See Appendix A for a summary of our methodology. Davis et al. (2009) provides more detailed information on how the accessibility measures were created.

Accessibility to Hospital and Primary Care Clinics Across the Four Counties. Parolees' potential access to health care facilities varies across counties and by facility type and race/ethnicity. Table 2.5 summarizes the results for hospitals and clinics by county.

In terms of potential access to general acute care hospitals, a larger share of parolees in Alameda County (63 percent) resided in areas with low levels of accessibility to hospitals than parolees in the other counties. In all three of the large urban counties (Alameda, Los Angeles, and San Diego), more than half of parolees resided in areas with the low levels of accessibility to hospitals. The higher levels of access for parolees in Kern County reflect the fact that most parolees reside in the city of Bakersfield, which alone has four general acute care hospitals.

With respect to clinics, more parolees in Los Angeles County (48 percent) tended to reside in areas with low levels of accessibility than was the case for parolees in the other three counties (Table 2.5). In each of the counties, a higher percentage of parolees resided in areas with low levels of accessibility to hospitals, as compared with the clinic results.

Accessibility to health care resources also varied by parolees' race/ethnicity (Table 2.6). In terms of accessibility to hospitals in Los Ange-

Table 2.5
Summary of Accessibility Results for Hospitals and Clinics, by County

Type of Facility	Percentage of Parolees Who Fell into the Two Lowest Accessibility Quartiles
Hospitals	
Alameda County	63
Kern County	37
Los Angeles County	53
San Diego County	54
Clinics	
Alameda County	38
Kern County	30
Los Angeles County[a]	48
San Diego County	27

[a] In Los Angeles County, the comparison represents accessibility to public/private partnership clinics and other primary care clinics. It differs from the other three counties whose measure of accessibility includes both medically indigent service program providers and other primary care clinics in a county.

NOTE: Numbers in the table have been rounded.

les County, more African-American parolees resided in areas with low levels of accessibility than Latino or white parolees. By comparison, Alameda County had a similar pattern, but in Kern and San Diego counties, more Latino parolees resided in areas with low levels of accessibility to hospitals than white and African-American parolees.

With respect to accessibility to primary care clinics by race/ethnicity, the story is more nuanced. In three counties, less than a quarter of African-American parolees resided in areas with low levels of accessibility to clinics. The exception was Los Angeles County, where 44 percent of African-American parolees resided in these areas. In comparison, for Latino parolees in Alameda and Los Angeles counties, the share residing in areas with low levels of accessibility to clinics was nearly 50 percent. This is significantly higher than the roughly 20 percent of Latino parolees residing in these areas in Kern and San Diego counties.

Table 2.6
Summary of Accessibility Results for Hospitals and Clinics, by County and Race/Ethnicity

	Percentage of Parolees by Race/Ethnicity Who Fell into the Two Lowest Accessibility Quartiles		
Type of Facility	**African-American**	**Latino**	**White**
Hospitals			
Alameda County	73	47	48
Kern County	31	40	37
Los Angeles County	60	51	47
San Diego County	51	59	53
Clinics			
Alameda County	24	48	59
Kern County	24	25	37
Los Angeles County[a]	44	47	57
San Diego County	21	20	36

[a] In Los Angeles County, the comparison represents accessibility to public/private partnership clinics and other primary care clinics. It differs from the other three counties whose measure of accessibility includes both medically indigent service program providers as well as other primary care clinics in a county.

NOTE: Numbers in the table have been rounded.

Accessibility to Mental Health and Substance Abuse Treatment Facilities Across the Four Counties. Similar to the results for hospitals and clinics, accessibility of parolees to mental health and substance abuse providers varied by county (Table 2.7). A larger share of parolees in Alameda and Los Angeles counties resided in areas with low levels of accessibility to mental health facilities than we see in Kern and San Diego counties.

In terms of accessibility to alcohol and drug treatment providers, we see a similar pattern. Approximately 40 percent of parolees in Alameda and Los Angeles counties resided in areas with low levels of accessibility to alcohol and drug treatment providers, compared with only about a third of parolees in Kern and San Diego counties (Table 2.7).

Table 2.7
Summary of Accessibility Results for Mental Health and Alcohol and Drug Treatment Providers, by County

Type of Treatment	Percentage of Parolees Who Fall into the Two Lowest Accessibility Quartiles
Mental Health Providers	
Alameda County	53
Kern County	27
Los Angeles County	51
San Diego County	38
Alcohol and Drug Treatment Providers	
Alameda County	42
Kern County	28
Los Angeles County	44
San Diego County	30

NOTE: Numbers in the table have been rounded.

Accessibility to mental health and alcohol and drug treatment providers also varied by race/ethnicity (Table 2.8). For example, in Kern and San Diego counties, between 15 and 22 percent of African-American parolees resided in areas with low levels of accessibility to alcohol and drug treatment resources, compared with 44 and 47 percent of African-American parolees in Alameda and Los Angeles counties, respectively. In terms of accessibility to mental health providers, more than half of African-American and Latino parolees in Alameda and Los Angeles counties resided in areas with low levels of accessibility. In comparison, a much lower percentage of African-American and Latino parolees in Kern and San Diego counties resided in areas with low levels of accessibility to mental health providers.

We found no difference in accessibility by race/ethnicity in San Diego County.

Table 2.8
Summary of Mental Health and Alcohol and Drug Treatment Accessibility Results by County and Race/Ethnicity

Type of Provider/ County	Percentage of Parolees by Race/ Ethnicity Who Fell into the Two Lowest Accessibility Quartiles		
	African-American	Latino	White
Mental Health Providers			
Alameda County	57	52	38
Kern County	20	30	26
Los Angeles County	57	49	47
San Diego County	38	36	38
Alcohol and Drug Treatment Providers			
Alameda County	44	38	39
Kern County	15	32	30
Los Angeles County	47	45	37
San Diego County	22	36	30

NOTE: Numbers in the table have been rounded.

Discussion

It is well known that the prison population tends to be sicker on average than the general population. Our analysis of the BJS survey's self-reported data for California inmates provides a rich understanding of the range of physical health, mental health, and substance abuse problems that this population brings upon return to local communities. We found that returning prisoners bear a high burden of chronic diseases, such as asthma, hypertension, and diabetes, as well as infectious diseases, such as hepatitis and tuberculosis—all conditions that require regular access to health care services for effective management. In addition, the burden of mental illness and drug abuse or dependence is especially high in this population, underscoring the importance of access to mental health and alcohol and drug treatment services and the importance of continuity of care for this population. But the likelihood of ex-prisoners receiving adequate health care once they are released is poor given the high rates of uninsurance among this population and other barriers to accessing care.

A number of trends complicate the successful reentry of parolees into communities. Our analysis of the geographic distribution and concentration of parolees across California and in the four focus counties showed that reentry particularly impacts 11 counties statewide and that, within counties, parolees tend to cluster in certain communities and neighborhoods. Such clustering has implications for linking to and providing health care services to this population and for considering how to effectively target reentry resources. As illustrated by Los Angeles County, which has a combination of both urban and more sparsely populated areas, there is a need to tailor outreach and service delivery strategies to areas where the reentry population is more concentrated versus areas where it tends to be more dispersed.

The fact that African-American and Latino parolees, in particular, tend to return to disadvantaged neighborhoods and communities—ones characterized by high poverty and unemployment rates—suggests that reentry will be especially challenging for these groups. Further, our analysis of the geographic distribution of safety-net resources illustrated that health care resources in these communities tend to be scarce.

Important study contributions are formally defining what the health care safety net is for the reentry population and developing measures to assess the ability of the safety net to meet ex-prisoners' needs. Across and within counties, the geographic distribution of safety-net facilities varied, and we identified geographic gaps in the location of health care facilities, including hospitals, clinics, mental health clinics, and alcohol and drug treatment providers vis-à-vis the concentration of parolees. Taking into account differences in capacity, the underlying demand for safety-net services, and travel distance, our analyses of accessibility (i.e., analysis of potential access) showed that parolees' access to health care safety-net facilities varies by facility type, by geographic area, and by race/ethnicity. As policymakers consider how to ensure access to services for the reentry population in California, they will need to take into account this variation in counties' safety nets.

Our analysis of the health care safety net presented here was conducted in 2009, just prior to the deep cuts made in rehabilitative programming for prisoners and in safety-net services within California. For example, the substance abuse network specific to parolees, the PSN, has had its funding reduced. CDCR has drastically cut its funding for community-based alcohol and drug treatment programs for ex-prisoners. And although Proposition 36 contracted treatment providers appear to be a viable source of care for the reentry population in each of the focus counties, these providers are no longer being funded by local counties. The impacts of these various changes are discussed further in subsequent chapters.

CHAPTER THREE

Understanding the Challenges of Reentry: Ex-Prisoner Focus Group Results

Introduction

To understand the health care needs of those released from California state prisons, their experiences in seeking care, and the role health plays in their efforts to reintegrate back into the community and reunite with their families, it is important to hear directly from those who have been incarcerated about their experiences in returning back to local communities. We also wanted to understand, from ex-prisoners' perspective, what factors facilitated or hindered their ability to meet their health care needs and other needs, their perceptions about access to care and quality of care, and their suggestions about how California can improve the provision of services to the reentry population.

In this chapter, our focus is on learning about the individual experiences of those who have gone through this process and are now focusing on rebuilding their lives out in the community.

Approach

We conducted six focus groups in three of the largest counties in our study: Los Angeles, Alameda, and San Diego.[1] These discussions were

1 Although our analysis of the capacity of the health care system included a rural county, Kern County, we elected to focus on the three largest urban counties in our study for these

intended to be exploratory in nature and to help suggest areas for further exploration.

To select the focus group participants, we considered several different sampling options. One option would have been to screen for and recruit individuals with specific health problems, either as they were about to leave prison or when they were out in the community (e.g., at parole offices or with community organizations). However, doing so would have been prohibitively expensive, because it would have required an extensive screening process to identify a sample of individuals with specific chronic health problems or infectious diseases. In addition, our interest was in understanding how health impacts the experience of prisoner reentry in general. We also knew that a high percentage of individuals would likely have a history of substance abuse and/or mental health problems. Therefore, given resource constraints and our overall study focus, we opted not to screen for specific health conditions.

To recruit the focus group participants, we worked with local organizations in each of the counties. Two were health care providers, and the other four were nonprofit organizations that provide a range of services to the reentry population, including employment training, housing assistance, mentoring, case management, and other activities to facilitate linkages with health care and social services. Two of the organizations were faith-based. These organizations were located in neighborhoods and communities that our analysis indicated had relatively high numbers of parolees. These organizations helped us with recruitment and also served as the location for the focus group discussions. Although these organizations provided space to conduct the focus groups, none of the organizations' staff members were allowed to observe or participate in the discussion (with one exception, when an individual came in midway through the focus group discussion).

We developed a recruitment flyer that these organizations helped to distribute. The recruitment flyer was distributed broadly. In one county, a health care provider also distributed the recruitment flyer to a

---

discussions since a larger share of ex-prisoners return to these counties, and thus the demand for safety-net services will be higher in these counties.

local parole office. In some instances, individuals who signed up for the focus groups also recruited their friends upon learning about the study.

In each site, we conducted two focus groups. The focus group discussions were co-led by RAND research team members and outside consultants chosen because of their experience with, and expertise in, facilitating focus group discussions with the formerly incarcerated. In addition, a project team member served as a notetaker. Focus group participants were provided an incentive payment at the end of the discussion to thank them for their participation. The focus group participants were promised confidentiality and were encouraged to use only their first names or nicknames. As part of the oral consent form, we asked participants for their permission to audio-record the discussion and provided the option of not doing so; none of the participants refused. The research team did not have access to any prior information about the participants. The focus group discussions were audio-recorded and transcribed for use only by the research team for analytic purposes.

We created a focus group protocol (see Appendix B) to be used as a guide for the discussions, which covered the following topics: participants' health care needs while incarcerated and experience in receiving care while in prison, experiences with prerelease planning, health care needs upon release and experience in accessing services, barriers and facilitators to receiving needed services while in prison and out in the community, views about the quality of care received, and suggestions for how to improve the prerelease planning process and access to services upon release. Participants were asked to also briefly state how long they had been out of prison (or jail), the last time they had been incarcerated, and whether they had been in prison previously.

A total of 39 ex-prisoners participated in the 90-minute focus group discussions. All participants were male. We did not specifically ask about race/ethnicity or age, but the participants appeared to be predominantly Latino/Hispanic or African-American. The focus group participants appeared to mostly range in age from their early 20s to 50s, with several being in their 70s. In terms of length of time these individuals had been out in the community, about two-thirds had been out less than one year, with the range being a few days to 30 years.[2] In terms of their history of incarceration, only one individual stated that this was his first time in prison. For the other focus group participants who offered this information, the typical answer was 2–3 prior incarcerations, with the maximum being seven times. The length of stay of their most recent incarceration ranged from less than one year to 36 years. We did not ask participants to report the reason for their incarceration, although many of the participants alluded to substance abuse as being the cause of the problems that led to them being incarcerated or that resulted in a parole violation. In one case, an individual had vandalized a parole office to get sent back into prison. One individual reported that his last incarceration was the result of having an unregistered firearm.

To analyze the focus group data, two researchers each reviewed the transcripts to identify general themes. We then compared our individual reviews and reached agreement on the key themes that emerged. We used a cutting-and-sorting technique to identify specific themes and to identify individual quotes or expressions that summarized the key discussion points.

The experiences and views of this sample of ex-offenders can by no means be generalized to the broader population of men who have been incarcerated in California state prisons and who have returned to local communities. Nonetheless, the themes and stories we heard are consistent with other findings from the literature. To provide the reader with an idea of how these findings relate to the broader literature in this field, we note this in the discussion section. Further, the issues these participants raised are similar to concerns that the providers also expressed in Chapter Four.

---

[2] Although we had requested that focus group participants be recently released from prison, in one instance, we learned that one participant had last been incarcerated in prison 30 years ago.

Key Findings from the Focus Groups

How Ex-Prisoners Think About Their Health Care Needs

Physical health care versus mental health and substance abuse treatment needs were not always linked in focus group participants' minds. They tended to think of these areas as distinct. This was reflected in how focus group participants answered questions related to whether they had health problems upon release, whether health impacted their ability to find employment or housing, and how health ranked in importance relative to other basic needs, such as employment and housing.

For example, *focus group participants typically ranked health lower than economic considerations,* such as housing and employment, which were described as the most important challenges they faced. *Yet, participants identified "getting sober" and finding regular care and support for mental health as critical.* Also, when asked whether they had any health problems, participants would often answer that they did not but then go on to talk about substance abuse problems.

Mental health and substance abuse treatment needs, and oral health needs were frequently mentioned. The most common physical health concerns reported were oral health problems. Participants reported problems with toothaches and loose teeth and experiences with having tooth extractions. In addition, participants mentioned having cancer, diabetes, hypertension, prostrate problems, and infectious diseases, such as HIV/AIDS, hepatitis, and STDs. Focus group participants also commonly conjectured that they may have been exposed to tuberculosis while in prison. Few had serious physical health problems, and so health care was not reported as being a critical challenge upon being released. "With me, coming home for the health care issue would be very low priority, because I get a cold once a year. I've never been shot, stabbed, had a broke bone, anything. The worst thing I had was my diverticulitis in about 45 years of living."

In the discussion, *a number of participants mentioned how low or depressed they felt at times during their incarceration* or about being away from their families. This finding is consistent with the survey results reported in our earlier report (Davis et al., 2009), where 55 percent of state prisoners reported a history or recent symptoms of mental illness;

of those with recent symptoms of mental illness, 20 percent reported symptoms of major depression. Only a few focus group participants talked specifically about mental health problems or concerns. For example, one individual who was receiving care from a local community clinic described how his overall health was and how mental health issues were the primary problem he now faced:

> [B]asically when there's a lot of people, I get nervous and I sweat, probably because of the situation me being in the jail a lot.
>
> *[When asked how he would rate his overall health now:]* I say it's about a 4 now, because as far as my health is good, but as far as my mental part, I say it's out of whack. Because if I've got to have these dreams every day and sit around people and sweat and trip, I believe I still have a problem.
>
> Now they're sending me to a psych. They gave me a date to go see him. But . . . as far as my health, my health is good. I'm strong, healthy, no high blood pressure, none of that. When I was in the penitentiary, I had high blood pressure, high cholesterol. So when I got out, I started eating right, started living right. But now, it's the mental thing.

Many participants talked about their struggles with substance abuse. In a number of cases, substance abuse problems were the underlying factor that led to them going to prison. Substance abuse problems often continued upon release and resulted in violations of their parole or new crimes that led to their being returned to prison.

> As far as substance abuse, I attend AA [Alcoholics Anonymous] and NA [Narcotics Anonymous] programs. That really helps me and that's real accessible as far as me getting to them. But as far as health . . . I have a problem. I'm a crack addict and alcoholic and I know I need help. And these programs, they do help me as long as I keep doing the things. . . .

> For me, I don't think I really cared about health because I was into drugs, alcohol, partying for the short time I was out. I've only been out like six years in like 25 years. . . . But I think that those six years that I was out, I don't think I really cared about my health. And now here I am. I think the most important thing for me would, yeah, my health . . . but I think the most important thing for me would be if I don't have a roof and trying to get a job, and at the same time while I'm trying to do that I've got to look out for my health now.

In general, the focus group participants who were older and who had been incarcerated multiple times were the group most interested in changing and addressing their substance abuse problems or other problems that may put them at risk for returning to prison (i.e., recidivating).

> Recovery, to me, is the foundation of me staying out of prison, it's where I'll start. I'd rather get deeply rooted in recovery, and I'm quite sure and it's been proven that it will keep me from drifting off into that situation that got me in prison [in the first place].

> The first time I got out of prison, I had been in there for probably four years and nine months straight, and while I was in there, I would go to a few [AA or NA] meetings, because I knew I had a little bit of information about recovery before I went in and it was because of the situation, I was under the influence of drugs and that I understood that was the reason that I committed the crime. So I accepted that in prison and I decided that on my own, I was going to stop and I'd had enough of it or whatever and it was just that there was no foundation. Everything was good while I was in prison—I was just done, that's what I told myself. I was done with that life, period.

> I got out, and things changed—it's like, I really didn't deal with the disease itself while I was in there, and that led me going back. I stayed out of prison six years, but I was just on the abstinence for probably about three of those years . . . . [I] gradually went back [to using drugs] until eventually I went back to prison again because of a drug-related issue. But this time was different, this time I had a lot more experience and

> I knew what I wanted this time. I had a couple of birthdays in there and you get a little bit more seasoned . . . so when I got out I knew what I immediately had to do, because I know it will affect me in my mind and just decide to go out and mess myself up. So I had to figure out where that came from, that's why I had to really jump into the 12 steps this time. I didn't waste no time getting deeply rooted in it. . . .

Views About Access to Substance Abuse Treatment Programs in Prison

Substance abuse treatment services in prison are provided through in-prison substance abuse programs (SAPs) that are overseen by CDCR's Division of Addiction and Recovery Services (DARS).[3] CDCR DARS contracts with community-based alcohol and drug treatment organizations[4] to provide most of the treatment services for inmates and for parolee offender participants. These organizations provide services to both men and women, to inmates in conservation camps, and to inmates in all four institutional security levels (I–IV) (CDCR Division of Addiction and Recovery Services, *Annual Report*, 2009, p. 30). Also, volunteers and inmates may run AA and NA meetings in the prison setting.

There are also community-based treatment programs.[5] These alcohol and drug programs provide continuing care services through substance abuse services coordination agencies (SASCAs). There are four

---

[3] In fiscal year 2007–2008, 21,684 inmates received in-prison substance abuse treatment services, and 10,946 parolees participated in community-based treatment services funded by CDCR. In fiscal year 2007–2008, 41.2 percent of in-prison SAP completions had as their governing offense property crimes, 37.0 percent had drug-related crimes, 12.4 percent had crimes against persons, and 9.4 percent had other crimes (CDCR Division of Addiction and Recovery Services, *Annual Report*, 2009).

[4] These providers include the Amity Foundation, Center Point, Community Education Centers, Inc., Mental Health Systems, Phoenix House, Walden House, West Care, and the Contra Costa County and Orange County Offices of Education.

[5] These community-based treatment programs include Community-Based Substance Abuse Programs, the Female Offender Treatment and Employment Program (FOTEP), the In-Custody Drug Treatment Program (ICDTP), the Parole Substance Abuse Program (PSAP) (Senate Bill 1453), and the PSN.

SASCAs, one in each parole region. Providers such as Amity Foundation, Phoenix House, or Walden House are contracted to provide the community-based treatment services. However, as noted in our Phase I report, the treatment capacity of these programs represents only a small percentage of the total demand for alcohol and drug treatment services by the reentry population.

Problems with access to substance abuse treatment programs in prison were an important topic of discussion, with SAPs seen as beneficial by a number of the focus group participants. For example, one individual who was not "clean" said that the six months during which he was in the SAP helped him to understand about the effects of marijuana on the mind and body. Another individual who had participated in the SAP program for nine months said he had tried for many years to get clean prior to participating in the program. He also talked about how the SAP program helped his spirit by also ensuring that his kids received Christmas presents, which helped his depression about not being able to provide for them. Another individual who wanted to participate in the SAP program was unable to get into one of the treatment slots. Discouraged, he said that instead he looks toward God for spiritual help and that "I don't look to programs. I'm self-motivated."

Gaining access to SAPs though was problematic for many participants. Recent budget cuts by CDCR in programming have meant cuts in substance abuse treatment programs in the prison system (and cuts in funding for community treatment providers). In California, about 40 percent of funds for rehabilitative programs have been cut. Nonprofit community alcohol and drug treatment providers had their funding substantially reduced or eliminated. These focus group discussions were conducted after these cuts had occurred, and, depending on how recently the participant had been released from prison, their comments reflect the impact of these cuts in limiting access to in-prison substance abuse treatment programs.

Participants who had trouble accessing substance abuse treatment programs in prison relied instead on Alcoholics Anonymous or Narcotics Anonymous groups run by volunteers, though, in some instances, even these programs had been cut. For some inmates, this meant that they went long periods without access to any substance abuse treatment services. One participant commented that he was without access to substance abuse treatment services for 6–7 months. As one individual commented, "People get tired. You ask for help and they say no." Another participant discussed how inmates organized their own 12-step meetings in prison. He was in a fire camp, and he said that they got their own AA books and would "pray in and pray out" of the meetings and discuss on their own "the book."

Focus group participants cited a number of examples of problems in gaining access to SAP programs. From their perspective, there is very little programming space available for substance abuse treatment. One participant asserted that there were only 12 slots for the AA program at one California prison facility, with 3,000 inmates on the waiting list. In the yard at the facility he was at, he said, there was only one dormitory with SAP programming. Another participant said that a facility he was at had two SAP dormitories that each housed 200 SAP participants, and both were fully occupied.

In addition, *focus group participants felt the decision about who gets substance abuse treatment programming is capricious* and often determined by correctional officers, without regard to whether one needed treatment. For example, one individual stated that in the prison yard, correctional officers were pulling inmates at random to go into the SAP dorms. He wanted access to SAP but was not permitted, whereas others who were not interested or had no substance abuse problems were still placed in a SAP dorm. Also, focus group participants commented that some inmates without substance abuse problems took up treatment slots because it was a way to get perks, such as being moved to a location closer to their family and because they believed that being in a program would look favorable when they came up for parole. In their view, these individuals were not motivated to change or to rehabilitate. Still, several other individuals commented that it is difficult when you have access to only 1–2-day treatment programs. They recognized that it was not sufficient to truly help them but said people still took them to get whatever programming they could.

Focus group participants also discussed the importance of having substance abuse programs available for those who were serving life sentences or lengthy sentences. They said that it was difficult to get access to these treatment programs if one was in this category. In their view, these programs also helped them in terms of rehabilitation and earning credits toward parole. In addition, inmates who served as mentors also said they needed SAP programming to help them be effective mentors.

Further, *if individuals were near their release dates, they were not eligible to participate in substance abuse treatment programming.* For example, one individual stated that he was incarcerated in a private contract prison facility in another state. Since he was within the 60–90-day window of being released, he was told that it was too short a time to give him SAP programming. CDCR DAR's policy is that individuals are ineligible for SAP programming if they have a release date within the next six months; this policy reflects the old treatment model based on at least a six-month program (CDCR Division of Addiction and Recovery Services, *Annual Report*, 2009).

Finally, one individual on parole realized he had a serious drug problem. His desire to change was even stronger than his desire to stay out of prison, as illustrated in the following exchange:

> **Participant:** What gets me about it is, man, you guys do it on your own. I did it on my own and I know I was out there bad. I'm the only person in San Diego that got high that was sick of it. I went down to the parole office and told the parole officer, 'Man, I need you to lock me up.' They wouldn't lock me up—you know what I did, you know how I got locked up? I knocked out the windows [of the parole office] with an ashtray. I knocked out the whole window and then they handcuffed me.
>
> **Moderator:** So you could go back to prison because you didn't want to do drugs?
>
> **Participant**: I needed help.

Views About Access to and Quality of Health Care in Prison

Focus group participants expressed a number of concerns about their ability to access health care within prison and about the indifference of the health care system and correctional system.

The focus group participants gave some examples of individuals experiencing a medical crisis (e.g., heart attack, severe asthma attack) where, in their view, the crisis was either ignored or there were delays in providing the needed care. We were unable to determine when these incidents occurred nor whether they occurred before or after the federal receivership had been put into place.

Focus group participants also talked about the *long waiting times to see a doctor or nurse or to get medications. They also discussed the indifference of the prison system toward the health care needs of inmates.* The participants reported that typically there is a long wait before being able to see a doctor, ranging anywhere from two weeks to a month from when an individual made their initial request. For those that wanted to see the doctor immediately, "You practically have to fall down in the yard to get help. You better not be faking it." Focus group participants also felt that the prison health care system was designed to get them through the system as quickly as possible. In addition, they sensed a lack of empathy among some of the medical staff:

> That's the mentality when you go through the health care system in prison. You're just pushed through there, let's get out, I don't really have time for you. But now, that's not to say that there aren't one or two people in there that you could develop a rapport with to try to maybe get something done or you have some concerns.

Focus group participants felt that medications were overused in prison and that often they were told medications were the solution to many of their problems:

> "The MTA [Medical Treatment Assistant] Office—all they tell you is to take ibuprofen and drink lots of water."

> "Ibuprofen is the cure-all for everything."

> "They have thousands and thousands of us in prison brainwashed that an aspirin would cure whatever it is. And I'm saying whatever it is. And this is what we do. When that MTA comes around, you say, 'Give me a couple aspirins,' they pour you a handful.

That means they don't have to see you for six months. You've got enough."

"And it's really sad that medications—and we're talking about psychotropic medications—are just being thrown at people. And then we're trusting the fact that these are professionals and they know what they're doing."

A number of factors play a role in limiting access to health care within prison. *From the focus group participants' perspective, some correctional staff lacked empathy or did not always react quickly enough when a medical crisis was occurring.* "There's a callousness in the prison system coming toward the prisoners. Part because they see so many, part because there's so many diverging personalities, and yes, it's a difficult job." One individual talked about the process of getting medications distributed. "In the medical yard, they would line you up across the driveway (have people in wheelchairs and on crutches) to get your medications. You'd get to the window and the MTAs would be very rude and say, 'Why do you need these meds now?'"

Another factor mentioned is the "informal" role that correctional officers appear to play as gatekeepers in terms of access to health care. Focus group participants discussed their experiences in requesting to see a doctor and having the correctional officer say it was not necessary. Again, the refrain of "if you can walk, you aren't sick." In one instance, an individual who had worn eyeglasses all his life had lost his glasses and asked a nurse about getting them replaced. The correctional officer said to him, "How many fingers am I holding up?" Because the inmate gave the right answer, the correctional officer said, "You don't need glasses." According to this individual, he went seven months with blurry vision before he was able to get a new pair of glasses.

Another concern expressed was correctional officers possibly influencing the medical staff about treatment decisions. As one focus group participant explained it, at times there can be as many correctional officers as medical staff in the correctional treatment centers (CTCs). He noted instances of correctional officers telling younger nursing staff or less seasoned nursing staff in CTCs how to do their job, whereas in his opinion that would not happen with more seasoned nurses.

Finally, the following case illustrates how *lack of coordination when an individual is being transferred to another prison facility or to a community provider can lead to problems with continuity of care.* In this case, an individual who suspected he had prostrate cancer had his medical records lost when he was transferred to another prison facility, which delayed his diagnosis and treatment. In this instance, the individual began having trouble with urination and was concerned that he may have prostrate cancer. The in-prison lab test showed that his Prostate-Specific Antigen (PSA) level was elevated to 54 ng/mL. "I did a lot of research and studies myself because I knew these folks didn't have my best interest at heart. And I found out a man's PSA level is only suppose to be 1 to 4. Anything over 4 up to 10 is considered serious, and anything after that, there's a possibility you got cancer."

In March 2007, while he was incarcerated, a biopsy was done, and the doctor told him that he would have his results within two weeks. However, three days later this individual was transferred to another prison facility and, according to him, his records got lost in the system. At the new facility, he began passing blood in his urine, and when he reported to the medical staff, he was told that they were awaiting his medical records. In July 2007, his medical records were still missing, and when he again saw a doctor (by this time his symptoms were getting worse), he was told this time that he did not have cancer. The individual questioned how the doctor could know without seeing his medical records.

Over the next three to four months, his PSA level kept creeping up. When it was in the high 70s, the prison staff sent him to a community urologist who then requested his medical records. Further lab tests were done. Approximately nine months after the initial lab test, on December 13, 2007, this individual was informed by a prison doctor that he had cancer. He was started on Luperon injections, which helped him somewhat in terms of alleviating his pain and discomfort. In this case, it was never clear to this individual what the treatment plan was,[6]

---

[6] The practice guidelines for elevated PSA levels are to monitor over time in order to make a determination about prostrate cancer.

and he wondered to what degree his missing medical records was a factor in delays in determining his course of treatment.

Experiences in Having Care Transitioned to Community Providers

Some participants with existing medical conditions discussed the process of having their care transitioned to community providers, and *they related both positive and negative experiences.* One individual with diabetes had an overall positive experience. He talked about being diagnosed in 1995 with diabetes while in prison and staying in the prison "hospital" for about 35 days to be stabilized. He was sent to classes to learn about managing his disease. Upon release, he was linked with a community provider. In 2004, he returned to prison, and this time was diagnosed with prostrate cancer. "But in my particular case, each time I've ever been sick to that point, when I was released, I came home with all my medical files and they had me set up right where to go with the diabetes and the prostate cancer, Day 1. Now, that's not the norm!"

Several other participants had negative experiences. For example, one individual was transferred to another prison facility when he had only eight months remaining on his sentence. Problems with infected gums and loose teeth led the dentist to decide to pull his teeth and provide him with dentures. When it was time for parole, his dentures were still not available, and he was released from prison without them. Instead, he was given a paper stating that he would have to go to a dentist's office in the community and have the dentist sign a written statement indicating he or she would accept his dentures, with responsibility for paying for shipping and handling falling to the former inmate:

> [T]he whole process is, when I was in there, they were supposed to provide me with everything and made sure I had my teeth before I left because I had enough time to get my teeth. So if they say they're not going to have enough time to do your teeth, they're not supposed to take my teeth out. But they said I had enough time. Some fine example. I'm still waiting for my teeth. . . .

Interest in Preventive Care

As summarized in Chapter Two, former inmates are a population that tends to be disproportionately sicker than the general population, with acute and chronic health conditions and infectious diseases. *Focus group participants talked about their interest in receiving preventive care.* Most said the extent of preventive care they received while incarcerated was a flu shot.

There is informal sharing of information about health among inmates, including what type of screening exams may be important. For example, one individual who was in his mid-40s reported that, while incarcerated at a California prison facility, he had requested a physical exam because he was working in the kitchen and wanted to see what his health was like. This request was denied. He then asked for a colonoscopy because a fellow inmate had told him that starting at age 40 one should get a colonoscopy every 1–2 years. His request was denied, and he was told that colonoscopy screening exams should begin at age 50 years. In fact, the colorectal cancer screening guidelines of the Centers for Disease Control and Prevention (CDC) recommend screening starting at age 50.[7] This individual was then sent to a private contract prison outside of the state and again requested a physical exam. This time, he was told that he could not have the exam because it was not included in the contract with CDCR. For this individual, these instances were examples of being denied access to care.

As noted earlier, focus group participants generally viewed access to care in prison to be poor. Given problems in accessing care within prison and the perceived indifference of custody staff to inmates' health problems, many individuals felt that it was up to them to stay healthy. As one participant put it, "I'm going to get my butt out there and take care of my damn self, exercise, whatever I need to do."

Prerelease Planning

Most of the focus group participants had not participated in any formal prerelease classes or planning. For those that had, there was a range

[7] For those at higher risk of developing colorectal cancer, it is also recommended that screening start at an earlier age (Centers for Disease Control and Prevention, 2011).

of intensity described by the focus group participants. The highest-intensity programs described were those where a week-long class was offered 3–4 months prior to release. The next highest-intensity program was having access to a prerelease counselor who could answer questions about the availability of services to help with the transition back into the community. The least intense, and most common, was the provision of a written packet of information about available programs or services.[8]

Most of the focus group participants felt the prerelease planning they had received was inadequate. They reported that it typically consisted of general information and a list of services but not information about how to access those services; nor were the listed services specific to the county that they would be returning to. As one participant noted,

> My experience at the state level with prerelease is not that the information is not good, but the information is basically superficial. If you don't know how to go and contact [the] motor vehicle department [or] the social security office to get those documents that you will need, then it doesn't help. Have that ready to go before you get out.

Instead, *offenders tend to rely on word of mouth, on mentors within prison, or on family members, or they were self-motivated to find out where they could go to seek services.* Some focus group participants who needed substance abuse treatment or help with housing or employment tended to rely on information from other offenders who had been released before and returned to prison. For example, in Los Angeles County, several ex-prisoners knew about the programs run by the Amity Foundation because their bunkmates had directed them to the foundation's program. Other treatment programs that focus group participants

---

8 In California, the CDCR provides each parolee with a *Parolee Information Handbook* that summarizes what a parolee needs to do upon release and provides general information about where they can to go get education, employment training, and mental health and alcohol and drug abuse counseling (CDCR, *Parolee Information Handbook*, no date). In addition, the handbook provides general information on applying for Social Security Income (SSI), Food Stamps, and General Assistance and eligibility for Medi-Cal or Medicare.

were told about by fellow inmates included the Volunteers of America "Think for a Change" program and the CLARE Foundation.

Some participants stated they were told they could not participate in a prerelease class because their confinement was too short. In one case, an individual had been transferred to another institution close to his release date and so was ineligible for the prerelease planning at that institution.

Prerelease planning for some health care needs was seen as spotty and inadequate. For example, offenders receiving treatment for such conditions as cancer or diabetes reported receiving little or no information about where they could go to get follow-up care upon release. Many lacked health insurance and had little prior contact with communities' health care systems, making it difficult for them to understand basic steps, such as how to identify a clinic or a physician out in the community.

Parole and Community Team (PACT) Meetings

The PACT meetings are one avenue by which a newly released individual can learn about and connect with different service organizations. Up until recently in California, when offenders were released from prison, the majority were placed on parole supervision and required to attend within a certain specified time period a PACT meeting in their county of residence. Different types of service providers (e.g., faith-based organizations, health care, housing assistance, employment placement or training, etc.) attend these meetings and briefly discuss what services are available and pass out information about their programs. After the announcements by service providers, parolees are then required to file past the tables of providers and have the provider mark an "X" on the parolee's sheet of paper indicating they received information from that provider. Which organizations are present at the PACT meetings varies widely from meeting to meeting, with participation being voluntary. Because a parolee is required to attend only one PACT meeting, it can be hit-or-miss as to which providers they learn about. If a parolee attends a PACT meeting where no health care providers are present, then the individual misses information altogether on how to access health care services.

Focus group participants varied in their knowledge about the PACT meetings and even whether they were required to attend them. Some individuals said there was a health care provider at their PACT meeting, although this was not common across the focus group participants. They also commented on the process in the PACT meeting and variation in the types of providers present. "You've got maybe 15 different stations. You've got all these various stations that we have to go to. You got the medical people, you got the AIDS people, you got the General Relief people there."[9] For instance, one individual said he wanted to know how to apply for Medi-Cal, but because there were no medical people at the PACT meeting; he did not know where else to go to get that information or how to apply.

In addition, several participants talked about a disconnect between where the PACT meetings are held and where they live. One individual commented that where the PACT meeting is held determines which organizations show up. Although he was assigned to a specific parole office in the region, he did not live in that area and so wanted information about health care resources and other services closer to where he was now living. Transportation challenges too were discussed. As one individual noted, "You gotta get there, transportation is get there on your own, man, get there, walk it, bicycle, bus . . . you better get there."

Several participants felt the parole officer was unable to help them with services. As one individual stated, "The parole office doesn't have anything to offer regarding health or transportation."

The focus group participants had recommendations about improving information about and access to health care providers at the PACT meetings. They suggested that providers regularly attend these meetings. *The type of information they were interested in included how to reinstate or obtain Medicaid (Medi-Cal in California) insurance, where they could go to get free health care, and where they should go to get treatment for different types of health care problems.* They suggested that inmates be provided all this information at the time of release rather than wait until they returned to communities. They also suggested having a uni-

---

[9] General Relief is where focus group participants said they could apply for food stamps and homeless services.

form prerelease class for everyone, regardless of what prison facility they were in or which county they would be returning to upon release. In addition, they suggested that there should be a packet of information tailored for every county.

Where the Focus Group Participants Sought Care and Other Services on Release

A majority of focus group participants had substance abuse problems, and so accessing treatment services in the community was important to them. They mentioned participation in self-help groups, such as AA or NA. Other programs and organizations named included the CLARE Foundation clinics; the Volunteers of America "Thinking for a Change" program;[10] Impact Drug and Alcohol Treatment Center in Pasadena, which offers residential and outpatient drug treatment; Roads to Recovery in San Francisco, which is an in-custody substance abuse treatment program; and Amity and "Amistad" (Amistad de Los Angeles is a long-term residential drug treatment program funded by the Amity Foundation).

They had positive views about these programs. For example, one individual who had participated in the SAP program for six months upon release went to Amity, a therapeutic community, where he was able to "dig deep to see what's really involved, what's really the issues you got going on in yourself. I graduated that program in about two months. It's a good experience. I get to see what others go through, the issues that other people have, and what they do to conquer the issues."

Another individual whose substance abuse problems resulted in him being incarcerated several times stated: "Because the years that I would get out, I didn't know how to be responsible out here and I didn't know how to function right. So within anywhere after two weeks, my mindset was already going back. It was just a matter of time." He had been in a six-month in-prison SAP program, and because he was near-

---

[10] The Thinking for a Change (T4C) program is an integrated, cognitive behavior change program for offenders that includes cognitive restructuring, social skills development, and development of problem solving skills (National Institute of Corrections, no date).

ing release, a counselor approached him and talked with him about going to a sober-living home:

> So she gave me a book and she started talking to me a little bit about it, explaining it to me about what the homes consist of and stuff like that. And I ended up doing it. But I only chose it because it was the closest to my parole office. Because I knew if I didn't make it, I wasn't going to make it, man. So I ended up picking the sober-living home where I'm at and I was there less than 30 days. And my SASCA rep, the people that are paying for me to be there at that sober-living home, he comes up to me—him and my counselor—and they tell me, "Because of the way you are right here out in society"—and I didn't know how to talk to people. I didn't know how to function. I didn't know how to communicate with them. I didn't know how to speak to them. And they tell me, "We know a program that would benefit you if you chose to do it." It wasn't mandated or nothing. So I thought about it for like three days and I say, "It's not going to hurt me. It'll only better me if I give it a chance." And I'm glad I did it.

Focus group participants also discussed what health issues they have had since being released and where they went go to seek treatment. Two individuals had gone to emergency rooms for treatment, one for a pinched nerve and the other for stomach problems. They were sent hospital bills for $5,000 and $30,000, respectively, as well as bills from the treating physicians. In the case of the individual with stomach problems, a social worker at the hospital explained to him how he and his family could apply for Medi-Cal insurance, which ended up covering these costs. This individual subsequently was able to obtain health insurance through his employer.

Health care providers or facilities mentioned by focus group participants included the University of Southern California Medical Center, Los Angeles; the Weingart Center JWCH Medical Clinic located on Skid Row in downtown Los Angeles; and county mental health clinics. In addition, focus group participants mentioned that the Amity Foundation staff and the Volunteers of America staff helped link them to health care providers or clinics when they had problems.

One individual commented that a lot of parolees come to Los Angeles's Skid Row area to get care from the Weingart Center's JWCH Medical Clinic. They know that this is the one place they can come to get help even if they don't have a medical insurance card. Another individual mentioned that the Outpatient Reduced-Cost Simplified Application (ORSA) "program" enabled him to get his medications.[11] Also mentioned were Healthy Oakland and Highland Hospital (the main county hospital) in Oakland, Healthy San Francisco, and the medical care providers that the Second Chance Program in San Diego County would bring in.

In terms of other types of health care services, one individual said he did not need any health care services, but then went onto to say that he was looking for dental services because of a toothache. When asked who was helping him find access to a dentist, his reply was "nobody." This same individual though also reported going to a health care clinic near Vermont and Vernon Avenues in his neighborhood in Los Angeles to get a physical examination and testing for HIV and other STDs.[12] He learned about the clinic from a "lady on the corner who had a flyer." She told him that he did not need Medi-Cal or Social Security to get help at the clinic.

Other programs mentioned were employment-related, including the Second Chance Program in San Diego County, WorkSource,[13] Labor Ready in Oakland, and the Urban League (Los Angeles Urban League's WorkSource Business and Career Center). The Urojas Community Services' outreach program that picks individuals up as they were released from prison was also mentioned.

---

[11] ORSA helps those unable to pay for outpatient medical care, tests, or medicines (Los Angeles County Department of Public Social Services, 2011).

[12] Likely he was referring to a nonprofit community health care clinic in this area of Los Angeles County.

[13] WorkSource is an employment and training program that includes One-Stop Centers. For example, Friends Outside in Los Angeles County operates the "Parole to Payroll" program, which provides employment and job training services to those with criminal convictions and are co-located with the WorkSource/One-Stop Centers.

Views About Cultural Competence

A number of the focus group participants expressed their desire to have access to support services (including health care) that were provided in a culturally competent manner. They expressed a desire to be treated with respect. Some expressed this as being treated like a person instead of as an offender. One focus group participant summarized the focus group discussion as follows: "What I hear in every one of our conversations and in every one of our stories is the sense of being recognized and acknowledged as a man and a human being." From their perspective, treatment provided with respect builds trust and allows the patients to become engaged in their health care and speak up on their own behalf. They often mentioned the programs they were currently involved with as examples of the types of care they preferred.[14] As one ex-prisoner expressed it,

> What Healthy Oakland will do for you is they will personalize you first. You're a person. And see, what that does for you, it makes you feel more comfortable to speak up. I'm 41. I need to start checking for my prostate now. Now, I wouldn't do that in prison. I wouldn't have liked letting them check for my prostate in prison because it's so impersonal in prison. You're just that number, your [Department of Corrections] number. Here, I want to take care of [my] health needs.

Another stated that he appreciated the individualized care he received at Healthy Oakland: "And the biggest thing I think they're doing is they're assessing each person individually, what their needs are, and then they focus on those things during the program."

The focus group participants also *wanted to be treated by providers and staff who were empathetic to their circumstances and needs.* As a result, they preferred staff who had been formally incarcerated themselves or who had substantial experience in working with the formerly

---

[14] These included Healthy Oakland and The Gamble Institute in Alameda County, Amity and Amistad de Los Angeles, the CLARE Foundation, and Volunteers of America's "Think for a Change" programs in Los Angeles, and Second Chance and UAAMAC in San Diego, among others.

incarcerated. Employing ex-prisoners was seen as in indication of how invested a clinic (in this case, Healthy Oakland) was in addressing their needs and those of their peers rather than simply being a place where care is provided. One individual stated:

> Everybody there is from the community. Now, the doctors may be from somewhere else, but they're right there onsite and they come and volunteer their time. The employees are there from the community. So the community has a sense of ownership, even though they don't own it, but they feel as though it's theirs.

This experience stands in opposition to that expressed by others about accessing care in other community health care settings (e.g., hospitals or physician offices). Some focus group participants indicated that they perceived these providers to be overly focused on insurance status and that, because they had no insurance, they would receive care of lower quality. As the following exchange illustrates, simply asking for insurance could be perceived as a slight:

> In my opinion and through my experience, when you're indigent and you go to these private hospitals, you don't get the same care that you would if you had insurance. . . . You get better service going to a county hospital [that provides indigent care] than you would going to [a private local hospital was named]. Yeah, because they asked me did I have health care insurance; I told them no. That's the first question they ask you, do you have health care insurance. That's right, before you start services. When you say no, I believe you got into a different file. Here's the health care care ones for people who have insurance. There's a jacket for that, then there's you, then there's us.

Some preferred not to have care that was apart from the general community. They did not want to go to clinics that were just for ex-prisoners, but instead thought that the care would be better if they were not the only population receiving it and also simply did not like the idea of being part of a segregated population. Focus group participants nevertheless recognized that they had very few choices for care. One expressed it this way: "Had it not been for the county hospitals, as overrun as they are, and had it not been for places like Healthy Oakland, many of us would be in a terrible state of health, period. That's the state of health care for us. If not for those two places, health care is nonexistent, period."

Ease of access to care also was considered to be important. For example, one employment training program brought in medical staff on a regular basis. Ease of access to care also meant offering care at convenient hours. As one individual stated, "Accessing Healthy Oakland is the easiest way to get your health care because you can stop in at . . . 8:00 in the morning or 8:30 in the morning, fill out all your paperwork and see a doctor that same day." For others, this meant being picked up at the prison so that they could go directly into programs.

Other strategies for providing services that the focus group participants mentioned as being important included locations that provide wraparound services, such as employment services in addition to health programs, preventive screenings, on-site mental health counseling, and access to drug treatment.

The Importance of Family

Our focus was on understanding ex-prisoners' needs and views about programs and services available to them. An important message we heard throughout the discussions was the importance of family. *Consistently, the participants commented on the critical role that family plays in providing internal motivators to change, encouraging them through the rehabilitative experience, and in helping them to meet the challenges of returning home.*

Focus group participants talked about the role of family in motivating them to participate in substance abuse treatment programs and inspiring them to change. One individual participated in a particular facility's SAP program because he wanted to be near his kids. Another individual commented that the one thing that really helped him was family, "who care about you and look out for you." He stated that his wife and kids were the main factors in helping him to focus and that their visits helped motivate him to continue getting treatment for substance abuse problems.

Family helped with such basic issues as providing food, housing, clothing, and helping out with paying the bills. Such gestures also helped ex-prisoners in terms of their own emotional well-being. When one individual was asked how important his family was in terms of his mental health, his response was:

> Oh, it's very important. I always believe in family, family is really a structure and a foundation that I believe in. I can always rely on them and they can always rely on me. Whatever the situation may be, they're there for me. So we're really tight. If I need emergency housing or something for some reason I don't pay my rent or something, to keep from being totally homeless. I can call one of them and they'll help me through because they know I'm about changing my life. I've got that support and I've always got to stay positive.

This individual went on to say that when he was released, "Family was right there. Before I was paroled, I stayed in contact with my family all the time. That was pretty much where my letters come from; it was family members. So when I'm paroled, they allowed me to come and stay as long as I'm showing some kind of energy to get my stuff in line. Like I said, it was an emergency situation and they were right there for me."

In addition, the focus group participants mentioned the importance of organizations that supported the family as also helping them to keep their spirits up and to motivate them to change. For example, one ex-prisoner talked about how emotionally low he felt because he could not be there for his kids at Christmas. The simple gesture of an organization providing his children gifts at Christmas helped to bring him out of his emotional "dumps": "The SAP program helped my spirits. I was feeling down. All three of my kids received Christmas gifts through this program, which helped with my depression."

A few participants commented that, for those who were not lucky enough to have family support, being able to access and link with programs was particularly important.

The Experience of Being Released

For some individuals, they were young men when they entered prison and now lacked knowledge about how to navigate a changing society and using technological innovations as basic as cell phones or the Internet to apply for jobs. For those who have been in prison a long period of time, they are especially vulnerable, relative to those that have "churned" through prison over short periods of time or those who have shorter sentences to serve. As one individual who had been incarcerated for 36 years put it, "You aren't savvy about society, and it makes you have emotional and anxiety issues upon release." He went on to say that he knew at least 30 guys who had been in prison for at least 30 years and now are out on the street. "They are struggling." Prisons don't equip those who have been incarcerated for a long period of time to reintegrate back into communities and society. Focus group participants who had been incarcerated for longer periods of time emphasized the need for availability of programs within prison for and upon release for those who are serving long sentences.

One participant commented on the challenge he faced in being released and the lack of preparation: "You know, [the prerelease program and prison system don't] get you prepared for the streets or anything. You get your $200 gate money, you spend your $78 to $80 buying your ticket to get to where you're going, and you're on the street. And it's a system designed to have you fail from the beginning. So I don't know what it's going to take to fix it."

One focus group participant poignantly described the difficulties he encountered upon release of getting from prison to the county he would be returning to and, specifically, to the provider he had heard about from other inmates. The following quote is a sobering reminder of the hurdles even those individuals motivated to change face:

> That's what happens to me when I'm paroled, this is my story. The day I paroled, I got out and prior to getting out, like I said, my bunky, he set me up the night before. He said, "You want to hear the good news or the bad news?" I said, "Give me the bad news." He said, "You won't be able to go tomorrow to Amistad, but as soon as you get to the parole office, call Amistad and they'll hook you up." I said, "What's the good news?" He said, "I got you in?"

I said, "Okay, I'm happy." And when I got out, coming down there, I was having a hell of a time because as soon as I got on the train coming down south, I wanted to talk to my sister, all I had was $200. I said f--- it, I got off at . . . I spent $7, after spending $47 on the train, and I talked to my sister, and she's like, "Hey brother, what are you doing?" I said, "I'm going to come and see you." She said, "I'm about 150 miles from where you're at right now. Just go down to L.A."—because she lives in Merced—"go to L.A. and report to your parole officer and we'll talk later on."

So, I had to catch a ride, I ended up paying a (inaudible) . . . to take me to the bus station and I missed the bus by two minutes, it was rolling off the track. So I had to spend another $30, but when I got down to L.A., I was so confused I didn't even know how to use the Metro. I didn't have no parole papers, I didn't have the address, I couldn't figure out what I was going to do. So I said "Lord, help me out." My think[ing] was I was going to take the parole paper and go to a motel and say I just got out of prison, can you give me a room, that's what I came up with. So I headed towards the city . . . and this guy came on the train with me and said. "Hey, you just got out, right?" I said "yeah," he said "you want to use my phone?" I said "what's that going to cost me?" I started looking out for his homeboys, because he was gonna rob me, real shady, you know. . . From Union Station to Metro Green Line, I probably spent another $7 trying to figure out the machine until somebody actually showed me how to do it.

My money was getting short, it was getting late, so finally I said all right, I used his phone and I called Mark [Faucette], who's the vice-president of Amistad, and he says, "Where you at?" I said, "I'm on a green Metro link going towards Norwalk, just trying to get a motel room." He said, "Are you gonna be all right?" and I said "No, I don't think so, but I'm going to give it a shot." He said, "When you get into Norwalk Station, turn around and come back all the way to Union Station." I was like, "Oh f---, I gotta spend more money?!" And I was frustrated, angry, excited, everything was just coming up and when I got to the Metro link I said, "All right, Lord, you gotta help me out here." So this dude walks me up there and he's trying to explain to me, well this girl

> walks up and gives me a ticket and she says, "Here." So I says, "What's that gonna cost me?" She says, "Nothing, me and my boyfriend's going home, and it was an all day ticket, you can get back to Union Station." . . .
>
> By the grace of God I made it to Amistad [de Los Angeles]. . . . The next day when I went to the parole officer, you know what he told me? "I don't have no tokens, I don't have no (inaudible) . . . I have nothing for you. I'm glad you went to that program because you would have been sleeping in the streets, ain't no motel would've took you in. They don't have nothing for you." It took me four tries to get a bag of tokens on a $10 (inaudible) . . . but it's only because he seen what I was doing in the program. He said, "I'll see what I can do," and after that he said, "I can't help you."

Discussion

The reentry population is vulnerable, not only because of their health care needs but also because they have been removed from society for long periods of time. The long quote immediately above—which describes one participant's experience in trying to make his way from a northern California prison to Los Angeles County and then to a recovery program (Amistad de Los Angeles) that his fellow inmates had directed him to—shows just how difficult this transition is.

Clearly, prerelease planning and initial postrelease support is important for helping individuals transition from prison back to communities, with some research indicating that prerelease planning is associated with reductions in offender recidivism (Nelson and Trone, 2000). Further, inmates upon release from prison are often unaware of what health care and other needed services may be available to them (Rossman, 2001). Most of the focus group participants had not participated in *any* formal prerelease classes or planning. This is consistent with other research findings that only a small minority of state prisoners released each year experience a multisession, formalized prerelease program (Mellow, 2007).

Instead, the individuals in our focus groups reported relying more on word of mouth among inmates, mentors in prison, or family members to learn about where they could seek drug treatment or other needed services upon release. It was clear they wanted more detailed written information about what services are available, how they can access them, where to go to get drug treatment services, and what they need to do to for other basic needs such as applying for General Relief, Food Stamps, and other benefits; and they also wanted assistance with housing and educational and employment training. In addition, they felt it important to have this information tailored to the individual counties to which they would be returning. Although some of this information may be available through their parole officer or at PACT meetings, they wanted the information in advance so they could be better prepared for release.

At the same time, given limited resources and staff time, it is not feasible for any correctional system to develop a prerelease plan for every individual leaving a state's prison system. As summarized in Chapter Six, CDCR instead does prerelease planning for individuals with chronic medical or mental health problems based on need and acuity. CDCR tries to arrange community-based care for soon-to-be-released prisoners in need of acute or subacute care, those who are unable to arrange for care because of disability, those in need of dialysis, and those who are unable to handle activities of daily living (ADLs) (CDCR Division of Correctional Health Services, "Release Planning Continuity of Mental Health and Medical Care," 2011). For example, individuals with less serious mental illness are provided information on health care services in the county to which they will be returning to; for individuals with more serious or acute mental illness, CDCR tries to get the individual's permission to send his or her medical records to county mental health agencies and/or facilitates linkage with a mental health provider. In terms of individuals with substance abuse problems, if they are participating in a SAP they may be eligible for one of the continuing care or community-based treatment programs funded by CDCR, though the eligibility rules vary from program to program (CDCR Division of Addiction and Recovery Services, *Annual Report*, 2009).

The focus group discussions were conducted prior to the implementation of California's new Public Safety Realignment Plan starting October 1, 2011. Under public safety realignment, CDCR will also provide prerelease packets to counties for individuals who will be placed on postrelease community supervision (PRCS). Specifically, for each individual who will be released on PRCS, CDCR will send counties a prerelease packet 120 days prior to the individual's release. The packet will include a variety of information, such as documentation on classification actions and inmate case factors, inmate's known gang affiliation and known nonconfidential enemies within CDCR, and victim's request for notification of release. Of importance here, the prerelease packets will also include medical information, such as whether the individual has tested positive for tuberculosis, medical clearance, disability information, and mental health information if applicable (CDCR "Implementation of Post-Release Community Supervision Act of 2011," 2011). Due to staff reductions as a result of realignment, CDCR will be unable to complete the risk and needs assessment instrument, called prerelease Correctional Offender Management Profiling for Alternative Sanctions (COMPAS),[15] on inmates released on PRCS but instead will include in the prerelease packets any assessment that is available in an inmate's file. Thus, counties will have some prerelease information about these offenders, including their medical needs, but, without COMPAS, counties will need to rely on other mechanisms to assess the rehabilitative needs of offenders to be managed at the county level.

The PACT meetings represent a potential place for those recently released from prison to learn about and obtain access to health care and other service providers. And it is a way for health care providers to access this population—a problem we heard about in our provider interviews in Chapter Four, where providers told us they want to serve

---

[15] COMPAS is a risk and needs assessment instrument used to inform prerelease planning decisions (CDCR, ""COMPAS Assessment Tool Launched—Evidence-Based Rehabilitation for Offender Success," 2009). COMPAS assesses individuals on seven criminogenic needs to determine offender rehabilitation treatment programming needs. COMPAS is to be administered to California inmates approximately six to eight months before their release as part of case planning for parole supervision (Farabee et al., 2010). According to a draft report by the California Rehabilitation Oversight Board, as of July 2011 only 42 percent of parolees have a reentry COMPAS assessment (California Rehabilitation Oversight Board, 2011).

this population but are uncertain about how to locate or access them. However, based on the focus group discussions and earlier interviews with parole officers and observations by the research team of a PACT meeting in southeast Los Angeles, these meetings are less than an ideal setting for engaging ex-prisoners and providing them with information about services available. Some parolees seemed confused and disoriented after recently being released from prison, making it difficult for them to process the information being provided at these meetings. In addition, for most, their highest concerns are getting information about housing and employment, with health care needs being a distant third. Further, some interviewees commented that they did not want to raise any health care concerns to their parole officer, fearing that it may label them as troublemakers or individuals for parole officers to watch closely.

More important, changes are occurring under realignment that will result in far fewer parolees that will be supervised by parole. Thus, the PACT meetings may reach fewer individuals than in the past. Instead, county probation departments and jails will need to serve this linkage function and develop the necessary community partnerships with service providers to effectively provide services to this population.

Thus, there is a need for parole, county probation, law enforcement, and community health care and reentry service providers to collaborate in developing tailored information guidebooks that can be distributed to individuals prior to release from prison and be readily available to them once they have returned to local communities. Such guidebooks will need to go beyond lists of services to include specific problem-solving strategies, highlight immediate needs critical to near-term successful reentry, identify providers committed to serving this population, take into account appropriate literacy levels, and be written in a linguistically and culturally competent manner (Mellow, 2007).

When it comes to health care problems, our focus group participants cited the types of problems that have been reported in other studies (e.g., National Commission on Correctional Health Care, 2002; Davis and Pacchiana, 2004; Mallik-Kane and Visher, 2008). As mentioned, our focus group participants tended to rank health needs as being lower than other needs, such as housing or employment. Substance abuse problems were reported by many of the focus group participants—a finding consistent with other research studies on returning prisoners (Mallik-Kane and Visher, 2008). Focus group participants also considered substance abuse problems as separate from health concerns, which suggests that corrections staff responsible for prerelease planning, parole and probation staff, and community providers responsible for helping develop prerelease plans or plans to transition their care should be sensitive to this distinction. In other words, when individuals are asked if they have any health concerns, they may say no, when in fact, their primary concerns may be how to access treatment in the community for their substance abuse problems.

Barriers to accessing substance abuse treatment programs and other health care in prison included long waiting times to see a physician or nurse, limited capacity of substance abuse programs within prison, perceived indifference of the health care and correctional staff, and the informal gatekeeper role some correctional officers played. The focus group participants' comments suggest that access to care in prison is problematic for at least some individuals and that it may be a contributing factor to the unmet needs among this population. In addition, the participants expressed a desire for care to be provided in a culturally competent manner, with providers being sensitive to the experience of incarceration.

The focus group participants discussed at length their desire to participate in in-prison substance abuse programs (SAPs); however, they reported a number of problems in doing so, including a limited number of treatment slots. As a result, some individuals went without treatment altogether or relied on self-help groups, such as AA or NA. Our focus group discussions were conducted after reductions in rehabilitative programming in California's prisons had occurred. Budget cuts began impacting rehabilitative services in 2009. The treatment capacity of CDCR's SAPs went from 10,119 treatment slots in June 2008 to only 2,350 slots, with only 2,162 inmates enrolled, in January 2010 (CDCR, Division of Addiction and Recovery Services, *Annual Report*, 2009; CDCR, "Adult Programs Key Performance Indicators January 2010–December 2010," 2010). As part of its efforts to preserve SAPs given budget cuts, CDCR announced that it would adopt a streamlined, three-month treatment model and phase it in at nine prisons for male inmates to replace CDCR's previous 6–36-month programs. The shorter treatment model is projected to enable CDCR to provide substance abuse treatment services annually to 8,450 inmates (CDCR, ""Adult Programs Key Performance Indicators January 2010–December 2010: In Prison Substance Abuse Treatment Enrollment %," 2010).

Focus group participants also expressed an interest in receiving health education and preventive care. Given that this population has significant health challenges, this interest represents an important opportunity to provide health education to inmates and to make preventive care a priority. Then again, the focus group discussions suggest there may be some misperceptions about what preventive care is needed and that having requests for routine screenings turned down, although perhaps consistent with the Centers for Disease Control and Prevention guidance, was viewed as being denied quality care. This too suggests that community health care providers should make preventive care and health education part of their treatment plan for ex-prisoners.

Focus group participants gave examples of where individual inmates were experiencing a crisis, but, in their view, the medical crisis was either ignored or the response of the correctional staff was too late. We are unable to verify or confirm that these incidents did occur. Importantly, as noted in Chapter One, a federal receiver was appointed in 2005 to oversee prison medical care to address preventable deaths and improve the quality of care provided to inmates. An analysis of inmate death reviews by the federal receiver's office found that although overall death rates between 2007 and 2009 have remained stable, there has been a reduction by 16 percent in the number of identified lapses in care and a reduction of 31 percent in the number of cases of preventable death (Imai, 2010).

There are several limitations of this analysis. These findings represent only the perspective of men who were formerly incarcerated in state prison. It does not include the perspective of the CDCR nor of the court-appointed federal receiver. In addition, we recognize that the focus group results are based on a relatively small sample of individuals. We therefore have compared these findings with other research about the health experiences of individuals returning from prison to place these findings into a broader context.

Lastly, in Chapter Five, we discuss the impact of incarceration on families and the challenges they have in staying connected with their incarcerated family members. The literature suggests that family contact during incarceration is associated with lower recidivism rates (Hairston, 2002; Klein, Bartholomew, and Hibbert, 2002). The focus group discussions provided real examples of how important family is to individuals in helping to motivate them while incarcerated to seek rehabilitative services, in helping them to overcome such basic challenges as housing and employment upon release, and in motivating them to get help upon release. In a real sense, the family is the safety net for those returning from prison. This finding is consistent with research by Naser and Visher (2006) about the concrete types of support families may provide. In addition, it underscores the importance of having in place corrections policies that support contact during incarceration, such as reducing the costs of phone calls and housing prisoners closer to their communities (Naser and Visher, 2006). In Chapter Six, we discuss the opportunity under public safety realignment to remove one key barrier to maintaining family contacts by having counties supervise, manage, and rehabilitate low-level offenders.

CHAPTER FOUR

Understanding the Challenges of Dealing with Released Prisoners: Provider Interview Results

Introduction

In Chapter Three, we provided the results from focus groups we conducted with ex-prisoners in three large California counties. The focus group discussions enabled us to hear directly from those who have experienced incarceration about how health influences the reentry process, factors that facilitated or hindered their ability to meet their health care and other needs, their perceptions about access to care and quality of care, and their suggestions about how California can improve its provision of services to the reentry population.

In this chapter, we summarize key findings from the literature about ex-prisoners' access to insurance, how the safety net is organized to meet ex-prisoners' needs, and the opportunity that health care reform represents to improve access to health insurance. We then provide the results from interviews we conducted with providers in Los Angeles, Alameda, and San Diego counties. The providers discussed the needs of the formerly incarcerated they see in their clinics, community health centers, drug treatment programs, and multiservice centers. They also discussed the challenges of providing services to these individuals, including addressing the complex range of other needs they may have in terms of housing, employment, transportation, and problems with family reunification.

Literature on Ex-Prisoners' Access to Insurance and Health Care Reform

Being in good health and having adequate access to health care services can be critical components in enabling ex-prisoners to successfully reintegrate into the community after incarceration. Health and health care affect all aspects of reentry, including employment, education, housing, and family reunification (Freudenberg, 2004; Mallik-Kane and Visher, 2008). And individuals with untreated substance abuse problems and mental and physical illnesses are less capable of finding and maintaining employment, staying in school, and finding or keeping housing. Thus, treating substance abuse problems and mental and physical illnesses better positions ex-prisoners to address the other concerns in their lives, thus potentially reducing the chances that they will commit new crimes (Mallik-Kane and Visher, 2008; Wenzlow et al., 2011; Bazelon Center for Mental Health Law, 2009; Mancuso and Felver, 2010).

As discussed in Chapter Two, ex-prisoners typically have poor health and poor access to health care services. Health concerns among ex-prisoners include chronic conditions, such as diabetes; infectious diseases, such as HIV; and substantial substance abuse and mental health issues (Davis et al., 2009). Upon release from prison, such individuals are at increased risk for death and face serious obstacles to accessing high-quality care (Wakeman, McKinney, and Rich, 2009). For many, these barriers are exacerbated or even caused by low insurance rates and overstretched safety-net resources in the communities they return to. Freudenberg (2004) succinctly summarizes this constellation of health and health care problems faced by ex-prisoners:

> Inmates enter the nation's jails and prisons with a disproportionate burden of illness, receive limited or inadequate treatment to address these problems while behind bars, then return to communities that face significant challenges in providing the health care and public health services that can promote health and prevent disease.

In addition, ex-prisoners face a number of other obstacles to care. For example, many face bureaucratic or procedural barriers to accessing care in a timely way, poor treatment from administrative staff, or long waiting times. Others perceive their providers to be uncaring. Together, these factors can make it frustrating and difficult for ex-prisoners to seek care (Marlow, White, and Chesla, 2010). At the same time, the fact that many prisoners have low education and low literacy may reduce how effectively they interact with their providers. They may not ask the right questions or understand the information they receive, and this may lead to poor follow-up to their care. Moreover, providers may perceive some of the institutionalized attitudes and behaviors of ex-prisoners as threatening, which may lead to or reinforce negative provider attitudes toward this population (Freudenberg, 2004). Such negative provider attitudes, in turn, may cause providers to be less likely to take on ex-prisoners as patients.

Freudenberg (2004) suggests that access to services is likely curtailed by three primary factors: low insurance rates, low levels of health care safety-net resources in communities, and prisoners' social demographic characteristics. In the following subsections, we examine two of these three factors—low insurance rates among ex-prisoners and low levels of health care safety-net resources in communities—and discuss the Patient Protection and Affordable Care Act (ACA) as an opportunity to help ameliorate these challenges for ex-prisoners and providers.

Ex-Prisoners' Access to Health Insurance

Current estimates find that between 57 percent (Heiser and Williams, 2008) and 85 percent (Visher, LaVigne, and Travis, 2004; Mallik-Kane, 2005) of ex-prisoners do not have health insurance, compared with about 16 percent of the general population (U.S. Census Bureau, 2011f). In the current system of health care financing, the primary pathways for gaining access to health care are employer-sponsored health insurance and public insurance programs offered by local, state, or federal government. For example, states and the federal government share costs for Medicaid, which is the nation's primary insurance program for low-income persons. However, because unemployment among ex-prisoners is high, very few ex-prisoners have been able to acquire private insurance. At the same time, while eligibility rules for public insurance programs differ from state to state, access to Medicaid is typically limited to families or parents with children who meet both income and categorical standards (Dorn et al., 2004). Many ex-prisoners do not meet these standards, and while states may cover these persons through a Medicaid waiver, few have. This is likely because such a waiver typically comes with no additional federal financing (Dorn et al., 2004).

Ex-prisoners' access to public insurance is further constrained by two additional factors. First, even when individuals in the reentry population are eligible for public health insurance because they have children and low incomes, they often face numerous challenges in applying for public insurance, including low literacy levels, poor mental health and functioning, incomplete personal identification, and lack of documentation (Bazelon Center for Mental Health Law, 2009; Mancuso and Felver, 2010).

Second, those who are eligible for and enrolled in Medicaid may have their benefits terminated when their confinement begins (Freudenberg, 2004; American Bar Association, 2011). Currently, states may not collect federal reimbursements for Medicaid expenditures for incarcerated persons. According to an American Bar Association (2007) review, many states have misinterpreted this to mean that such persons must be terminated from Medicaid, despite the fact that several federal agencies have called for states to simply *suspend* these benefits. This process of terminating benefits is particularly problematic for those in and out of jail in a matter of days. Not only have they lost access to public insurance for care outside jail, but they also are unlikely to be able to get health care services in jail, given their short stay. Upon release, ex-prisoners are not automatically qualified for Medicaid and must reapply on their own. But in the time it takes to reestablish benefits, they will have lost access to necessary medications or other treatments (Freudenberg, 2004; American Bar Association, 2007).

Safety-Net Health Care Resources in California

Because ex-prisoners are most likely to be uninsured or insured in public programs, they typically receive care through the health care safety net. This safety net in California is multifaceted and comprises several different components. Providers of care include both public and nonprofit hospitals, community clinics, and some private physicians. County-run public hospitals provide the greatest share of hospital care for the uninsured population, while private nonprofit hospitals provide most of the hospital care received by patients with public insurance. Three-quarters of all the patients seen at community clinics for primary care visits are on Medi-Cal or are uninsured. In addition, there are several different insurance programs that safety-net patients may qualify for. These are primarily the state and federally run Medi-Cal for adults and Healthy Families for children and the county-run medically indigent adult (MIA) programs (Tuttle and Wulsin, 2008; California Health Care Foundation, 2011).

In California, counties have primary responsibility for ensuring access to health care for indigent populations. The safety net encompasses a diverse set of providers and financing mechanisms, and counties have varying resources to support and maintain the safety net. As a result, there are different county models of organization of safety-net care, but two major subtypes prevail. First, larger California counties operate separate county-specific systems, whereas the smaller California counties pool their resources together into a centrally run system. Second, larger counties may own and operate hospitals, clinics, and other facilities, in addition to supporting any private resources that are available; they may purchase services by contract through private providers; or they may operate a hybrid of these two models. Of the four counties discussed in detail in this report, three (Alameda, Kern, and Los Angeles) operate their own hospitals and clinics, while San Diego primarily contracts for services (Kelch, 2011).

County resources used to support the safety net are largely derived from a dedicated sales tax, motor vehicle license fees, and county general funds. However, safety-net providers also receive a large portion of their funding from Medi-Cal and other government grants. In some communities, clinics specialize in providing both social and health care services specifically to the ex-prisoner population (Kelch, 2011). Regardless of insurance status, ex-prisoners likely rely more on public and nonprofit providers that on private for-profit ones because of the challenges they face in accessing any services and because their appearance and demeanor make them less desirable and harder to treat than other patients (Davis et al., 2009).

In addition, in California, separate networks of health care providers in the areas of mental health and substance abuse treatment are contracted with to provide community-based treatment for individuals released from prison. These networks are small in size, and access to them typically depends on referral by CDCR or by parole officers. In terms of mental health services, parolees are eligible for care from the 72 parole outpatient clinics (POCs) throughout the state.[1] These clinics provide basic mental health services to the parolee population, including medication management and some individual or group therapy. Parolees with more-severe mental health conditions will often be referred by the POC to other county or community mental health programs for more extensive treatment (California State Auditor, 2001).

In terms of substance abuse treatment, several separate networks provide community-based treatment services to ex-prisoners, primarily funded by CDCR. Similar to mental health, these networks have limited capacity. For example, the Parolee Services Network (PSN) provides community-based alcohol and drug treatment and recovery services to parolees in 17 counties statewide (including the four focus counties in our study). The PSN program provides up to 180 days of treatment and recovery services, with parolees being placed in these programs immediately upon release from prison or by parole. The PSN program serves a relatively small number of parolees. For example, for our four focus counties, the number of parolees served in fiscal year 2005–2006 ranged from 148 in Kern County to 375 in Los Angeles County (Davis et al., 2009). Local assistance funding for the PSN has remained about the same over the years (Davis et al., 2009); however, in fiscal year 2011, funding for the PSN was reduced because of state budget cuts.[2]

---

[1] POCs include social workers, psychiatrists, and psychologists and are often co-located with the parole offices or headquarters in each region of the state.

[2] The other community-based substance abuse treatment programs available to parolees is the In-Custody Drug Treatment Program (ICDTP), a 150-day program; the Senate Bill 1453 program, in which inmates who have participated in the SAPs may complete 150 days of residential, community-based substance abuse treatment as a voluntary condition of their

Finally, ex-prisoners may also be eligible to take advantage of the Substance Abuse and Crime Prevention Act (SACPA, also known as Proposition 36), passed in 2001. Specifically, the act increased state funding for drug treatment and allowed eligible nonviolent drug offenders to be diverted to drug treatment instead of receiving a traditional sentence. If individuals commit a violation while on parole that meets the criteria for Proposition 36 (e.g., nonviolent drug offenses or drug-related parole violations), they are technically eligible to participate in this program in lieu of incarceration (Gardiner, 2008). Proposition 36 allows for dismissal of charges upon successful completion of treatment. Proposition 36 was an important program for ex-prisoners, with parolee participation in Proposition 36 being greater than that in the PSN program. In Los Angeles County, for example, more parolees participated in the Proposition 36 program (1,684 parolees) than in the PSN program (375 parolees) in fiscal year 2005–2006 (Davis et al., 2009). In July 2009, funding for Proposition 36 was eliminated under the SACPA, although the legal mandate requiring treatment to be offered to defendants in lieu of incarceration remained (Los Angeles County Department of Public Health, Substance Abuse Prevention and Control, 2011). Beginning in October 2011, Proposition 36 was revised to create a fee-based, participant self-pay counseling program (Los Angeles County Department of Public Health, Substance Abuse Prevention and Control, 2011).

The differences in care that result from these varied local systems can be important for health and outcomes. Details of this variation are summarized in Chapter Two. However, one result consistent across counties is that ex-prisoners are often released into communities that have poor access to providers because of both low provider availability (Freudenberg, 2004) and increased demand for safety-net services by the other disadvantaged residents in a community (Davis et al., 2009). Moreover, community-based services for mental health, substance

---

parole; the Female Offender Treatment and Employment Program (FOTEP), which provides female parolees with up to 15 months of residential treatment services; and the Community-Based Substance Abuse Programs, for which CDCR contracts directly with treatment providers throughout California (CDCR OARS, undated).

abuse, and physical health services are provided in separate systems and are not coordinated. This means that even if ex-prisoners have access to health care through insurance, they might find it difficult to get all their care needs met in primary care settings in their communities.

New cuts in state and local funding in California further exacerbate poor access to providers and low insurance rates among California's ex-prisoners. In 2010, for example, CDCR reduced its funding for rehabilitative programs by 40 percent, which translated into about a $200 million reduction in funding for education, vocational, and substance abuse programs. In fiscal year 2011/2012, California's governor proposed an additional one-time cut of $150 million to CDCR rehabilitative programs. These reductions include a 39 percent reduction to substance abuse contracts.[3]

Potential Impact of Health Care Reform in Improving Ex-Prisoners' Access to Health Care

By 2014, the ACA (Pub. Law 111-148) will provide a historic opportunity to address a key barrier to care for ex-prisoners—lack of health care insurance. As previously described, ex-prisoners are largely uninsured because they often lack access to employer-sponsored health insurance plans and because many are ineligible for public programs. The ACA addresses these concerns, with one of the major provisions of the act being the expansion of eligibility to all non-Medicare eligible citizens and legal residents[4] under age 65 with incomes up to 133 percent of the FPL.[5] It also will provide subsidies to individuals

[3] Of this, $75 million (50 percent) will be from adult programs, $44 million (30 percent) from Division of Adult Parole Operations (DAPO), and $31 million (20 percent) from Female Offender and Program Services (FOPS). This translates to the following reductions in contracted services: (1) reductions in Substance Abuse Services Coordination Agencies (SASCA) contracts, including eliminating Sober Living and Out-Patient Services ($25.9 million in savings); (2) suspension of the PSN and Bay Area Services Network contracts for one year ($11.7 million in savings); and (3) reductions in-prison substance abuse programs ($3.7 million in savings) (CDCR, "$150 Million Reduction Fiscal Year 2011/12: Program-Related Savings," 2011).

[4] That is, legal residents who have been in the country five years or longer.

[5] The ACA specifies that childless adults are eligible for Medicaid with modified adjusted gross income at or below 133 percent of the FPL. However, the ACA also adds a 5 percentage-

with incomes between 133 and 400 percent of the FPL if they do not have a qualifying offer of coverage from an employer (Kaiser, 2011a). Moreover, the law penalizes large employers for not offering coverage and provides temporary tax incentives to induce small employers with low-wage workers to offer coverage.[6]

The net effect of the ACA is that there will be more options available to low-income populations, either through an employer, the exchanges, or Medicaid. Importantly, these changes open up the possibility for many ex-prisoners and other individuals involved with the criminal justice system to become eligible for Medicaid (California's Medicaid program is referred to as Medi-Cal) or will enable them to purchase private health insurance at a much cheaper rate, thus, removing a key barrier to access to care. It is expected that persons with a history of involvement in the criminal justice system will likely represent a large component of the Medicaid expansion population (Mancuso and Felver, 2010).

While most of the coverage expansions set forth by the ACA are not required to take effect until 2014, the state of California applied for and received a waiver to begin the Medicaid expansions immediately. This new program, called the Low Income Health Program (LIHP), is optional to counties and allows them to cover single adults with incomes up to 200 percent of the FPL (Kaiser, 2011b; CDHCS, 2011).

Further, Medicaid will be expanded to more fully cover drug treatment, prevention services, and wellness programs—services important to the reentry population. Primary among these is the support of several new grant programs to fund community-based organizations to develop or expand health care services. For example, the ACA establishes the Community Health Center Fund, which provides $11 billion over four years from 2011 to 2015 to build new centers and improve or expand on services offered at current centers. The act also provides funding in 2011 to grow the National Health Service Corps,

---

point deduction from the FPL, which effectively makes the Medicaid eligibility threshold 138 percent of the FPL (State Health Access Data Assistance Center, 2011).

6 These temporary tax incentives apply only to businesses with 25 or fewer workers who pay average annual wages below $50,000.

which works to expand the number of health professionals working in various communities across the United States (Kaiser, 2011b). There is also increased support for wellness and education programs to help all persons understand and maintain good health (Kaiser, 2011b).

Currently, most states' Medicaid programs have limited coverage of substance abuse treatment services (Buck, 2011). Health care reform will improve coverage for substance abuse treatment services. Under the ACA, the essential health benefit (EHB) requires that substance abuse treatment services be covered (among other categories of items and services) and that the scope of health benefits provided must be "equal to the scope of health benefits under a typical employer plan."[7] The Secretary of Health and Human Services is tasked with identifying the essential health benefits and will have considerable leeway in determining what will be included. A key question is what will be the scope of benefits within these specified categories of services and to what degree cost-sharing or other utilization limits may be put into place to help ensure plan affordability. Thus, although substance abuse treatment services will be more fully covered, there could be substantial cost-sharing or other utilization limits that may make it difficult for ex-prisoners to afford care. In addition, these new requirements may change the nature of substance abuse treatment services so that it is less focused on residential treatment programs and more integrated into outpatient programs and into more integrated programs or care systems (Buck, 2011).

Lastly, states are required to expand Medicaid coverage. However, this change should not be overly burdensome to California given the federal matching rates for the expansion population (i.e., 100–138 percent of the FPL) (Somers et al., 2010).[8]

Beyond these issues, there are also some other challenges. Expansion of Medicaid eligibility could lead to increased demand for health

---

7 The EHB requirement applies to qualified health plans offered in state health benefit insurance exchanges, all new individual and group health plans, and benchmark or benchmark-equivalent benefit packages for the newly eligible Medi-Cal population (California Department of Alcohol and Drug Programs, 2011).

8 For states that had lower thresholds previously, the federal government will reimburse newly eligible populations at 100 percent initially, declining to 90 percent over time. For

care safety-net services that are already stretched thin, thus possibly affecting access to care given limited capacity at the county level. In addition, Disproportionate Share Hospital (DSH) payments[9] are being cut, which means that fewer resources will be available for individuals who remain uninsured. Noncitizens will not necessarily qualify for Medicaid. Finally, under the ACA, individuals can be penalized for not having health insurance, which likely will include a portion of the reentry population.[10] Combined, these changes and restrictions suggest both opportunities as well as challenges under health care reform. They also underscore the importance of facilitating Medicaid enrollment for eligible ex-prisoners and soon-to-be-released prisoners.

In summary, because of the current patchwork quilt of health care services available to ex-prisoners, few individuals returning from prison have a stable medical home. As a result, they are at risk for increased health problems and for recidivating. They may go without care or overuse the emergency department with expensive and inefficient care. However, improving access to insurance and increasing the number of providers is not enough. Ex-prisoners' social disadvantages, such as low education, low health literacy, and institutionalized attitudes, mean that education among patients and providers is necessary to ensure these patients receive the best care possible.

Many of the problems raised in this review of the literature were discussed in the interviews we conducted with health care providers. The approach we used for the provider interviews is summarized below, followed by the interview findings and a discussion of those findings.

---

states that previously provided coverage to individuals with incomes between 100 and 138 percent of the FPL, federal reimbursements starts out lower and then increases over time.

9 Disproportionate Share Hospital (DSH) adjustment payments provide additional help to those hospitals that serve a significantly disproportionate number of low-income patients. States receive an annual DSH allotment to cover the costs of DSH hospitals that provide care to low-income patients that are not paid by other payers, such as Medicare, Medicaid, or other health insurance (U.S. Department of Health and Human Services, no date).

10 Although penalties are waived for the lowest income groups (non–tax filers).

Provider Interviews: Approach

In addition to reviewing the literature, we conducted interviews with different types of providers in Alameda, Los Angeles, and San Diego counties. These interviews were intended to be exploratory in nature and to help identify possible areas for further exploration.

We selected interviewees who led or played a key role in their organization in terms of providing treatment services to the reentry population. The interviewees included a large county provider of indigent care, health care or mental health care providers co-located with nonprofit community organizations, a large nonprofit provider of drug treatment services (interviews included the organizational head and a case manager), an organization of health centers that provides primary health care services to the uninsured, a community assessment service center that serves as an entry point for individuals in need of alcohol or drug treatment services, and a community health center that serves as a medical home for the formerly incarcerated. In addition, we interviewed two public health directors, a deputy director of a county alcohol and drug program, and a representative from the Department of Veterans Affairs. We conducted a total of 12 provider interviews.

We created a semi-structured interview protocol (see Appendix B) to help guide the discussion. The following topics were addressed: views about the health care needs of individuals returning from prison, type of health care services and other services the organization provides, the organizations' service capacity to meet the needs of this population, the impact of budget cuts on the organization's ability to serve this population, factors that facilitate or hinder individuals' ability to access services, collaborations with other service providers or organizations, challenges the organization has faced in providing care to this population, and the interviewee's recommendations for improving access to care for this population.

Project team research staff conducted the interviews. As part of the provider oral consent form, each interviewee was promised confidentiality, and in some instances (when a notetaker was not available), they were also asked for permission to audio-record the interviews. None of the participants refused. Interviews that were audio-recorded were transcribed for use only by the research team for analytic purposes. The transcripts were augmented by the manual notes.

To analyze these data, we first reviewed the interview notes and transcripts to identify general themes. We then used a cutting-and-sorting technique to identify specific themes and to identify individual quotes or expressions that summarized the key discussion points. Our analysis of these qualitative data was intended to identify similarities and differences between interviewees with respect to the following domains: views about the treatment needs of this population; factors that facilitated or hindered access to care, challenges in providing services to this population and problems with continuity of care; effects of budget cuts; the role of communication and the role of patient navigators; and suggestions for improving access to services and transitioning care to community providers.

The experiences of this sample of providers by no means covers the range of perspectives from the provider community. But the themes and stories we heard are consistent with other findings from the literature. To provide the reader with an idea of how these findings relate to the broader literature in this field, we note in the discussion section how these findings compare with results from other research on providers vis-à-vis meeting the health care and other needs of the reentry population.

Provider Interviews: Results

From the Provider's Perspective, the Reentry Population Has a Wide Range of Treatment Needs

In Chapter Two, we summarized the survey results about the self-reported health care needs of inmates in California's prisons. Our provider interviews provide additional context for understanding the range of health care problems that providers encounter when treating this population. We asked them what type of treatment needs they see among the reentry population. One interviewee characterized *the treatment needs of the reentry population as the same kind of conditions any community health center may encounter,* including illnesses from neglect and lack of access to care, such as uncontrolled diabetes, asthma, or hypertension. Several providers commented on the chronic conditions seen among this population, including diabetes, hypertension, chronic obstructive pulmonary disease, and chronic pain. They also mentioned infectious diseases, such as hepatitis C and sexually transmitted diseases (STDs). In addition, a provider noted that in their clinics they were increasingly seeing dental and vision problems among the reentry population. Several providers also commented on the impact of unmet dental needs that can affect one's appearance (e.g., missing teeth) and an ex-prisoner's ability to find a job.

Providers also cited the need for mental health care and alcohol and drug treatment. For example, a mental health counselor who works with a community organization that provides wraparound services for the formerly incarcerated described the large need for mental health services among the clients she served. She estimated that approximately 65–70 percent of their clients were dealing with posttraumatic stress disorder, depression, and/or anxiety. A provider whose network includes a number of health centers similarly commented that ex-prisoners' mental health needs are large, with anxiety and depression being common among this population. Several interviewees also mentioned the need for medication management. Behavioral issues such as anger management were also cited. Substance abuse problems, including drug-seeking behavior (i.e., individuals trying to obtain narcotics), were noted by the provider of a network with a number of health centers.

Given their complex set of needs and untreated health conditions, *the reentry population tends to be more resource-intensive to treat.* An interviewee from a community assessment service center felt that one of the key issues is that ex-prisoners often present with medical problems that have gone untreated and undiagnosed for longer periods of time than is true for the general population. Thus, when they enter the health care system, assessing their treatment needs and stabilizing their conditions is a priority that can require substantial resources and time. Another provider similarly noted that when an ex-prisoner presents at one of their clinics, the individual tends to have a constellation of both health care and social services needs that require upfront a number of resources to do a comprehensive assessment and develop a treatment plan.

One of the challenges that health care providers face is how to link these individuals with other needed services (e.g., employment, housing, transportation). Several providers commented on the multitude of needs that ex-prisoners may have. For example, in addition to their health care needs, other concerns that must be addressed include whether that individual has eaten today, has transportation problems, or whether he or she has a place to sleep. From a health care perspective, one provider summarized the dilemma as follows:

> If an individual does not have housing, then [do] you need to consider where the patient can keep his or her prescriptions? If an individual has a hearing aid, could it be stolen? If an individual has an infection or a wound that will require periodically cleaning and fresh dressings applied, does he or she have a place where they can do so?

In the case of the community assessment treatment center, the center staff also make referrals to other community organizations for non-health-care-related needs and maintain a community resource guide and list of contacts to facilitate referrals. However, it is difficult to keep the information up to date as community programs experience budget cuts or have changes in space availability. The ability to link an individual to other services can be time-consuming and depends on having established in advance informal or formal relationships with other health care and community organizations.

Lack of Medications and Medical Records Can Affect Continuity of Care

The provider interviewees all commented on the problems associated with individuals being released from prison without an adequate supply of medications (especially those on psychiatric medications). For example, a mental health counselor stated that ex-prisoners she has treated with mental illness are supposed to be given a 30-day supply or a prescription that they can fill upon release from prison. However, in her experience, a number of individuals who are released have neither.

Further, ex-prisoners may be reluctant to use the limited funds (e.g., $200) they are given upon release from prison to buy medications, because they also need that money for transportation or a hotel room and other basic needs.

Several other providers also commented on this issue. In their view, prisoners are often released with only a few days' or a two-week supply of medications, and sometimes no prescription. This means that the ex-prisoner needs to have his or her medications refilled quickly upon release; yet it often takes time to get an appointment with a health care provider—a situation that can be anxiety-provoking for the individual. As a result, ex-prisoners may walk into a clinic the same day they need psychiatric medications refilled, yet the clinic may have no medical history information about them.

Two of the interviewees—one who is a large provider of indigent care and the other who oversees a large network of health centers—expressed *a desire to work with the California prison system to facilitate the postrelease transition of ex-prisoners.* Both had attempted in the past to do so but without success. In one case, the interviewee had previously tried but was unsuccessful, characterizing the process for doing so as being "very convoluted." The other provider discussed his organization's attempt to work with a local prison in the region to establish bridging services for those about to be released from prison and who likely would be seeking care from their community network of health centers. Although the prison's leadership was receptive to the idea, the social worker to whom the provider was transferred never contacted him to discuss further what could be done.

Differences in the drug formularies used by community providers versus the correctional health care system can also be problematic. Ex-prisoners expect that they will be able to continue on the same medications they were taking while in prison. However, differences in drug formularies may require them to change medications. For example, one interviewee noted that some of these medications may not be covered for their health center—that, instead, the center has to follow its own drug formularies in prescribing medications. This can prove frustrating to some individuals. A community health center provider similarly noted that their clinic has to provide patients with the medications that their county's drug formulary offers for them that may differ from what they had received from the correctional health care system.

Lack of medical records for those being released from prison is an important problem in terms of ensuring continuity of care. For example, a provider of indigent care noted that for those with HIV/AIDS or hepatitis—important public health concerns—it would be helpful to know what kind of care and education these individuals had received while incarcerated. Trying to get the medical records for a client can be difficult; and as another interviewee noted, relying on the individual to provide a detailed medical history is a poor substitute, because in general "patients are not good historians."

One interviewee in the context of discussing problems with continuity of care summarized the issue as follows:

> I think coordinated care needs to occur because if it doesn't then, you know, we're just going to throw them [ex-prisoners] into a [health care] system that is not, number one, equipped to deal with them and, number two, where behavioral issues and challenges are probably going to end up getting them connected again with law enforcement.

Individuals May Be Reluctant to Seek Help from Parole

For ex-prisoners with mental health problems, the parole outpatient clinic (POC) is a basic but important way for them to obtain the psychiatric medications they need. Individuals with mental illness and those on psychiatric medications upon release from prison are referred to the POC, or their parole officer can also make the referral. However, this process may not include the full range of prisoners who may need access to mental health treatment and medications upon release. These individuals may be reluctant to tell their parole officers that they need mental health care, for several reasons. A mental health counselor we spoke to commented that, in her view, the parole system penalizes individuals for making known that they have mental health or alcohol and drug treatment needs. The counselor noted that ex-prisoners she has counseled have reported concerns that the parole officer may see them as being a troublemaker or someone that needs to be watched more closely if they report needing mental health or drug treatment. As a result, ex-prisoners, in her experience, tend to avoid going to the POC altogether. In addition, she noted there is often little or no communication between the health care clinic or provider and the parole officer, which results in lack of documentation and lack of contact information; thus, ex-prisoners are often on their own in terms of getting linked to mental health care services.

Low Levels of Health Insurance and Lack of Finances Limit Treatment Options

One interviewee summarized the major factors limiting access to health care as lack of knowledge among ex-prisoners about what resources are available to them, lack of transportation, lack of insurance and inability to pay for health care, and an inability to meet eligibility requirements. In addition, lack of medications (and a plan for obtaining them upon release) and lack of medical records were cited as the type of problems that providers typically encounter.

Lack of health insurance and finances is an important barrier to accessing care for many ex-prisoners. The challenges it presents to community organizations trying to facilitate linkage to services is illustrated by the mental health counselor we interviewed. In her view, although her county has residential treatment programs for those with substance abuse problems, the cost is often prohibitively expensive for the reentry population. She estimated that residential treatment programs for those with substance abuse problems cost approximately $3,700 per month. In addition, although nonprofit counseling clinics, such as one run by a local college and another by a nonprofit charity organization, may provide services on a sliding fee scale, the mental health counselor rarely refers her reentry clients to these clinics because they simply lack the ability to pay anything at all.

Another provider who runs a network of health centers tried to give us a sense of the complex set of challenges faced by a community health center in trying to meet the needs of this population when they lack adequate insurance or funding:

Fourteen individuals between June 8th and June 20th came in that were prisoner reentry: seven for pain meds, which is a huge issue, legitimate or not; five with known mental health issues; four with hypertension; three with diabetes; and three requesting or needing, you know, just assistance in terms of . . . just some kind of help. The patients report being released from prison, jail, or probation with 10 days' worth of psych meds and they need help with getting more. But sometimes if an individual calls for an appointment, our first available [one] might be in 10 days [to] three weeks [out]. . . .

Thirteen of them were deemed eligible for our Health Care for the Homeless program, but there's a limitation of three visits per year; and two were CMS [County Medical Services, San Diego County], which is getting ready to be transitioned to something else that maybe they will or they won't qualify [for]; of those two that were in CMS, mental health and health education was being provided through our Health Care for the Homeless program and only one was a Medi-Cal patient. So, basically, we have one that's funded at an acceptable level, the 14th [individual].

Many of these patients who had Medi-Cal, CMS, SSI [Supplemental Security Income], all of that stuff before being incarcerated, they lost it while they were incarcerated. Many of the patients don't have basic IDs and birth certificates needed to apply for [health care] funding. . . . So, three of those 14 didn't even have identifications, and being on the outside presents these patients with a challenge of lack of stable food, shelter, medical care [which they had] while they were incarcerated. They also have, and the best I can describe it, is kind of a post-traumatic stress syndrome. . . . [A]nd, of course, as I mentioned, some of the patients exhibit aggressive behavior and it could be because they are drug-seeking. . . . So, that kind of gives you a snapshot at one site.

Interviewer: That's just one of your clinics.

Yeah, that's just a two-week period.

Challenge of Linking Individuals to Mental Health Treatment

As summarized in Chapter Two, many individuals returning from prison also bring with them mental health treatment needs. From the providers' perspective, *these individuals face a number of challenges in accessing care, including limited mental health treatment resources, delays in being seen by a health care professional, and lack of health insurance.* The discussion below illustrates the challenges from the perspective of a mental health counselor trying to link her clients to mental health services.

The mental health counselor characterized her county's mental health treatment resources as lacking beds, mental health professionals, and funding. To place an ex-prisoner who is in need of psychiatric treatment, she often will spend a lot of time calling various providers in the county to see whether there are any residential treatment program slots available. For example, she recently attempted to place a female ex-prisoner with severe post-traumatic stress disorder. The counselor called ten different mental health providers, only to be told there were no treatments slots available, because this ex-prisoner lacked health insurance. Eventually, the counselor was able to get the female ex-prisoner into a crisis home. As a result, this mental health counselor said that she tends to rely on crisis homes for the clients she serves. Yet crisis homes are only a temporary solution, with maximum lengths of stay of 7–14 days. And although crisis homes provide medications and some access to counseling, they often release an individual without medications. In addition, she noted that individuals with dual diagnoses (mental illness and substance abuse) or those with serious mental illness, such as schizophrenia, are especially difficult to place. Because the waiting lists to be seen by a psychiatrist or to get into a residential treatment facility can be long, the counselor noted that many individuals end up self-medicating or going without their medications and destabilizing.

The counselor said that she will refer less acutely ill patients to county mental health, where they will briefly see a psychiatrist (usually a resident) who will prescreen them and give them a two-week prescription of medications to tide them over until they can get an appointment with the psychiatrist. However, the wait time for an appointment is typically 3–8 weeks, which means that patients run the risk of running out of medications during that period or needing to again attempt to see a psychiatric resident to obtain another two-week supply of medications. And if a patient tests positive for drugs, then the psychiatric resident will not provide them with a prescription for medications.

The counselor noted that, complicating this process, *individuals who are coming out of prison often may not report mental health problems* or will wait until they are getting worse or destabilizing to do so. She felt this was the result of several factors, including the stigma associated with mental illness and the fact that some did not like the effect the psychiatric medications had on them. Thus, when the mental counselor learns of an individual's need to refill his psychiatric medications, it is often when that individual has already run out or is very near to running out of his medications.

Communication Problems on Both the Individual and Provider Sides

Adaptive behaviors that may have worked in an incarcerated setting such as not trusting and intimidating others are seen as maladaptive and even threatening in a health care setting. A number of providers commented on this issue. As one interviewee noted, ex-prisoners often have a cluster of issues, including feelings of isolation and depression, along with drug and alcohol abuse. Not being in society for a long period of time can hinder their ability to effectively communicate and advocate for themselves. Thus, individuals released from prison may misinterpret delays in appointments or long waiting times as a sign of disrespect or rejection. Low levels of literacy can also complicate communications.

Interviewees recognized the *need for treatment providers to become culturally competent* and more sensitive to the experience of incarceration and how that may affect an individual, echoing some of the focus group comments from ex-prisoners summarized in Chapter Three. Several of the providers considered it important to train staff to help them understand the characteristics of those returning from prison and what impact the experience of being in prison for 5– 20 years has on an individual. They said that a related challenge is finding the right staff and volunteers to work with the reentry population. Then again, several other providers had differing viewpoints. One interviewee felt that their network of providers were generally sensitive to the circumstances of these individuals and tried to work with the situation. Another interviewee representing a community health center did not consider communication problems to be an issue given their mission, which emphasizes cultural competency and the diversity of their staff and multicultural nature of their community and patient population. This provider also has staff members who were formerly incarcerated who assist individuals returning from prison to navigate the local health care system.

Difficulties in Navigating Health Care and Social Services Systems

Coming from a highly structured prison environment, where little is left up to the individual, to a community environment, where the health care and social services systems vary in their complexity and organization, can be challenging. Interviewees commented on the difficulties that those released from prison encounter in navigating the health care system. One interviewee noted it is not uncommon for ex-prisoners to miss appointments or not understand why a referral requires prior authorization or that a single visit to a primary care provider may not be sufficient to address all their needs.

All the interviewees commented on *the need for patient advocates or navigators to help ex-prisoners navigate the health care and social services systems.* Preferably, these individuals would have experience in working with the reentry population or would have been formerly incarcerated themselves. For example, the different silos in the health care and social services systems can complicate the referral process for individuals with a complex set of needs. If an ex-prisoner needs a consult with a cardiologist, the individual may require prior authorization and the cardiologist may be located far away, requiring the ex-prisoner to travel some distance for the consultation. And if an individual needs other referrals, such as to social services, then the individual will need to go other locations to access those services. This can be frustrating to individuals who may not understand why they need to go to multiple locations to receive services. In providers' view, this underscores the importance of providing assistance to the reentry population to navigate these various systems.

The *need for bridging services for individuals about to be released from prison* was considered especially important for those with mental health problems, or infectious diseases, such as hepatitis C or HIV/AIDS. As one provider put it, having someone who can go over with an individual all their medications and their past medical history as part of the prerelease process and then develop a tailored plan for accessing health care services upon release would be important. Another provider commented that the most immediate needs would be helping individuals get medications refilled and, in terms of navigational services, helping individuals understand what resources are available, how to access them, and how to behave in a health care setting. As he put it, the key questions for someone about to be released should be, "Do they have behavioral needs? Do they have psych med needs? Are [they] actively in a continuation program or transition program for alcohol and drug abuse? Do [they] have a place to live?"

Uncertainty Among Safety-Net Providers About How to Access Reentry Population

Extrapolating primarily from anecdotal information, *providers have a sense that they are increasingly serving the reentry population, but they do not necessarily have the statistics to quantify this assessment.* Safety-net health care providers in general often do not know which patients are former prisoners unless an individual self-identifies or there is another mechanism of disclosure. For example, one shelter/transitional home for ex-prisoners provides its clients with passes to seek services at local health centers. When an individual arrives at the health center with a pass, the clinic staff will then know he or she is an ex-prisoner. Another provider explicitly links with individuals prior to release who will be returning to the county from prison. In the case of the community assessment service center, they will know if an individual is an ex-prisoner; if the individual is referred to them by the courts, probation, or parole; or if an individual self-identifies.

Nonprofit community organizations are often important referral mechanisms for health care providers. As one CEO of a large group of health centers commented, "We don't have specific outreach to the [reentry] population. However, what we have done is we have a partnership with some agencies, such as the United African American Ministerial Action Council." Other organizations cited by the providers as making referrals to them included halfway houses; nonprofit community organizations that provide employment, housing, or wraparound services for the reentry population; and, in general, community assessment service centers (CASCs) and other health care providers. One community health center has a transportation program that picks up individuals as they are released from prison or jail and brings them to the center for an initial checkup.

Impact of Budget Cuts on Providers

When providers were asked what impact, if any, state, county, or city budget cuts have had on their organization's ability to provide services in general and specifically to the reentry population, the response we received was "huge." One provider of a network of health care clinics that serves the uninsured commented said they were just starting to see the tip of the iceberg. In this case, the provider eliminated its HIV programs and dental care programs and drastically cut back its mental health services.

The budget cuts have led one community assessment service center, which provide linkages for individuals to health care and other services, to reassess and shift priorities and to make tough decisions about what services they can provide: For example, should they focus just on conducting assessments, or should they also provide substance abuse, mental health, and medical treatment services? In addition, they also reassessed the external environment and their community partners to understand what may be changing for them and with respect to cuts in capacity and services.

For a nonprofit drug treatment provider, the budget cuts by CDCR for in-custody and community-based substance abuse treatment services have had a large impact. Whereas this provider used to have programs in 11 prison facilities, it now has programs in only two. Budget cuts also have led this provider to close its sober living facility. Further, there is no new county funding available to replace the funding lost from the state. In this provider's view, some of the *budget cuts may have resulted in perverse incentives for some patients.* For example, prior to CDCR's budget cuts, eligible ex-prisoners with substance abuse problems would leave prison with a funding stream for both residential drug treatment services and outpatient follow-up care (sober living). The cuts to sober living though have meant that the only continued treatment options are now residential drug treatment services, which many patients can only access through the criminal justice system. As a result, some individuals may purposely commit new crimes to gain access to treatment. This interviewee also commented that cuts in the Medi-Cal program have also had an impact on dental programs—a high-priority issue for many ex-prisoners.

Another effect of the budget cuts at the state and county levels for alcohol and drug treatment is an increase in administrative costs for treatment providers. In the case of the nonprofit drug treatment provider, its organization has had to try and replace funding lost from the state with new funding from a variety of sources. This has resulted in a patchwork quilt of some 65 different funders, each of which has its own auditors and guidelines that this single provider must comply with. Further, residential drug treatment now has to be authorized in seven-day increments, with the maximum limits being far below the norms provided in treatment guidelines.

More important in this provider's view, *the overall changes have resulted in dramatic decreases in the length of stay in residential drug treatment programs.* Whereas before an individual may have stayed 1–2 years in a residential drug treatment program, the average stay now is only 90 days. She was concerned that this new shortened model, driven by budget cuts, may impact the effectiveness of these treatment programs. A case manager for this treatment program echoed this view, stating that in many cases it can take an individual at least 1–2 months to detox before being able to effectively participate in a treatment program.

Another interviewee commented about the general lack of political will to allocate the resources needed for the reentry population. She referred to meeting the service needs of the reentry population as an unfunded mandate:

> [W]hat happens after our tax dollars and when they leave prison—while they're in prison, while they're being charged, while they're being picked up, profiled, all that. There's funding for that, but there's no funding once they've served their time and it's time to come back home. So it's an unfunded mandate, an unfunded phase of the criminal justice process. That's the biggest burden.

Providers' Recommendations for Improving Access to Services for the Reentry Population

The providers had a number of recommendations for improving access to services. The first set focused on transitioning their care from the prison system to community health care providers—the *prerelease phase*—and included the following:

- Have correctional health care staff notify clinic directors in advance about individuals soon to be released who may be on medications or who have serious health care problems that will require ongoing medical management; this would enable providers to help set up appointments in advance of an individual's release from prison. For individuals who are connected with halfway houses or transition programs, have the clinic director meet with these residents to facilitate the transition of their care.
- For those with mental illness or other serious health conditions, have the correctional health care system release individuals with an adequate supply of medications (e.g., at least 30 days); for individuals being released from county jail, provide them with at least a 3–5-day supply of medications.
- Have the correctional health care system provide individuals (or community clinics) with copies of their patient medical record prior to being released from prison; alternatively, have community clinicians go inside the prison prior to release to take a detailed medical history, including documenting what medications an individual is on, facilitating setting up an initial appointment, and helping create a chart that can go with the individual to the clinic where he or she will be seen.
- Provide individuals with information about where they can go to seek care and phone numbers of health care providers and clinics

available to serve them; tailor this information to the counties to which individuals will be returning.
- Assist individuals to begin completing the paperwork to have health insurance and other benefits reinstated at least 30 days prior to release from prison.

Recommendations for the *postrelease phase* include the following:

- Have communities' clinic staff conduct outreach activities with the reentry population to facilitate their linkage to health care services and to ensure that they have an adequate supply of medications (one possible solution is for providers to attend monthly PACT meetings to provide information about services available and how to access them).
- Have on staff individuals who have experience working with the reentry population and/or who themselves were formerly incarcerated to serve as patient navigators.
- Provide linguistic and interpretation services in community health care settings.
- Have community health care providers and nonprofit organizations seek grant funding to support identification of best practices in terms of patient navigational services and to assess how associated costs may be covered.

Discussion

From community health care providers' perspective, the reentry population has substantial mental health and substance abuse treatment needs, as well as significant chronic health problems, including diabetes, hypertension, renal disease, and infectious diseases, such as HIV/AIDS and hepatitis C. The findings in Chapter Two and the literature cited in this chapter support these assertions. In addition, providers recognize that ex-prisoners have a range of other needs, such as transportation, employment, and housing, which are important to take into account in treating these patients. Given newly released prisoners' complex set of needs and the prevalence of untreated health conditions among them, this is a population that often is more resource-intensive to treat, from the providers' perspective. The providers we interviewed did not comment on whether the health needs of ex-prisoners exceeded treatment capacity, as did Rhode Island providers who were interviewed in a separate study (LaVigne et al., 2004). Instead, the California providers discussed that, given the complex needs of these individuals, providing care would require multiple visits and referrals for specialty care, in addition to referrals to social services.

Providers also cited as a critical issue ensuring continuity of care for those being released from prison, especially those with chronic health care conditions or mental health or substance abuse treatment needs. Lack of adequate medications upon release can be problematic, because it often takes time for an individual to see a primary care or mental health provider out in the community. As a result, ex-prisoners are at risk of self-medicating or destabilizing. In addition, lack of medical history records makes it difficult for providers to treat this population, because providers essentially have to start from the beginning and undertake a comprehensive assessment. This, in turn, can contribute to this population being more resource-intensive to treat.

The providers we interviewed had recommendations for the correctional health system to release individuals, particularly those on psychiatric medications, with at least a 30-day supply of medications, because it can take time for an ex-prisoner to get an appointment with a community provider. In addition, the providers emphasized the need for ex-prisoners to be given copies of their medical records prior to release or to have community health care staff go into the prisons and take a detailed medical history to create a chart for the individual who will be seen by their clinic and facilitate setting up the initial appointment.

The providers we interviewed were not familiar with what type of prerelease planning is currently being done by CDCR. In general, CDCR's prerelease planning is based on need and acuity. For example, for individuals who require ongoing mental health care, especially those with more serious illnesses, CDCR will attempt to have the soon-to-be-released prisoner sign a release form so that their mental health information can be sent to county departments of mental health. (See Chapter Six for a more detailed discussion of prerelease planning by CDCR and recommendations for improving it.) The critical point here is that, from the community providers' perspectives, there are very few mechanisms in place to ensure continuity of care.

In addition, several providers had tried unsuccessfully to coordinate with local prisons to facilitate the transition of care for those about to leave prison. A key recommendation by the providers we interviewed was that California's correctional health care system notify community clinic directors in advance about individuals soon to be released from prison who may be on medications or who have serious health care problems that will require ongoing medical management. LaVigne et al. (2004) heard similar concerns from Rhode Island providers who participated in a focus group and felt that corrections staff did not try to incorporate them into the prerelease planning process. In addition, the Rhode Island providers noted lack of coordination among service providers in general that can result in a numbers of ex-prisoners with acute health care needs slipping through the cracks. The Rhode Island providers recommended that corrections staff, health care providers in the community, and soon-to-be-released prisoners work together to coordinate and develop pre- and postrelease health care plans.

A number of factors make it difficult for ex-prisoners to access care. These include lack of health insurance and finances, which serves as major barriers for providers and nonprofit community services to link an individual to needed services. Other factors include communication barriers, a lack of understanding of how the health care system is organized, and difficulties in navigating the different silos that make up the health care and social services systems. Combined, these factors also make it difficult for health care providers and community organizations to facilitate linkages to health care and other needed services.

Meeting the mental health needs of ex-prisoners, including individuals with co-occurring disorders (e.g., substance abuse problems and mental illness), was particularly emphasized by the mental health counselor interviewed for our study. The description of the level of effort required to place an individual in a treatment program or at least a crisis home and the lack of treatment options with dual-diagnoses have also been noted by other studies. For example, providers interviewed in LaVigne et al. (2004) commented that in Rhode Island, few residential treatment centers are set up to handle individuals with both substance abuse problems and serious mental illness; as a result, many individuals with co-occurring disorders end up at health centers and clinics that are equipped to handle only one issue or the other. Hiller et al. (2005) examined the use of health care services by prisoners with co-occurring disorders (substance abuse and mental health problems) and found that this group reported significantly greater use of the emergency room and more hospital stays, both for their lifetime and in the year prior to their current incarceration. Interviewees also recognized the importance of providers being sensitive to the experiences of the reentry population and trained on culturally competent care. The Health Resources and Service Administration (HRSA) provides a range of resources on cultural competence, including guidelines and toolkits (Health Resources Service Administration, no date-a). However, to our knowledge, none of these specifically address the criminal justice-involved population. Rotter et al. (2005) developed an approach to client engagement called Sensitizing Providers to the Effects of Correctional Incarceration on Treatment and Risk Management (SPECTRM) that could be used to train providers working with the reentry population. SPECTRM consists of a half-day training workshop for providers, which reviews potential behaviors considered adaptive in jail and prison and uses a cultural competence approach to address them and help providers to understand how these behaviors are often misinterpreted in community treatment settings (Rotter et al., 2005).

In Chapter Three, we discussed the cuts that have occurred with respect to state-level funded in-prison and community treatment services. In this chapter, our interviewees provided important insights about the impact of budget cuts on community health care providers in terms of having to reduce services, which could limit treatment options for the reentry population. These cuts included eliminating some services, such as mental health and sober living beds; reducing the number of treatment slots; and changing treatment models to much shorter courses of treatment. One provider also expressed concern about the impact of budget cuts on organizations to which they make referrals.

As for suggestions on how to improve access to care and facilitate better the transition of their care to community health care providers, our interviewees had a number of recommendations. We already summarized several of them above. In addition, the providers recognized the critical need for patient navigators who can assist ex-prisoners with understanding the health care system, assist with communications and medications, assist with health insurance issues, and help individuals access other health care and social services.

Two examples of clinics in California using this concept to assist the formerly incarcerated are the Transitions Clinic in San Francisco (National Reentry Resource Center and U.S. Department of Justice Bureau of Justice Assistance, 2010) and Healthy Oakland in Oakland (Healthy Oakland, no date; the official name is Healthy Communities, Inc.). The Transitions Clinics uses community health workers whose responsibilities include outreach to individuals returning from prison or jail and serving as patient navigators. Healthy Oakland similarly uses patient navigators who have been formerly incarcerated to conduct outreach and assist individuals returning from prison and jail to access health care services and other needed services. Both the Transitions Clinic and Healthy Oakland have ties to the public health departments in their respective counties. As discussed in Chapter Six, health care reform provides California with an important chance to further develop the medical home or health home concept for this population.

Lastly, a limitation of this analysis is that it represents only the perspective of community and some county health care providers. It does not include the perspectives of the CDCR California Correctional Health Care Services responsible for providing mental health and dental services to prison inmates, nor of the California Prison Health Care Services, overseen by the court-appointed federal receiver. In addition, we recognize that the provider results are based on a small sample of individuals. We therefore have compared these findings with other research on the challenges communities face in trying to serve this population to place these findings into a broader context.

CHAPTER FIVE

The Impact of Incarceration on Families: Key Findings

Introduction

As of 2000, an estimated 856,000 California children—approximately 1 in 9—have a parent involved in the adult criminal justice system (Simmons, 2000). Fifty percent of African-American inmates, 60 percent of Latino inmates, and 53 percent of white inmates in state prison have children under the age of 18 years (Davis et al., 2009). Approximately 21 percent of California prisoners (or 41 percent of those who reported minor children at the time of the BJS Survey of Inmates interview) were living with their children at the time of their latest arrest.

These children often face a set of odds that makes them especially vulnerable and at risk for poor outcomes as young adults. Children of incarcerated parents are more likely to exhibit low self-esteem, depression, emotional withdrawal from friends and family, and inappropriate or disruptive behavior at home and in school, and they are at increased risk of future delinquency and/or criminal behavior (Travis and Waul, 2003; Murray and Farrington, 2008). Incarceration also tends to place new burdens on governmental resources that are important for meeting the needs of these children and their families, including schools, foster care, adoption agencies, and other services (Travis, McBride, and Solomon, 2005).

In this chapter, we summarize key findings from the literature about what is known with respect to the impact of incarceration on children and families. We also present the results of a focus group discussion with women who serve as caregivers for their children and grandchildren while the children's parents serve time in California's state prison system.

Literature on the Impact of Incarceration on Children and Families

Impact of Individual-Level Effects of Parental Incarceration

As the U.S. prison population has grown, the number of children with an incarcerated parent has grown along with it. Between 1991 and 2007, the share of children who had incarcerated parents rose 79 percent. Today, nearly half the prisoners in state prison are parents. All told, the Bureau of Justice Statistics estimates that 1.7 million minor children in the United States—representing 2.3 percent of those 18 years or younger—have an incarcerated parent (Glaze and Maruschak, 2008). In 2004, nationally half of minor children with an incarcerated parent in state prisons were between the ages of 1 and 9 (Glaze and Maruschak, 2008).

The types of offenses that lead to incarceration vary among fathers and mothers. Nationally, parents incarcerated in state and federal prisons are more likely to be incarcerated for drug-related or nonviolent offenses than nonparents in correctional institutions (Glaze and Maruschak, 2008). Among the previously incarcerated, prisoners with a prior drug conviction (62 percent) have a higher likelihood of being a parent than prisoners with a prior conviction of a violent crime (52 percent).

Nationally, about half of parents in state prison provide the primary financial support for their minor children. More than a third of mothers in state prison report government transfers, such as welfare, Social Security, or compensation payment as income. Mothers are more likely than fathers to report receiving government transfers, regardless of who provided the primary financial support for their children (Glaze and Maruschak, 2008).

When a parent is incarcerated, the impact on the children is large and often hidden. Not only do such children lose a parent, they must also cope with altered systems of care—such as having to live with grandparents, having a new adult in the home, or even having to go into foster care. The incarceration of a mother is especially disruptive for a child. Mothers in prison most commonly are the primary caregiver for their children, whereas fathers most commonly report the child's mother as being the caregiver of their children. In these families, when a mother is incarcerated, grandparents play an important caregiver role. Forty-two percent of mothers incarcerated in state prisons identified the child's grandmother as the current caregiver and 12 percent reported the child's grandfather as the current caregiver (Glaze and Maruschak, 2008). In addition, more mothers than fathers had their child(ren) being cared for by a foster home or agency (11 percent versus 2 percent) (Glaze and Maruschak, 2008).

Parental incarceration can have a range of negative effects on children, effects that are similar to what one might expect in terms of the impact of any traumatic event on child development. The immediate effects of incarceration and the loss of a parent can include feelings of shame, social stigma, loss of financial support, weakened ties to the parent, poor school performance, increased delinquency, and increased risk of abuse or neglect (Travis, McBride, and Solomon, 2005). Longer-term effects may include questioning of parental authority, negative perceptions of the police and the legal system, impaired ability to cope with future stress or trauma, disruption of development, and intergenerational patterns of criminal behavior (Travis, McBride, and Solomon, 2005). Further, the needs of these children may vary by such factors as age at separation from their parent, the length of separation, the level of disruption to the family, and the availability of family or community support (Travis and Waul, 2003). In a study of children of mothers involved with the criminal justice system, Phillips et al. (2006) identified four subgroups of these children: (1) children with only isolated risks, (2) children with histories of abuse, (3) children with multiple parents/caregivers who have histories of drug abuse and/or mental health problems, and (4) children whose parents have few problems but are living in economically deprived, single-parent households. It is important to view incarceration not as a single event but rather as a process that unfolds over time, from the arrest phase to the conviction and imprisonment phase and then to the return of the parent (Parke and Clarke-Stewart, 2003).

Incarceration tends to disrupt parent-child relationships, because prison-visiting policies and practices are often not designed to reflect the needs of these children and are not geared toward maintaining the parent-child relationship (Hairston, 2007). Incarcerated parents may be housed far away from where their children and families live, thus making visits by family members difficult to achieve. For example, Travis, McBride, and Solomon (2003) report that women are housed in prisons that are, on average, 160 miles from their children, whereas men are housed in prisons that are, on average, 100 miles away. Other barriers to maintaining contact between a parent and child include corrections policies that may limit the number of calls or letters an inmate may receive, unaffordable collect call charges for phone calls made from prison, and restrictive prison visitation policies and harsh rules that make prison visits a negative experience for families and children (Hairston, 2007).

Finally, kinship caregivers, whether formal or informal, face a range of challenges, including helping the children cope with the emotional trauma of having a parent incarcerated, coping with different systems (such as the child welfare, educational, or legal systems), providing the financial support for the children, arranging visits with incarcerated parents, and dealing with the stigma of having a relative who is incarcerated (Nickel, Garland, and Kane, 2009). Given this, kinship caregivers have a range of support needs, including help with child care, housing, and financial support and assistance in navigating the various social services and systems (e.g., health care, mental health care, legal) that these families come in contact with. Grandparents who are caregivers must also address their own health care and other needs. For example, a study of 39 grandparent caregivers in Illinois found that 9 out of 10 were over the age of 50 and that 80 percent reported one or more health problems, such as arthritis, high blood pressure, or diabetes (Smithgall et al., 2006). Half said that they needed or participated in mental health services. Fifty-six percent of the grandparent caregivers said that the children under their care had emotional or behavioral concerns, and 41 percent said that the children had learning or developmental disabilities (Smithgall et al., 2006). In this particular study, one-fifth of grandparent caregivers reported that the leading circumstance that led to their caring for their grandchildren was that one or both of the biological parents were incarcerated, and nearly half said that the leading circumstance was alcohol and/or drug use by the biological parent(s).

The Impact of Child Welfare Laws and Other Legislation

In addition to the individual-level effects of parental incarceration, at the policy level, *child welfare laws and other legislation can have a disproportional impact on this population.* The federal Adoption and Safe Families Act of 1997 (AFSA) (Pub. Law 105-89) has provisions that accelerate the termination of parental rights for those who are incarcerated, because the law requires states to seek termination of parental rights when a child has been in foster care 15 of the previous 22 months. Yet this is a short time period for incarcerated parents, many of whom may be serving sentences of more than 18 months. Thus, incarcerated parents are disproportionately more likely than other parents to have their parental rights terminated if their children are placed in the foster care system. In California, for example, courts may terminate the rights of a parent convicted of a felony indicating parental unfitness (Nieto, 2002). Although courts are allowed to make exceptions if there is a "compelling reason" to retain parental rights, many parents and welfare agencies are often unaware of their options in this regard.

Welfare regulations also can impact parents' abilities to take care of their children upon release from prison. The Personal Responsibility and Work Opportunity Reconciliation Act (Pub. Law 104-93) permanently bars those with a drug-related felony conviction from receiving federal cash assistance and food stamps during their lifetime, unless their state has opted out of this provision. Federal welfare law also prohibits states from providing Temporary Assistance for Needy Families, Supplementary Security Income, housing, and food stamps to individuals who have violated a condition of probation or parole. Further, many localities also impose workfare requirements on public assistance recipients. At the same time, it can be difficult for a woman ex-offender, for example, to get an exemption from workfare assignments to participate in drug treatment. A missed appointment for either program can result in termination of benefits.

Incarcerated parents also continue to owe child support while incarcerated. While incarcerated, parents' ability to earn the required income is usually very limited. Upon release, then, the formerly incarcerated parent is faced with substantial child support debts. In some cases, the debts can lead to re-incarceration and/or incentives to engage in illegal activity, and can also interfere with the parent's relationship with his or her child (Cammett, 2006). Without modification, child support arrearages can grow significantly while a parent is in prison, and, upon release, wages can be garnished. For example, in Colorado, the average inmate with a child support order experiences a 63 percent increase in arrears balance during their term in prison. The average amount of child support owed upon release was $16,651 (Pearson, 2004).

There is wide variation across states in inmates' ability to modify their child support orders as a result of their imprisonment. State courts differ in whether incarceration should be considered "voluntary unemployment." Some state judges have concluded that if the inmate willingly committed criminal behavior, then he is responsible for his change in ability to pay child support; such judges have thus argued that the child support order should remain the same. Other states have come to the opposite conclusion by recognizing that inmates' ability to pay has changed, thus allowing for changes in the child support order. However, even if the state allows for changes in the child support order, there are often additional barriers. In general, parents have to petition the court to modify child support orders, which can be a lengthy and cumbersome process (Pearson, 2004). For example, a lack of coordination between corrections agencies and child support enforcement agencies leads to poor communication of rights and responsibilities to the inmate. It is also difficult to identify and communicate with incarcerated parents about their child support obligations and options. No state automatically modifies an obligor's child support order when the parent enters prison. Either the noncustodial parent or the custodial parent must request a review and adjustment.

What Is Known About Programs to Help Children and Incarcerated Parents

Approaches to providing services and support to these families and parents fall into three broad categories: (1) addressing the needs of parents and children, (2) addressing child support issues, and (3) addressing child welfare issues. Programs that have been tried focus either on the parent as the target of intervention, on the family unit, or on the child him/herself. In general, interventions focused on children of incarcerated parents have tended to be limited in number, to have involved small sample sizes, and to not have been rigorously evaluated (Hairston, 2007). In addition, many of these programs have had short life spans, and they often have small budgets, tend to rely on volunteers, and tend not to be part of established social services programs or agencies (Hairston, 2007).

In-prison programs to address the needs of children of incarcerated parents have included such activities as parent education classes, parent-child visitation programs, child-in-residence programs, mentoring programs, and support groups for children. Parent education classes can cover a range of different topics, from basic child development and the development of parenting skills, to the realities of parenting from prison and dealing with children's reactions to parental incarceration (Hairston, 2007). Parent education classes aimed at fathers also may cover such issues as child support, anger management. and domestic violence. In general, these programs tend to vary widely in content, number of sessions offered, the target population (incarcerated mothers, fathers, or both), and their level of financial and institutional support (Loper and Tuerk, 2009). Evaluations of these programs vary in their rigor, and outcome evaluations on the impact of these programs in improving parenting skills and child outcomes have been very limited (Hairston, 2007). Further, as noted above, many of these programs have been short-lived, partly because they are not part of established social services' programs or agencies; thus, when correctional programming cuts occur, these programs often are among the first to be cut.

Child-parent visitation programs are designed to enable incarcerated parents, often mothers, to spend extended time with their children. These programs can include daylong visits, overnight visits, and child-in-residence programs. The goal is to maintain the child-parent relationship during incarceration and decrease the negative impact of parental incarceration and separation (Hairston, 2007). Girls Scouts Beyond Bars is one example of an enhanced visitation program that allows girls to participate with their mothers in structured troop activities and provides counseling and support to the girls (Hairston, 2007). An evaluation of the Girl Scouts Beyond Bars program found that it led to more frequent prison visits by these children, improved communication between the mothers and daughters, and helped to decrease the stress children felt because of separation from their mothers (Block and Potthast, 1998; Miller, 2006). In addition, such programs can help decrease caregivers' stress (Miller, 2006). Child-in-residence programs allow mothers to keep their infants or young children with them while they serve their sentence. Typically, these mothers and children are housed in a separate part of the correctional facility or in a secure community setting (Hairston, 2007). These programs are intended to foster mother-child bonding and also provide the mothers with opportunities to learn and practice good parenting skills.

Mentoring programs for children and youth include the Amachi Program, a community-based program started in Philadelphia as a partnership of secular and faith-based institutions that recruits volunteer from congregations who mentor children of prisoners. The Amachi mentoring model is based on the notion that effective mentoring can help prevent risky behavior and promote achievement among children, and the program has been replicated in a number of other cities (Goode and Smith, 2005). Similar to other mentoring programs, the Amachi program model matches children with mentors who commit to spend a certain amount of time each week over at least a year with the child. In addition, the federal government has funded an initiative called the Mentoring Children of Prisoners (MCP) Program, which has funded a number of mentoring programs throughout the United States. However, evaluation results are not yet available to assess the impact of these programs. There is also a broader literature that addresses the needs of at-risk youth that we can draw on, because children with incarcerated parents are generally considered to have many of the same risk factors. In terms of mentoring programs, evaluations of the Big Brothers Big

Sisters of America mentoring program have shown positive outcomes in such areas as reductions in antisocial behaviors (e.g., use of illicit drugs) and improvements in academic outcomes (e.g., higher grade point averages, less school absenteeism) (Promising Practices Network, 2009). However, one large-scale evaluation of the Big Brothers Big Sisters of America program cautioned that short-term mentoring of youth may not lead to long-term changes (Hairston, 2007).

There also have been efforts in various states to address the policy and legislative issues in the area of child support. For example, there have been initiatives to educate and support incarcerated parents about child support issues, such as in the state of New York, where child support enforcement workers train correctional counselors as part of prerelease programs. Some states, such as Massachusetts and Texas, are experimenting with ways to streamline the review process to expedite modification requests to child support orders filed by incarcerated parents. California and other states include information about child support requirements as part of the prerelease process. In addition, some community programs that offer a range of services to the reentry population also offer services to help parents understand and address their child support requirements.

Finally, there are programs focused on grandparents as caregivers in general. For example, various states, including California, have kinship navigator programs intended to facilitate linkage with local resources, such as caregiver support groups, training, or respite care (Nickel, Garland, and Kane, 2009). California's kinship navigator program lists services available at the individual county level (California Kinship, undated). The intent of these programs is to help caregivers navigate through various systems such as child welfare, child care, Temporary Assistance for Needy Families, health, legal/judicial, and education.

Family Caregiver Focus Group: Approach

In addition to reviewing the literature, we conducted a focus group with seven caregivers of children whose parents are incarcerated. This discussion was intended to be exploratory in nature and to help suggest areas for further exploration.

To select the focus group participants, we worked with a community-based organization in San Diego County that provides services to children of incarcerated parents. We developed a recruitment flyer that the community organization sent home with the children participating in the organization's program inviting caregivers to participate in our focus group discussion. The community organization staff also called individual caregivers to encourage their participation in the focus group. The community organization served as the location for the focus group discussion. A RAND researcher led the focus group discussion, with a project team member serving as the notetaker; both had extensive experience in qualitative research. Focus group participants were provided an incentive payment at the end of the discussion to thank them for their participation. We also bought dinner for them to eat during the discussion. The focus group participants were promised confidentiality and were encouraged to use their first name only or a nickname. As part of the oral consent form, we asked participants for their permission to audio-record the discussion and provided the option of not doing so; none of the participants refused. The research team did not have access to any prior information about the participants. Although the community organization provided space to conduct the focus groups, none of the organization's staff members were allowed to observe or participate in the discussion. The focus group discussion was audio-recorded and transcribed for use only by the research team for analytic purposes.

Table 5.1 summarizes the characteristics of the children's families. A total of seven caregivers agreed to participate in the focus group. Six of the caregivers were grandmothers, while one was a mother with two daughters. In five of the families, both of the children's parents were or had previously been incarcerated.

A focus group protocol was created (see Appendix B) to help guide the discussion. The following topics were addressed: the child's initial concerns about being separated from his or her parent; whether the child had any contact with his or her parent; behavioral problems or other problems, such as with school, that the child has experienced; the

Table 5.1
Characteristics of the Families

Focus Group Participant	Children	Incarcerated Parent
Participant #1	Two teenage grandsons (ages 11 and 14)	Both parents
Participant #2	One granddaughter (in middle school)	Both parents
Participant #3	One grandson (in middle school)	Information not available
Participant #4	Two teenage granddaughters	Father is on parole; mother is in prison
Participant #5	One great-nephew (under the age of 5)	Both parents
Participant #6	Two grandsons (under the age of 5)	Both parents; father is serving a life sentence
Participant #7	Two daughters (under the age of 18)	Father

type of help or assistance that children and caregivers needed and barriers and facilitators to receiving this help; the needs of the caregivers and what issues they encountered; the experience of the caregivers in seeking help; views about support needs of the children; and caregivers' suggestions for how to access to services and support for these children and for the caregivers.

The focus group discussion was transcribed and the transcripts were augmented by the manual notes. To analyze the focus group data, we first reviewed the transcript to identify general themes. We then used a cutting-and-sorting technique to identify specific themes and to identify individual quotes or expressions that summarized the key discussion points.

Our analysis of this qualitative data is intended to draw out the major themes discussed by these seven participants. The experiences of this small sample of caregivers by no means can be considered to cover the range of experiences, but the themes and stories we heard are consistent with other findings from the literature. To provide the reader with an idea of how these findings relate to the broader literature in this field, we note in the discussion section how much these findings are consistent or not with the results from other research on grandparents as caregivers.

Family Caregivers Focus Group: Results

The Challenges Incarcerated Parents Face Upon Release

The focus group participants talked about the *challenges incarcerated parents faced upon release, such as problems finding employment or housing.* For example, one participant shared, "I've noticed a lot of times when they come home, it's very hard to find a job. They go and they look for a job, then they're turned down." The same focus group participant noted,

> And when my son went and applied for a job, they said, "If you haven't had anything on your record in the last seven years, then you can work here." But when it came right down to it, and they're [the employers] checking—he had been working there about three months and then when they finally checked it . . . then they said they had to let him go. So that was very depressing for him.

Another focus group participant who had been previously incarcerated herself also talked about how difficult it was to find a job if you have a felony on your record. She was currently not working, waiting for the felony to be purged from her record.

Another issue identified was the problem of ineligibility for Section 8 housing if an incarcerated parent has a drug felony on his or her record. One focus group participant's son had been recently released from prison but was still unemployed. The mother of his two daughters was still incarcerated but would be released within the year. The focus group participant hoped that the mother, when she was released, would be able to find a job, but also noted that Section 8 housing would be problematic and so likely the grandmother would still have to care for the grandchildren.

Another participant discussed the impact of having her son violate a technical condition of parole and how minor infractions, such as missing an appointment, were enough for an individual to be sent back to jail or prison. In this instance, her son was living with his sister in northern San Diego County and had to travel by bus over an hour to meet with his parole officer. When his parole officer told him that he had missed an earlier appointment, he was stunned. According to the focus group participant, it was difficult for him to understand the reasons for sending him back to prison. As she put it, "It's almost like the system is setting them up to fail."

In another case, a focus group participant discussed the requirement for a parolee to have an address. In her view, if individuals were not able to provide an address to their parole officers, then it was seen as a "strike" against them. As she put it, "How can you tell a person you have to have an address if they don't have a job?" In her case, her son put down her address, and the parole officers would come to her house looking for him. She disliked them doing so, especially because she herself had never been in jail or prison before.

The Suddenness of Being Thrust into a Caregiver Role

The focus group participants talked about the challenges of raising a young child or a teenager when they themselves were now in their 40s, 50s, or 60s. As noted above, all but one of the participants was a grandmother. One grandmother found herself suddenly caring for a young baby. She spoke about the trauma of having a police officer show up at her door late at night to bring her the ten-day-old baby, telling her that either she took the baby or the child would be put in to the child welfare system. She commented on how difficult it was to dress the child and get him to daycare, etc., now that she is older: "And then now he [her son] got another one that's two or three days old. And that theory of family, but I'm old. I don't know what I'm going to do. I saw my mother go through it. I don't know. I don't want to see my grandkids in the system."

In the suddenness of being thrust into a caregiver role, a common theme expressed was *the stress of not knowing where to turn to for help or what services might be available to them.* Another focus group participant described how someone showed up at her house with her nine-month-old and three-year-old grandchildren and gave them to her. "I didn't let them go into the [foster care] system." In this case, the mother of the two children initially gave the grandmother her welfare check to help the grandmother take care of them, but that was a long time ago (more than 12–13 years ago). In the suddenness of being thrust into a caregiver role, a common theme heard was the stress of not knowing where to turn to for help or what services might be available to them.

The decision to take these children into their homes was because they were family and because the *caregivers did not want these children to go into foster care and become part of the child welfare system.* One individual felt that she did not have any choice. In another instance, a participant was struggling with the issue that her son continued to have children. She mentioned earlier in the discussion that she was caring for two of the grandchildren, but she then said that her son's girlfriend also had two other children, one of which was her son's. When his girlfriend was incarcerated, the grandmother also ended up taking care of her two children.

From the caregivers' point of view, being with family helped these children feel some sense of stability. One participant discussed when her grandchildren were in foster care. She could see a difference in how they acted and their fear about what might happen to them. While in foster care, they did not know whether they would eventually be placed back with their family or would be with their parent again. From her perspective, her grandchildren were better off being with her and felt more comfortable in this setting because they were use to being around their grandmother. Also, she felt that, as a result, these children felt less acutely the loss of their parent.

The focus group participants all had the same goal of trying to keep their families together and the children out of the child welfare system, but it was becoming increasingly difficult for some of them. As one participant, with a large family and who had been taking care of her 14-year-old grandson since he was a year old, noted, "I don't really know how I feel. I look forward to being in a senior center complex." Another commented, "I'm struggling with that now because my son keeps having kids. I'm getting older and he keeps having them."

The Degree to Which the Children Want to Have Contact with Their Parents

The focus group participants reported that the *children had mixed feelings about seeing their parents when they returned from prison.* A common experience was children going back to live with the parents but eventually returning to the grandmothers because of the unstable living situation they found themselves in. For example, one participant's teenage granddaughter went to live with her father when he was released from prison. However, his situation was unstable, both in terms of employment and because he was living with a girlfriend who had her own children. The granddaughter liked living with them, but when her father and his girlfriend broke up, she did not want to spend any more time with her father and ended up going back to live with her grandmother. The father would call at least once a week, but seldom did the grandmother hear her granddaughter talking to him. The grandmother felt it was up to the father to make contact with his child.

Another grandmother whose grandson went to live with his father and his girlfriend and her children described a similar scenario. The grandson saw them as being a family unit, and he got to spend nights at his father's house and got to be part of a "real" family. However, when his father broke up with his girlfriend, this young man blamed his father for messing up everything. The grandmother explained, "So he doesn't give him [the father] the time of day anymore. He doesn't want to [see him]."

Another focus group participant talked about how her two granddaughters did not want to have anything to do with their father after trying several times to live with him and his girlfriend when he was released from prison. One of her granddaughters, in particular, felt a lot of anger toward her father:

> She's angry with her father. She hates his actions. And she uses the word 'hate' and I told her, 'Hate is a strong word.' But she hates his actions because he's lazy, won't get a job. He's not taking care of them. Grandma and grandpa are taking care of them: getting their hair done, buying their clothes, doing this, doing that.

Another grandmother talked about the difficulties her two grandsons had when their mother returned. As she put it, it is difficult for her oldest grandson because his mother was in and out of prison a great deal. When she was released, she would promise things to him but would not carry through, which would then upset him: "He's angry with everyone because of his mom. He loves her, but he hurts inside because she's in and out, in and out." However, his younger brother has had a different experience. The younger brother has lived with his grandmother since he was three weeks old. So to him, although he knows who his mother is and that she is often incarcerated, her absences when she is sent back to prison do not affect him as much as they upset his older brother.

Another grandmother talked about how her grandson wanted to have contact with his mother and that she lived nearby but does not call him. He had called his mother several times. "She doesn't come down to visit him or anything," the grandmother said. He has other siblings, however, whom his mother does visit occasionally. "So when he talked to his sister, she said, 'Mom came by. Did she come by to see you?' That kind of hurts." His other grandmother (on his mother's side of the family) also had promised to have him come spend time with her during the summer months, when he is out of school. "It never happened. And when you tell kids things like that, they expect it." This young man never said anything about it, but the grandmother said she sensed how hurt he was. She went on to say that she let him spend one Christmas with his sister, and that was all he talked about for a while. "That's the most he's ever spent with his family on his mother's side. That was for a week."

In several cases, the incarcerated parent had been released but was having trouble finding a job or staying out of trouble. The children would temporarily live with the parent but eventually end up back with the grandparent. For example, in one instance, although a focus group participant's son had been released from prison, he was having difficulty finding work and so unable to provide a home for his children. His children went to live with him temporarily but eventually ended up coming back to the grandmother. She commented that her son tried several times to make it work but failed.

The focus group participants also had mixed feelings about letting their sons or daughters come live with them. Several did not expect their son or daughter to live with them upon release from prison. Two individuals said they would let their son or daughter live with them. In one case, although her son had failed to provide for his children, the focus group participant planned to let her son's girlfriend come live with her for a while to help her get back on her feet. However, the grandmother's program sponsor cautioned about being too optimistic about how this would turn out, especially since the girlfriend had been in prison a long time: "Hopefully she's not institutionalized, but I don't know. But I say she's a good girl. I still believe in her and have faith in her."

Children's Support Needs

One individual talked about the struggle her granddaughter had with school and the limited nature of the school's tutoring support. Her understanding was that a child could only be tutored in one subject per semester and for only an hour and a half at a time. She also commented that the school was slow in putting tutoring services into place. She gave the example that the semester would be halfway over by the time the school had finished the FBI background check and paperwork necessary to hire individuals who had applied to be tutors. Another focus group participant who had volunteered to become a tutor commented on the lengthy process for background checks. She had volunteered in September, but it was not until November that she was "cleared" to begin tutoring.

Another grandmother was interested in having her grandson evaluated for attention deficit hyperactivity disorder (ADHD) and learning disabilities. She talked about the disconnect between, on the one hand, receiving a letter from the school saying that the child is failing but, on the other hand, talking with his teachers and hearing them say that nothing was wrong with him and that he was just "defiant." This grandmother knew that her grandson was able to verbally answer questions but was having trouble with homework and writing. She wondered if he had a learning disability and wanted the school to evaluate him, but she was uncertain as to how to get an evaluation done.

The focus group participants felt that Project Live, a program run by a nonprofit organization that focuses on providing services to children of incarcerated parents, had a number of benefits. One key benefit was that it helped these children feel that they were not alone.

The grandmother also went on to talk about how this program also made a difference to her in terms of the "kinship." She also felt the same way about another mentoring program called Village of Promise.

In addition, the focus group participants talked about how Project Live staff had helped the children in a number of positive ways, including helping them with school and homework, doing problem-solving, linking them to counseling services, providing bus tickets, helping them and their families with clothing and furnishings, and taking the kids on outings. Another important, but less tangible, benefit that participants highlighted was the following: "The kinship, the caring. I think the caring and the kids recognizing that somebody loves them. . . . [T]hey do fun activities and something different for the kids whenever they might get a chance to be able to do so. But for the most part, I think it's just the caring part that they [the program staff] show and the kids reciprocate to that, they grasp it."

They also talked about the Village of Promise, which is a "collective" mentoring project in Southeast San Diego for children in 6th, 7th, and 8th grades with incarcerated parents. The Village of Promise's overarching goal is to "break the cycle of incarceration by providing a supportive environment to children of incarcerated parents through support of their mental, spiritual, emotional, social and physical well-being" (Village of Promise Collective Mentoring Project, no date). Several of the focus group participants were members of the Village of Promise and had high praise for the program: "We're in a program that I love, Village of Promise. It's educated us a lot about our rights as parents and grandparents."

The grandmothers also commented on the *importance, as their grandsons became teenagers, of having male mentors for these young men and for them to know that someone cares.* They discussed the challenges of dealing with teenagers who were beginning to act out, were getting into trouble at school, or were emulating the behavior of their peers. Although they could laugh at some of the antics of these teenagers, they recognized that as these young men were growing up, they needed a strong male role model that, as grandmothers, they could not provide. They feared that, without a strong male role model or mentor, these young men would begin to run with the wrong crowd or begin following a similar pathway as their incarcerated parent.

Another theme was the *desire for timely feedback from the schools* if their grandchild or child was having trouble in class, so they could intervene earlier on than wait to discover a child was failing a class. In one instance, a focus group participant's grandson had been expelled earlier that week and had just returned to school. She talked about dreading every time the phone rang, expecting it to be the school calling her about a problem with her grandson and how it would help to occasionally hear some positive feedback:

> He went back today and then they called me again. And it's like, oh my God, am I going to school or is he going to school? Sometimes I feel like they call me for the least little nothing and it's very, very frustrating. And sometimes, it makes you feel like—you ever had bill collectors? Like a bill collector's calling, but it's the school? And you hate to have to answer the phone because you know it's not good? Well, anytime he does something good, nobody never calls and say anything.

At the same time, the grandmother also had a sense of humor about the types of issues that arise with teenagers, but she also reinforced the importance of caregivers also needing to receive positive feedback from the school as well:

> So don't feel bad because when I got the phone call [to recruit her for the focus group], I'm like, "Oh, what did he do today?" And they said, "Oh, it's nothing he did, it's nothing he did today. We wanted to ask you if you would participate in this meeting [the focus group discussion]." I'm like, [SIGHS] "Okay, good. So you're not alone."
>
> When he got all those A's, nobody called and said, "Well, he got A's in this class. He got A's in that class." Nobody said that.
>
> But as a matter of fact, nobody called when he got F's either.
>
> I mean, even though we're adults, we're like children in a sense. We like to hear the good things as well as the bad things.

Along similar lines, focus group participants discussed that *they wanted their grandchildren to understand the reality of what it would be like to be in juvenile hall or a group home if they continued to act out or got into trouble.* One participant stated, "My 14-year-old, he's at a point where he thinks he knows everything. But he really doesn't. He wants to be grown, but he's not."

Another participant explained, "I was talking to him today and that kind of bothered me, because when I was talking to him, I was telling him something; I said, 'You know, you may think that you're bad, but there's someone out there worse than you and they can beat you and hurt you.' And he kind of smirked. . . . and that bothered me."

Given these concerns, the focus group participants discussed having their teenage grandchildren take a tour of one of the juvenile halls in the county to give them a sense of what it would be like. The desire was for it to be a wake-up call for the grandchildren who were acting out or who might be susceptible to getting in with the wrong crowd. Several of the participants' grandsons and granddaughters had gone on a tour of a local juvenile detention facility. Others in the group were interested in finding out how they could sign their grandchild up for the tour. "So just letting them feel what the [juvenile justice] system is like to try to prevent them from getting in the system."

Caregivers' Support Needs

The focus group participants discussed the *need for "respite care,"* not only for those taking care of young grandchildren but also for those dealing with teenagers. They talked about the county providing respite care for three days in the form of a licensed childcare provider who would take care of the kids during that time period to give the grandparent (or caregiver) time off. They were uncertain whether it was available through the court system or the foster care system.

They also went onto say that there was no form of "respite care" for grandparents taking care of teenagers. They were interested in learning about programs that might offer a 1–2-week overnight camp for teenagers, such as a boys' camp or some other specialty camp, that would give the grandparents time off, as well as provide a learning experience for the children they cared for.

In terms of *where they received help,* the focus group participants were appreciative of the support that the community-based organization that put together this focus group had provided them. One participant remarked, "I didn't have a lot of money and they have [bus] vouchers that they give to families to help them along the way to support those children for the immediate things they need, especially for attending school." Another individual talked about not having family nearby, but said that the few she did have (along with friends) had really stepped up to the plate, saying, "If you need me to babysit, call me." At Christmas, at her job, at the hospital where she works makes donations and does gift exchanges for different families. She was asked if they could make donations to her family that year, for which she was grateful.

Another individual mentioned belonging to a 12-step program that helped her a great deal. In addition, she worked for a resource center. The center's staff got together to help her when she first started taking care of her grandchildren.

The focus group participants used the discussion as an opportunity to share information among themselves about programs or services they had found or have had success with. For example, for the grandmother who was concerned that her grandson had ADHD and was finding it difficult to get an evaluation done, one of the focus group participants let her know that she could request that the school do an evaluation of him for learning disabilities and the school would be required to conduct the evaluation within a certain period of time: "There's all different types [of tests for learning disabilities]. [If] it's not ADHD, there's other types of learning disabilities because we learn visually, auditory, and kinesthetically. And he may need all three or maybe just one or two of them, but it's a certain type of test they have." The other participants urged this grandmother to talk to the director of Project Live, who they felt would be able to help her. With respect to the discussion of tutoring, one focus group participant suggested the Village of Promise program, for which San Diego State students serve as mentors, and suggested that perhaps they could help out at the school that their grandchildren attended.

Importantly, one of the benefits of gathering these caregivers together to discuss the needs of these children was that hearing about the experiences of the other focus group participants helped them to feel less isolated. Hearing others talk about similar situations made them feel like they were not the only one dealing with these problems. One individual said she had been feeling alone because her grandson had just been expelled from school, and she was in the process of dealing with this situation. Participating in the focus group discussion helped her to realize she was not alone:

> [W]hen you asked about some of the services that would be nice, you know like this [dinner and gathering for the focus group]—sometimes we know that we're not alone, but sometimes things happen, you feel like you are alone. But then when you come here and hear it [the experiences of others], then you come back to reality. Okay, I'm not really alone.

Finally, we asked what *advice they would give to others in their situation.* One individual said she would recommend to other caregivers that they try and get other family members involved in helping with the children. She gave the example of her son recently having another child. When her son was being sent back to prison for another term, she reached out to his brother to ask if he would be willing to care for this new child. Another focus group participant said she would tell others to remember there is hope: "With me, I look at it as if the parent who's incarcerated doesn't have life in prison, that their stay away from their children is only temporary. . . . So there's hope."

Another individual offered the following advice: "Sometimes it can be overwhelming. . . . If you need help, ask for help. You'd be surprised what people will do if you just ask."

Discussion

We know that the impact of parental incarceration on children likely varies across California counties, with some localities having higher rates of incarceration than other localities. In our earlier report, we found that even within counties, certain neighborhoods are particularly impacted by incarceration (Davis et al., 2009). Although we have an idea of where programs for children of incarcerated parents will likely be in greatest need, a fundamental problem we face is lack of information about the exact number of California children who are affected by parental incarceration.

Although we did not specifically set out to focus on grandparents who care for their children while their parents are incarcerated, this is how the composition of our focus group turned out. It provided us with some important insights about the experiences of grandmothers who were providing this type of kinship care, including the challenges of raising young children and teenagers, of coping with behavioral problems among these children, and of trying to keep their families together yet not knowing where to turn to for help. As was true about caregivers in other studies (Nickel, Garland, and Kane, 2009), our focus group participants were motivated to try and keep their families together.

Davies et al. (2008) reported similar results from focus groups conducted with 31 mentors of children with incarcerated parents. In their study, the mentors similarly commented on the behavioral problems observed with children, especially boys, including anger and rebellious behaviors. Some of the children who were being mentored also experienced problems with school, including poor academic performance, suspensions, and truancy. The mentors also noted the involvement of grandmothers—among other family members such as aunts and mothers when the father was incarcerated—who tried to provide a normal structure for these children.

The focus group participants in our study also discussed their unwillingness or lack of knowledge about how to seek care from the child welfare system and not knowing what resources might be available to them. This is consistent with other studies on kinship caregivers (Nickel, Garland, and Kane, 2009). In addition, grandparents who are raising their grandchildren are not automatically eligible to receive financial support and may experience difficulty in establishing eligibility for assistance (Waldrop and Weber, 2005).

For caregivers who were middle aged and older, the experience of being thrust into a caregiver role later in life was emotionally and physically trying. For some of the focus group participants, the change to becoming a caregiver was very sudden and unexpected. They expressed a need for a week or two of respite care, be it child care or a sleepover camp for teenagers. However, the only respite care they were aware of was that offered by the foster care system. In some instances, family members helped out for brief periods of time. Other forms of support caregivers needed were information on the range of services available to them; assistance in obtaining help for children with learning disabilities; and information about other social services or programs.

These caregivers were caring for grandchildren as a result of parental incarceration; however, they also shared the similar support needs of grandparents in general who find themselves caring for their grandchildren when parents are no longer able to care for their children for a variety of factors, including incarceration, substance abuse, physical or mental illness, or economic problems (Pebley and Rudkin, 1999). Similar to the caregivers who participated in this focus group, many grandparents agree to care for a grandchild because they do not want them to go to a foster home.

The support needs for children mentioned by the caregivers included assistance with school and tutoring services; mentoring opportunities; role models, particularly for teenage boys; and programs aimed specifically at children with incarcerated parents that enable them to feel less isolated. The caregivers specifically commented on the stigma that the children felt of having an incarcerated parent and that having a program similar to the one in San Diego was important for enabling these children to realize that other kids are also going through similar experiences. In addition, the caregivers felt it was important to provide the children, especially teenagers, with a realistic experience of what involvement in the juvenile justice system would mean through field trips to juvenile hall. These results are consistent with the literature, which similarly found the need for male role models for teenage boys, the benefit of having mentors who regularly visited and did routine activities with the child, the importance of helping these children understand the negative consequences of getting involved in crime, and the need for these children to be given structure and boundaries and to know that someone had high expectations of them (Davies et al., 2008).

In addition, the mentors in Davies et al. (2008) study commented on the financial strain that caregivers and these children might experience because of the loss of financial support by the incarcerated parent. The financial strain of grandparents taking care of grandchildren can involve strain from additional expenses, difficulty applying for governmental assistance, poverty, and underemployment (Waldrop and Weber, 2005).

The challenges that a parent recently released from prison faces in terms of finding employment and stable housing had a ripple effect on their children, who experienced firsthand the instability of reuniting with a parent who is struggling to find housing and a job. In this case, the end result was that often the child returned to live with their grandparent(s). The Davies et al. (2008) study of mentors of children with incarcerated parents similarly discussed the instability a child may face when the incarcerated parent returns.

There is also a need for services in support of family reunification that can address the multiple needs of these families. As discussed in Chapter Four, providers note that these tend to be families that touch multiple systems of care, including social services, child welfare, mental health, alcohol and drug, and health care safety-net services, as well as the criminal justice and juvenile justice systems. Our focus group of caregivers commented on how family reunification is often stressful and can raise feelings of hurt, anger, or resentment toward the individual returning from prison. This perspective was also reinforced in the provider interviews.

A limitation of our study is that we did not explicitly examine the large and complex issues of child welfare laws and other legislation and their impact on parents in California who are incarcerated, although our focus group discussion touched briefly on some of these issues. Nor did we explore the disproportionate impact welfare laws have on these families in terms of terminating the rights of parents, moving these children into the welfare system, and placing a number of almost insurmountable barriers on their release.

The results of these laws and legislation are felt directly by parents who wish to reunite with their children but face a number of barriers, including (1) not knowing where the child is if he or she is now in the foster care system; (2) dealing with termination of parental rights; (3) having a drug felony on one's record, which may limit a parent's ability to get food stamps or Section 8 housing or other support needed to be able to provide for their children; or (4) trying to find employment while also dealing with child support arrears.

In addition, the system is designed to discourage caregivers from seeking help from child welfare agencies or from public assistance, for fear that the child welfare system may investigate whether they meet all the criteria for being a foster parent. Caregivers are also unaware of their rights or what resources are available to them to help care for these children. As so poignantly expressed by our focus group participants, the result is often a feeling of isolation and not knowing where to turn for help.

Another limitation is that our discussion with caregivers was based on a small sample of seven individuals, and thus these findings can only be considered exploratory and not indicative of the range of experiences of caregivers. That said, the themes and issues the caregivers in our focus group raised were consistent with those reported in the research literature.

What emerges clearly from our focus group discussions is that when a parent is imprisoned for a crime, the innocent children of that parent are also punished. As a result, such children are at increased risk of experiencing a host of negative outcomes.

CHAPTER SIX

Conclusions and Recommendations

Our report explores the public health implications of prisoner reentry in California and the challenges that reentry creates for individuals returning from prison, for their families, and for their communities. In this chapter, we provide recommendations for how to address these challenges, while considering the overall policy and economic contexts. We argue that the economic crisis, reductions in prison rehabilitative services, the increased numbers of individuals who will be housed and supervised at the county level, and a weakened safety net in the communities receiving these individuals all pose serious challenges to addressing the health needs of the reentry population, but that California's new public safety realignment plan and health care reform create important opportunities for meeting those challenges. The state and counties within it must be ready to take advantage of these opportunities. Our recommendations below suggest specific ways that they can do this.

California at a Crossroads

The weakening of California's health care safety net and the substantial cuts in the state's corrections budget for rehabilitative services have occurred within a larger context of the ongoing economic crisis. In the past three years, the nation has experienced the most severe fiscal crisis since the Great Depression. The recession has brought about the largest collapse in state revenues on record (McNichol, Oliff, and Johnson, 2011). California is working hard to address its large budget shortfalls, with a projected $23 billion budget gap in fiscal year 2012, and is also struggling to find the revenue needed to support such critical services as health care, education, and human services, something that may take years to accomplish.

The capacity of the health care safety net varies across California communities and has become even more constrained, while demand has grown. When we completed our 2009 analysis of the capacity of the health care safety net to meet the needs of the reentry population, we concluded that the safety net was sparse in some services and that parolees' potential access to health care services varied by county, type of service, and race/ethnicity. Since our analysis, the capacity of the health care safety net has shrunk substantially because of state budget cuts, while the demand for services has increased because of growth in the number of uninsured or underinsured persons (Girion and Medina, 2009). Also, within the state prison system, rehabilitative services have been substantially reduced. Substance abuse programming in California's state prison system has been cut to just one-fifth of its capacity of just a few years ago (CDCR Division of Addiction and Recovery Services, *Annual Report*, 2009). Alcohol and drug treatment models in place in the prison system and out in the community have now adopted much shorter length-of-stay models, without strong evidence about whether such models are effective. Community-based treatment programs have also faced substantial cutbacks in funding, and although Proposition 36—which diverted nonviolent drug offenders to treatment instead of incarceration—remains in effect, it is no longer being funded. Given these changes, individuals leaving state prison are returning to California's communities having received less and less rehabilitative programming. This means that the reentry population will have greater unmet needs and will have to be even more self-determined than previously, because transition points and linkages to care will become even more difficult to navigate (Zack, 2002).

California's new Public Safety Realignment Plan represents an almost tectonic shift in the state's criminal justice system that will have a number of implications for thinking about how to meet the health care and rehabilitative needs of the reentry population. In May 2011, the U.S. Supreme Court ordered California to reduce its prison population to 137.5 percent of design capacity within two years (CDCR, "Three-Judge Panel and California Inmate Population Reduction," 2011)—a mandate requiring the reduction of approximately 33,000 inmates. California's 2011 Public Safety Justice Realignment Plan will help to close the revolving door of low-level inmates cycling in and out of prison and reduce the size of the prison population. Beginning in October 2011, low-level offenders will no longer serve their sentence in state prison, instead serving their time in county jails.[1] For those offenders with split sentences, upon completing jail sentences, they will be supervised by individual counties' probation departments rather than by the state-level parole system.[2] And those who violate their parole will serve their revocation time in county jails instead of prison. In addition, low-level offenders released from prison beginning October 1, 2011, will be placed on county-level postrelease community supervision (PRCS), to be supervised by county probation departments instead of by state parole. CDCR will retain responsibility for parole supervision for offenders released on parole prior to October 1, 2011, and for violent and serious offenders, high-risk sex offenders, mentally disordered offenders, and inmates paroled from a sentence of life, including three-strikes offenders (CDCR, "2011 Public Safety Realignment," 2011).

Public safety realignment presents some challenges. For example, traditional mechanisms for linking ex-prisoners to health care and social services—e.g., parole officers, PACT meetings, POCs—will change dramatically for individuals placed on county-level postrelease community supervision and for low-level offenders who will serve their time in county jail.[3] CDCR will no longer have jurisdiction over indi-

---

1 "Low-level offenders" are those who have been sentenced for nonviolent, nonserious, and nonsex offenses.

2 The length of time in which individuals will be under probation supervision is estimated to be only one year, compared with three years under parole supervision in the state system (Stoltze, 2011).

3 It is unclear what the future of POCs—a basic way parolees with mental illness can obtain their psychiatric medications and access basic treatment services—will be as CDCR prepares to lay off almost 80 percent of its parole officers as part of the new public safety realignment plan; presumably, some parole offices and clinics may be closed as a result.

viduals placed on county-level postrelease community supervision or who serve their sentence at the local level. Instead, county probation departments will have this responsibility and will now need to fulfill this linkage function. This means that probation departments will need to develop partnerships with other county agencies, such as mental health agencies, and with local community providers (including community-based and faith-based organizations) to enhance services provided to this population. For low-level offenders who will serve their sentence within county jail systems, a key concern is that many of these systems have little or limited rehabilitative programming. Because individuals will be spending more time in jails than in the past, programming within the jails also may need to be enhanced. This will require that county jail systems also develop partnerships with county health care agencies and community organizations to meet the needs of these offenders and to facilitate their transition back to the community.

Counties are concerned about their capacity to meet this increased demand for mental health and drug treatment services (Stoltze, 2011). Under public safety realignment, a number of low-level offenders to be housed and monitored at the county level are expected to include individuals convicted of drug-related offenses, some proportion of whom will require treatment programs. In Los Angeles County—the county with the state's largest number of parolees—the Board of Supervisors, for example, has expressed concerns about the county's ability to provide the mental health care and drug treatment services that low-level offenders may require. County probation also has expressed reservations about the county's ability to provide the rehabilitative programming needed for this population (Stoltze, 2011). In general, counties are concerned that the funding from the state to house, supervise, and provide rehabilitative services for these individuals may be short-lived, despite promises from the governor (Kahn, 2011; Gonzales, 2011).

California's Public Safety Justice Realignment Plan also presents an important opportunity to address the public health needs associated with reentry. Specifically, the realignment plan not only provides the opportunity to reduce the size of the state's prison population and reduce the state's high parole revocation rates, it also focuses attention on the need to improve prerelease planning, build better mechanisms to transition care from correctional health to safety-net providers, and create local partnerships among probation, law enforcement, county agencies, and community- and faith-based organizations to better serve the needs of ex-prisoners returning to communities. Realignment will enable low-level offenders to serve their time closer to home, thus enabling them to have better access to family members, employers, and community organizations, which can possibly aid them with the reentry process. Under public safety realignment, counties may be able to do a better job of rehabilitating offenders and helping them to reintegrate into communities. However, this will depend on sufficient funding for counties to implement realignment and on counties' ability to develop the necessary expertise and service delivery systems to effectively manage and rehabilitate this population.

Given these changes, California is at an important crossroads. The reentry population will be returning to local communities from state prison having received fewer rehabilitative services and programming than in the past. Counties will have to deal with sentenced inmates that previously would have served their term in state prison. These individuals will have to rely even more on counties' health care and social services safety nets and on community- and faith-based organizations that serve the medically indigent, the uninsured, and the reentry population. Despite these challenges, there is also reason for hope in addressing the health care needs of California's reentry population.

An Historic Opportunity to Improve Access to Health Care for the Reentry Population

The Patient Protection and Affordable Care Act provides important opportunities to expand health insurance coverage for the reentry/criminal justice population, improve access to drug treatment, and improve management of their care. As discussed in Chapter Four, under health care reform, the ACA will expand Medicaid eligibility to all non-Medicare-eligible citizens and legal residents[4]

[4] That is, legal residents who have been in the country five years or longer.

under age 65 with incomes up to 133 percent of the FPL.[5] It also will provide subsidies to individuals with incomes between 133 and 400 percent of the FPL if they do not have a qualifying offer of coverage from an employer (Kaiser, 2011a). Moreover, the law penalizes large employers for not offering coverage and provides temporary tax incentives to induce small employers with low-wage workers to offer coverage.[6] The net effect of the ACA is that there will be more options available to low-income populations, either through an employer, California's Health Benefit Exchange, or Medicaid.[7]

This change opens up the possibility for many ex-prisoners and other individuals involved with the criminal justice system to become eligible for California's Medicaid program (i.e., Medi-Cal).[8] Ahead of full implementation of the elements of the ACA by 2014, California is moving forward with efforts to expand coverage to larger proportions of low-income persons through a Federal Medicaid Waiver for 2010–2015. This waiver is intended to serve as a bridge to health care reform and allow California to accelerate the enrollment of a significant portion of "newly eligible" adults through county-based coverage initiatives. Establishing a health home for Medicaid beneficiaries with chronic conditions is a central component of the waiver. Alameda County is using these funds to extend the medical home concept (e.g., Healthy Oakland) for the reentry population in Alameda County. Other counties, especially those with large numbers of parolees, are also considering a similar strategy.

---

[5] The ACA specifies that childless adults are eligible for Medicaid with modified adjusted gross income (AGI) at or below 133 percent of the FPL. However, the ACA also adds a 5-percentage-point deduction from the FPL, which effectively makes the Medicaid eligibility threshold 138 percent of the FPL (State Health Access Data Assistance Center, 2011).

[6] These temporary tax incentives apply only to businesses with 25 or fewer workers who pay average annual wages below $50,000.

[7] Noncitizens will not necessarily qualify for Medicaid.

[8] It is important to understand that Medicaid expansion in this context pertains to more than just the reentry population returning from state prisons; it also pertains to individuals in general who are involved with the criminal justice system, such as those in county jails, those on probation, and those on parole. We refer to this broader group in this section as the reentry/criminal justice population.

In addition, Medicaid will be expanded to more fully cover drug treatment, prevention services, and wellness programs. As discussed in Chapter Four, under the ACA, the essential health benefit (EHB) requires that treatment for substance abuse be covered, with integration of these (and other) services with general health care being facilitated. The ACA also aims to improve the health status of all Americans through prevention and wellness strategies (California Health Care Reform, 2010b). Two key ways of doing so are ensuring access to preventive care services by eliminating copayments and coinsurance and by providing grants to states and local health departments to conduct pilot prevention and wellness programs for 55–64-year-olds.[9]

The ACA also contains a number of provisions and incentives to strengthen and expand the nation's health care workforce, which could provide additional resources for the reentry population. For example, in 2010, the ACA provided $250 million nationwide to boost the supply of primary care providers (California Health Care Reform, 2010a). This includes funds to increase the number of nurse practitioners and physician assistants and to provide states with resources to plan for and address health professional workforce needs. In August 2010, California's Workforce Investment Board established a Health Workforce Development Council, which received a state health care workforce planning grant. In addition, state departments, universities, colleges, and local agencies have received grants to expand education and training opportunities.[10]

As part of health care reform, states are required to expand Medicaid coverage. However, this change should not be overly burdensome to California given the federal matching rates for the expansion population (i.e., 100–138 percent of the FPL) (Somers et al., 2010).[11]

---

[9] The other areas include (1) promoting healthier eating habits and greater physical activity through community grants, (2) requiring new food labeling for chain restaurants and vending machines, and (3) making grants to small businesses to provide employees with access to comprehensive workforce wellness programs.

[10] For a summary of grants received, see California Health Care Reform (2010c).

[11] For states that had lower thresholds previously, the federal government will reimburse newly eligible populations at 100 percent initially, declining to 90 percent over time. For

Combined, these changes and, in particular, the prospect of improved access to Medicaid insurance for low-income, childless adults create a critical opportunity for California to improve access to care (primary care, preventive services, mental health care, alcohol and drug treatment) for the reentry/criminal justice population and to put into place those elements of health care delivery systems needed to effectively manage their care, including those that

- provide care/case management (including patient navigators) for this population (this population tends to have a host of unmet needs—both health care and social services—that makes them more costly to treat, so improved access to care/case management will be important)
- establish health homes for the reentry/criminal justice population that will enable providers to develop the expertise and provider teams (e.g., patient navigators, culturally competent trained staff) needed to serve this population
- provide incentives for all relevant stakeholders—corrections and other criminal justice agencies, health providers, social services providers, and nonprofit community organizations—to work together to effectively transition the care of individuals returning to communities from prison or jails and to plan for and put in place wraparound services to address this population's multitude of needs
- reduce the costs of treating the reentry population in emergency rooms and hospitals
- improve health outcomes among the reentry population.

Lastly, health care reform also presents some challenges. Expansion of Medicaid eligibility could lead to increased demand for health care safety-net services that are already stretched thin, thus, possibly affecting access to care if provider capacity at the county level is not increased. Although treatment for substance abuse problems will be

states that previously provided coverage to individuals with incomes between 100 and 138 percent of the FPL, federal reimbursements start out lower and then increase over time.

more fully covered, there could be substantial cost-sharing or other utilization limits that may make it difficult for some of the reentry/criminal justice population to afford this care. In addition, Disproportionate Share Hospital (DSH) payments to hospitals are being cut which means that fewer resources will be available for individuals who remain uninsured. Finally, under the ACA individuals can be penalized for not having health insurance, which likely will include a portion of the reentry population.[12] Combined, these changes and restrictions suggest both opportunities as well as challenges for California.

What Can California Do to Prepare?

Below, we summarize our recommendations for how California and its counties can take advantage of this historic opportunity to improve services and outcomes for the reentry/criminal justice population amid the challenges posed by budget constraints and public safety realignment. These recommendations are based on a combination of our review of the literature and analyses of the inmate survey, parolee data, data on the health care safety net in four counties, provider interviews, and focus group discussions with formerly incarcerated men and family members.

Many of the steps we outline will also help California and its counties better plan for inclusion of the reentry/criminal justice population as part of the expansion of Medicaid. These recommendations also apply to other states facing similar problems about how to improve access to care for this population.

The first set of recommendations below pertain to the state-level departments and agencies that have a role to play in preparing California for public safety realignment and health care reform. Some also pertain to county agencies and departments.

---

[12] Although penalties are waived for the lowest income groups (non–tax filers).

Develop Informed Estimates About the Percentage of the Medicaid Expansion Population That the Reentry/Criminal Justice Population Will Represent

It is important to understand how the complex changes under public safety realignment may impact the size of the reentry/criminal justice population eligible for Medicaid, the likelihood of them enrolling, the expected demand for services, projected costs, and how under different scenarios (e.g., different enrollment practices) these estimates may change. These estimates will also need to take into account citizenship status and what percent of the reentry/criminal justice population will be eligible for subsidies as part of California's Health Benefit Exchange.

To inform planning for health care reform, **California will need to develop informed estimates of the likely number of ex-prisoners and others involved in the criminal justice system that will become part of the Medicaid expansion population.** The literature (Heiser and Williams, 2008; Visher, LaVigne, and Travis, 2004; and Mallik-Kane, 2005) provides preliminary estimates that suggest that the percentage of persons leaving California prisons who are uninsured could range between 57 and 85 percent of parolees (Malcolm Williams, unpublished). This analysis, however, does not account for the changes expected under public safety realignment in terms of reductions in the size of the prison population (nor take into account the size of the other components of the criminal justice population in California).

Develop Medicaid Enrollment Strategies

To prepare for the implementation of health care reform, California will need to develop strategies to enroll or reinstate Medicaid benefits for the reentry/criminal justice population. Such strategies should be part of prerelease planning and postrelease activities. The participation of this population in Medicaid will largely depend on how much CDCR (and county probabtion and jails) facilitates their enrollment (or applications to reinstate benefits) in California's Medi-Cal program. Correctional facilities can serve as an entry point for bringing persons involved with the criminal justice system into the health care system and connecting them with community health care providers (Center for Health Care Strategies, Inc., 2011).

Implementing a multipronged enrollment strategy will require that criminal justice, health care, and community stakeholders work together collaboratively. For instance, Somers et al. (2010) analyzed ten selected states' prior experience with covering low-income childless adults under Medicaid and concluded that hospitals, emergency rooms, clinics, and other providers that serve low-income adults without dependent children will likely be proactive in Medicaid enrollment for the expansion population. Further, because new Medicaid enrollees can obtain retroactive eligibility for up to three months prior to applying for benefits, hospitals and emergency rooms will have an additional incentive to facilitate enrollment of the uninsured (Somers et al., 2010). County mental health and alcohol and drug departments and local community organizations can also help facilitate Medicaid enrollment. Because the reentry/criminal justice population tends to have low literacy rates, trained specialists will be needed to assist individuals with applying for Medi-Cal and other benefits.

Leverage the Experience of Other States That Have Previously Expanded Coverage to Childless Adults Under Medicaid

Somers et al. (2010) examined the experience of ten states that had previously expanded coverage to childless adults. The experience of these states provides a rich source of information on issues California may want to consider. For example, Somers et al. (2010) suggest additional exploration in the following areas:

- Examine morbidity and cost profiles by factors, including income level, age, and employment status.
- Evaluate the effectiveness of different outreach efforts and enrollment practices on participation rates.
- Assess the influence of participation rates on overall morbidity and cost levels.
- Analyze demographics, health needs, and costs by year following coverage expansion.

Although their recommendations pertain to the Medicaid expansion population in general, they also suggest analyses that California might wish to undertake to understand the effectiveness of insurance expansion for the reentry/criminal justice population.

Develop Health Homes for the Reentry/Criminal Justice Population

The Medicaid expansion population is expected to include a number of individuals with multiple comorbidities and high rates of mental illness and substance abuse—all of which suggest likely high levels of service utilization (Somers et al., 2010). This suggests that health homes may be valuable in managing the complex care of these individuals.

The types of services that health homes provide could greatly benefit ex-prisoners (and other criminal justice-involved individuals) with chronic health problems and substance abuse and mental health problems. Health homes, funded by Medicaid under the ACA, can provide the following services to eligible beneficiaries: (1) comprehensive care management, (2) care coordination and health promotion, (3) comprehensive transitional care/follow-up, (4) patient and family support, (5) referral to community and social services, and (6) use of health information technology to link services.

States have flexibility in determining who is designated a health home provider, including

- a designated provider (e.g., physician, community health center, community mental health center, clinical/group practice)
- a team of health care professionals (e.g., physician, nurse care coordinator, social worker, behavioral health professional) which, for example, can be part of a freestanding clinic or practice, a community mental health center, or hospital-based
- a health team that provides health home services and meets established standards as a health home (e.g., medical specialists, social workers, nurses, behavioral health providers, etc.).

In comparison, a medical home is a health care setting, such as a community clinic or primary care clinic, that provides patients with comprehensive primary care and enhanced access to providers. Under the ACA, health homes will provide a broader range of services than a medical home. Further, a health home may or may not be provided within the walls of a primary care practice. "That said, states recognize the value of the existing infrastructure of a medical home and may choose to enhance the medical home with the new health home services" (Center for Health Care Strategies, Inc., 2011).

The ACA includes several opportunities to use Medicaid funding (Medi-Cal in California) to develop health homes for beneficiaries who have (1) two or more chronic conditions, (2) one chronic condition and are at risk for a second, or (3) a serious and persistent mental health condition (Center for Health Care Strategies, Inc., 2011). Chronic conditions are defined as including mental health, substance abuse, asthma, diabetes, heart disease, and being overweight—conditions we have identified as being common in the reentry population. In developing health homes, populations, diseases, and geographic locations can be targeted.

State participation in health homes is optional; however, states can apply to the Centers for Medicare and Medicaid Services to use Medicaid funding to pay for health homes. Health homes may be one way to effectively manage the care of the reentry (and criminal justice) population. Federal agencies such as SAMHSA provide detailed information on the implications of health homes for behavioral health services, including a guidance document to inform states' planning process (Substance Abuse and Mental Health Services Administration, 2011).

Lessons learned from California counties' early experiences with medical homes for the reentry/criminal justice population and from correctional program models to improve coordination of care can help inform state and local planning to establish health homes for this population. To date, there are several examples of medical homes being implemented in California, including Healthy Oakland[13] in Oakland and the Transitions Clinic in San Francisco that provide primary care to ex-prisoners and facilitate linkage to other health care and social services. There are also other models for linking ex-offenders to local health care services that can inform the development of health homes in California. The Hampden County Correctional Center (HCCC)

---

[13] Healthy Communities, Inc., does business as "Healthy Oakland."

Public Health Model of Community Corrections is an oft-cited model where inmates at a medium-security jail are assigned to neighborhood health centers. In addition to working closely with correctional staff, the health centers have developed partnerships with community organizations to provide a range of reentry support services, such as housing or employment (Conklin et al., 2002).

To help replicate this model and to facilitate partnerships between local correctional facilities and local community health care services, the Community Oriented Correctional Health Services received funding from the Robert Wood Johnson Foundation to expand the HCCC model and to provide technical assistance to communities interested in coordinating the care of offenders (Community Oriented Correctional Health Services, 2011).

Finally, there are a number of opportunities enacted through health care reform for states to receive enhanced federal support, including planning grants and enhanced federal match for developing health homes and grants. **California may wish to seek federal funding to support the planning for health homes for this component of the Medicaid expansion population.** In addition, over time, California might also apply for federal funding to evaluate the effectiveness of health homes for the reentry/criminal justice (and other special) population, in terms of improving health outcomes and access to care (and other needed services) and in reducing health care costs.

Develop Care/Case Management Systems That Can Account for Special Populations' Needs, Including the Reentry/Criminal Justice Population

Even with expanded access to health insurance, drug treatment, and prevention services, the reentry/criminal justice population is expected to have a range of unmet health care needs and require assistance with housing, employment, transportation, and access to other reentry services. Under health care reform, states can also apply for federal support to design and implement effective care management programs

(Somers et al., 2010).[14] **California may wish to consider applying for planning grants to support the development of tailored care/case management programs** that will include coordination with social services and community organizations that serve this population.

Assess Workforce-Development Strategies for Alcohol, Drug, and Mental Health Treatment

The reentry and criminal justice populations have relatively high rates of alcohol and drug problems and high mental health care needs; as a result, they may overwhelm existing publicly funded treatment provider networks (Mancuso and Felver, 2010). This, in turn, argues that alcohol and drug treatment providers and mental health providers should be preparing for the likely increased demand for services as Medicaid coverage is expanded.

The state may wish to establish a health task force to identify workforce-development strategies that will help build provider capacity for alcohol and drug treatment and for mental health care in general, and specifically for the reentry/criminal justice component of the Medicaid expansion population.

Further, the state and individual providers or systems of care might consider coupling access to physical health services with alcohol and drug and mental health treatment for the reentry/criminal justice population. This will enable a single point of entry in the health care system and make it easier to ensure continuity of care. Much work has been done on different models for integrating behavioral health and primary care, including behavioral health homes, which can inform California's planning process (see SAMHSA-HRSA Center for Integrated Health Solutions, no date). In addition, the National Council for Behavioral Healthcare is disseminating information that may be an important resource for planning in this area (SAMHSA-HRSA Center for Integrated Health Solutions, 2011).

---

[14] For example, planning grants, enhanced federal match for developing health homes, and grants to support the development of community health teams.

Consider Developing Electronic Medical Records

In California, responsibility for prison health care resides with two entities. CDCR's California Correctional Health Care Services is responsible for providing mental health and dental services to prison inmates. California Prison Health Care Services, overseen by the court-appointed federal receiver, is responsible for medical care provided to prison inmates. Both entities have a role to play in ensuring the effective transition from prison health care to care in the community. In addition, at the county level, jail systems also have a role to play in this area.

In this effort, electronic medical records (EMRs) are one tool to help improve continuity of care. Adopting EMRs will enable county jail systems and county health agencies, as well as community providers, to more effectively treat this population and help promote continuity of care. The federal receiver has plans to computerize inmate medical records. In addition, agencies within some counties, such the Los Angeles County Sheriff's Department, have already implemented information systems to enable the creation of EMRs or charts for jail inmates (Los Angeles County Sheriff's Department, Correctional Services Division, Medical Services Bureau, no date).

We recognize that this will be a very costly undertaking and that the electronic transfer of inmate medical records will take time to develop. However, in the long run, EMRs could improve continuity of care and patient outcomes and potentially reduce costs (Hillestad et al., 2005). To begin making headway, California may wish to consider applying for a grant from the federal government to conduct a pilot study to assess the feasibility of creating EMRs for the reentry/criminal justice population. The study could focus on specific components of this population, such as those individuals in state prison or county jails in need of mental health care or with specific chronic health conditions and who will likely become part of the Medicaid expansion population.

Finally, the development of health homes for chronically ill ex-prisoners may also be an impetus for developing EMRs to facilitate the transfer of care of these individuals to local community health care centers and clinics.

Consider Expanding Prerelease Planning Efforts

Prisoners who receive prerelease planning tend to have better outcomes. For example, Farabee et al. (2006) conducted an evaluation of CDCR's Mental Health Services Continuum Program. When background characteristics and parole region were controlled for, receiving a prerelease assessment by a social worker was associated with a 13 percent reduction in the odds of a parolee being returned to custody within 12 months and with a 34 percent reduction in the odds of being returned to prison within 12 months for those that had one or more POC contacts following release (Farabee et al., 2006).

In terms of prerelease planning, CDCR tries to arrange community-based care for soon-to-be released prisoners in need of acute or subacute care, those who are unable to arrange for care because of disability, those in need of dialysis, and those who are unable to handle activities of daily living (CDCR, "Release Planning Continuity of Mental Health and Medical Care," 2011). In addition, CDCR recently released new guidance for prerelease planning for individuals with mental health problems (CDCR, "Post Release Community Supervision Release Planning for Mental Health," 2011).[15] Individuals with a lower level of mental health care needs will be provided information on where they can seek mental health services out in the community; individuals with a higher level of mental health care needs will be asked to sign a release form so that CDCR can send their mental health information to a county mental health department.

Under public safety realignment, in addition, CDCR will now provide prerelease packets to counties for *low-level offenders* who will be placed on postrelease community supervision (PRCS). Specifically, for each individual who will be released on PRCS, CDCR will send counties a prerelease packet on the individual 120 days prior to his or her release. The packet will include a variety of information, such

---

[15] Individuals in need of a lower level of mental health care receive an information packet that provides them with information about where within their county of residence they can seek mental health services. Individuals who require high levels of mental health care will be asked to sign a consent release form so that their mental health information can be sent to the receiving county's department of mental health. Counties' departments of mental health can "opt in" or "opt out" of receiving such information.

as classification actions and inmate case factors, known gang affiliation, and available medical information (e.g., if an individual has tested positive for tuberculosis, medical clearance, disability information, and mental health information if applicable) (CDCR "Implementation of Post-Release Community Supervision Act of 2011," 2011). The prerelease packets are intended to assist counties in developing individual treatment plans, case plans, and referrals to services (Los Angeles County Probation Department, 2011). Some of these individuals may or may not be in need of community treatment services.

However, not all prisoners will fit under either of the above two categories, yet may still have health care needs that require linking to community treatment services upon release. We know from this study and other research that there is a large amount of unmet need among the prison population in general. For example, an individual may have substance abuse problems that are not currently being treated by an in-prison substance abuse program. Therefore, they would not necessarily be part of the first category of prerelease planning. Depending on their offense, they may or may not be part of the PRCS.

CDCR (and counties) may want to consider expanding prerelease planning to include all inmates with chronic medical, mental health, or substance abuse problems that are not currently covered. To help facilitate their transition of care, prerelease planning for prisoners, in particular those in immediate need of access to care by community-based treatment providers should include providing these individuals with a summary of pertinent information—for example, a problem list, medications, results of laboratory and diagnostic tests, scheduled tests or visits, third-party coverage for medical care (if known or arranged) and information about resources in the county they will be returning to. Also of importance will be coordination between the correctional health care system and community health care providers to ensure that individuals are released with an adequate supply medications and/or prescriptions and that they have scheduled a visit with a community health care provider to facilitate continuity of care.

Undertake a Comprehensive Assessment of California's New Public Safety Realignment Plan to Inform Future Policy Refinements

California's Public Safety Realignment Plan represents a profound change to the state's criminal justice system. Counties have developed their individual plans for implementing realignment; thus, in a sense, the state could potentially have 58 distinct experiments under way. However, to inform policy refinements at the state and local levels over time, there are a number of questions that will need to be answered:

- What impact, if any, has public safety realignment had on overall crime rates and recidivism rates?
- How effective are counties at meeting the health care and rehabilitative needs of this population?
- What types of service delivery and supervision/management models implemented at the local level result in better outcomes for this population?
- Do different groups of offenders fare better or worse under realignment (e.g., those with chronic mental health problems or substance abuse problems)?
- What are the postrelease experiences of individuals under realignment?
- What additional adjustments, if any, may be needed to improve realignment and to mitigate unintended effects?
- What cost savings have been achieved at the state and local levels?
- What costs have been incurred at the county level that current funding for realignment has not accounted for? Which costs should be the responsibility of the state versus the counties?
- What are the costs and benefits associated with realignment?
- What options are available to ensure long-term funding for realignment?
- What impact has realignment had on the remaining prison population in terms of access and quality of care, other rehabilitative programming provided, and security within the prisons?

This argues for investing in a comprehensive assessment of the impact of public safety realignment. In addition, the legislature may wish to consider having a standard set of metrics that counties will be required to track to enable cross-county comparisons and to facilitate assessments of the overall impact of the 2011 Public Safety Justice Realignment Plan.

There is a precedent for investing in a comprehensive assessment of such a significant policy change. The California's legislature set aside funds for a comprehensive evaluation of the Substance Abuse and Crime Prevention Act of 2000 that changed state law to allow qualifying defendants convicted of non-violent drug possession offenses to receive a probationary sentence and drug treatment in lieu of incarceration. Given the profound change to our criminal justice system that California's 2011 Public Safety Realignment Plan represents, the legislature may want to consider allocating funds for a comprehensive assessment of this new policy.

What Can Counties and Providers Do to Prepare?

County probation and law enforcement, as well as community leaders and organizations, are already preparing for the changes that will occur under public safety realignment. As noted above, counties will have an important incentive to establish new partnerships to improve rehabilitative services and enable individuals to successfully reintegrate back into communities.

Counties and treatment providers also are preparing for the likelihood of newly eligible adults enrolling in Medicaid in 2014. The Medicaid expansion population (which will include the reentry population and other criminal justice-involved individuals) is expected to have multiple chronic health conditions; thus, counties and providers can expect a high demand for primary and specialty care, especially in the initial months following enrollment (Somers et al., 2010).

Here, we offer some recommendations for counties to inform their preparations to meet the rehabilitative needs of the reentry population and this new demand for health care services by the Medicaid expansion population. These recommendations pertain to county criminal justice and health care stakeholders, as well as to community organizations involved in health care or who provide other services to the reentry population. Our recommendations are based on a combination of our review of the literature and analyses of the inmate survey, parolee data, data on the health care safety net in four counties, provider interviews, and focus group discussions with formerly incarcerated men and family members.

Develop County-Level Estimates to Inform Planning for Rehabilitative Services and for Increased Demand for Mental Health and Alcohol Care and Drug Treatment

CDCR has provided counties with estimates of the number of offenders who will be housed and supervised at the local level under public safety realignment. As part of their plans for implementing the new realignment plan, counties are working with county mental health and alcohol and drug programs to assess the needs of individuals returning to counties and to consider ways to transition their care from the state correctional mental health system to county mental health systems. We know from this study and from other research (Farabee et al., 2006) that the number of individuals in the state's Mental Health Services Continuum Program (the correctional mental health system) may not fully represent the total number of ex-prisoners in need of mental health and alcohol and drug treatment services. Nor does it include the other components of the criminal justice–involved population. Further, the possibility of enrolling many of these individuals in Medi-Cal under health care reform will increase demand for services by this population.

County departments of mental health and alcohol and drug treatment, as well as safety-net providers, need to be prepared for this increase in demand for services and consider ways that they can more effectively reach out to these individuals, assess their treatment needs, and provide services to this population. **A starting point is for counties to develop more informed estimates about the number of individuals that will make up the reentry and criminal justice population and their expected demand for services.**

Convene All Relevant Stakeholders for Planning and Coordination of Services

Counties have already developed their initial plans for public safety realignment. Their Community Corrections Partnership was required to develop and recommend to their county's Board of Supervisors a plan for the implementation of the Public Safety Realignment Plan. The planning committees included the chief probation officer, chief of police, sheriff, district attorney, public defender, the presiding judge (or their designee) of the superior court, and a representative from the county department of social services, mental health, or alcohol and substance abuse programs.

Counties also are planning for the implementation of health care reform and the expansion of Medicaid. As part of this planning process, counties may wish to consider establishing specific working groups tasked to assess the expected demand for services by the reentry/criminal justice population and options for meeting that demand. Many of the same stakeholders involved in realignment are also relevant to planning for the increased demand for services from this population and for their enrollment into Medicaid.

However, often-overlooked stakeholders are community- and faith-based organizations that have been actively involved for some time in serving the reentry population. In communities that will be especially affected by realignment, there are a number of such organizations that have experience in providing services in a culturally and linguistically competent manner and who have earned the trust of the local community (National Center for Cultural Competence, 2001). Thus, in light of the findings from this report, **we recommend that counties refine their plans for public safety realignment and health care reform by broadening the group of stakeholders involved to include community- and faith-based organizations.**

Public safety realignment will include funding for rehabilitative services. County policymakers and agencies will want to consider ways to ensure that community- and faith-based organizations are included in the bid and proposal process for reentry services. In the long term, counties and communities will need to develop strategies for building and sustaining local capacity in reentry services.

Assess Local Capacity to Meet New Demands for Health Care

Our analysis of the geographic distribution of health care facilities relative to the concentrations of parolees within counties highlighted that in areas with the highest numbers of parolees, there were gaps in some services and that access to health care providers varied considerably.

Counties and providers will need to assess whether there is sufficient local capacity to meet these new demands, especially in those communities that are particularly impacted by reentry and realignment. As noted above, demand for alcohol and drug treatment and mental health care, in particular, is expected to increase and may swamp the existing capacity of counties' alcohol and drug treatment programs and mental health programs.

Local public health departments and agencies can play an important role in assessing the capacity for care and identifying strategies for addressing service gaps for the reentry/criminal justice population. Public health agencies can convene other stakeholders (safety-net, substance abuse, and mental health providers, as well as corrections and community-based organizations that serve the reentry population) to address collectively the health care needs of the reentry/criminal justice population. Public health agencies also play an important role in ensuring that individuals get the care they need (whether they themselves provide the care or not). This assurance function could be executed through strategies such as mapping of health needs and available health care and reentry resources, facilitating outreach and enrollment in Medi-Cal, and providing information to the reentry/criminal justice population about where they can get culturally competent care (Derose, Gresenz, and Ringel, 2011).

Partnerships between health care providers (safety-net, substance abuse, and mental health providers) and community- and faith-based organizations that serve the reentry/criminal justice population could expand local capacity. For example, faith-based organizations often provide housing, social services, job training, health education, and counseling (sometimes to the reentry population), but these services function largely outside of counties' human service delivery system (Watson et al., 2008). Systematic inventories and oversight of such resources could serve both to increase local capacity and ensure the quality of these services.

Develop "Welcome Home" Guidebooks Tailored to Individual Counties, Particularly for Counties and Communities with High Rates of Return

In the focus group discussions with ex-prisoners, we learned that few had participated in prerelease planning classes. Many of them felt that what information they had received was inadequate and consisted only of general information and lists of services, with few details on how to access those services and on what specific services were available in the county to which they would be returning.

Typically, welcome home guidebooks include information on

- where to go to apply for general relief, Medi-Cal, Supplemental Security Income, food stamps, and other benefits
- where to go for housing assistance
- educational and employment training services
- transportation services
- how to access mental health and drug treatment services.

Many counties have developed such guidebooks. However, they vary in content and in the degree of specificity with respect to services available, and they can quickly become out of date.

Counties can use realignment as an opportunity to update and improve the utility of these guidebooks. Such guidebooks will need to go beyond simple lists of services to include problem-solving strategies, highlight services that address immediate needs (such as finding housing, applying for benefits, or accessing drug treatment services), and be written at an appropriate literacy level (Mellow, 2007). The guidebooks should contain detailed information about local resources and organizations, especially for those communities that will be most affected by realignment. The guidebooks also should be written in a culturally competent manner and (where important) translated into Spanish and other languages. Although guidebooks can be made available on county websites, hard-copy versions of a guidebook are important because many ex-prisoners may not have access to computers or be computer-literate.

The use of 211 listing of services is a starting point, but it is not comprehensive with respect to the range of organizations providing reentry services. Counties will want to develop a process by which local community- and faith-based organizations and other nonprofit community providers can provide information about their services and capacity. This may require establishing a local task force to develop the guidebook and include plans for regularly updating it. Compiling a comprehensive list will also provide counties with information to help assess where there are gaps in services and where capacity may be insufficient.

Key stakeholders—including community leaders, probation, law enforcement, county and city services, and community- and faith-based organizations—should collaborate on developing these guidebooks. This will require working with CDCR and local jail systems, as well as parole and probation, to facilitate the timely distribution of this information to individuals about to be released from prison or county jails. CDCR may want to consider assigning correctional staff to work with local counties in preparing and distributing this information in a timely manner. In addition, these guidebooks should be made widely available to local communities.

Train Providers on Cultural Competence

To improve individual health and build healthy communities, health care providers need to recognize and address the unique culture, language, and health literacy of diverse populations (HRSA, undated-b). The Institute of Medicine highlighted the importance of patient-centered care and cultural competence in improving quality and eliminating racial/ethnic health care disparities (Betancourt et al., 2005). The goal of cultural competence is to create a health care system and workforce that can deliver care to every patient, regardless of race, ethnicity, culture, or language proficiency (Betancourt et al., 2005). From the perspective of our focus group participants, culturally competent care includes respectful and empathetic staff and providers who understand the experience of incarceration.

Many health care providers do not have experience in providing services to the reentry/criminal justice population. **Counties may want to implement provider training to improve their cultural competence**, especially in primary care/public health clinics and in other settings where the primary care and specialty care needs of the reentry/criminal justice population will be addressed. HRSA has developed training tools and guides to assist providers in developing cultural competence for various special populations, such as the homeless, individuals with limited English proficiency, or those with HIV/AIDS (see Health Resources Service Administration, no date-a). However, HRSA's website does not include information specific to the reentry/criminal justice population, although their needs overlap with those of some of the special populations noted here. We recommend that county health care systems develop training materials for county and community treatment providers and work with local community- and faith-based organizations who serve the reentry population to ensure that training materials developed reflect the experiences and perspective of formerly incarcerated individuals.

Consider the Role of Patient Navigators

One way to increase cultural competency is to have staff that can serve as case managers or patient navigators and assist the reentry/criminal justice population in navigating health care and other needed services. Staff experienced in working with this population or who have been formerly incarcerated themselves may be particularly well suited for these positions. As part of planning for delivery systems of care, counties might wish to consider the potential role of care/case managers and patient navigators and such issues as training needed, numbers needed, how these individuals will be integrated into delivery care systems being developed for the Medicaid expansion population, and how these services will be reimbursed. **A demonstration project to explore the use of patient navigators, particularly in counties with large reentry populations, may be a worthwhile undertaking.**

Address the Needs of Families and Those That Care for Children of Incarcerated Parents

From the perspectives of both ex-prisoners and their families, staying in touch with family helps motivate individuals to rehabilitate and can facilitate the reentry process. Research has shown that those individuals who stay connected with their families have lower rates of recidivism than those of ex-prisoners who do not (Hairston, 2002; Klein, Bartholomew, and Hibbert, 2002). As noted above, public safety realignment will allow a number of offenders to serve their time closer to home, thus enabling them to have better access to family members (as well as employers, and community organizations) that can aid them with the reentry process.

To support prisoners' connections to family and facilitate entry, various types of programs and strategies are needed. First, **counties may wish to consider applying for federal grant funding to support programs that focus on children with incarcerated parents,** and, as noted in Chapter Five, research is needed on the size of this population and which programs are effective. Evidence-based programs for at-risk youth could be tailored and applied to this population, such as mentoring programs, cognitive behavioral interventions, or multisystemic therapy[16] that can address the range of risk factors for these children. In the case of multisystemic therapy, for example, funding can come from a variety of sources, including Medicaid reimbursement, state children's services funding, program-level grants to reduce recidivism, funds diverted as an alternative to out-of-home placements for youth, and state reimbursements to managed care organizations that treat emotionally disturbed youth (Promising Practices Network, 2011). The Administration for Children and Families' (ACF's) Administration on Children, Youth and Families' (ACYF's) Family and Youth Services Bureau has recently funded mentoring programs as part of its Mentoring Children of Prisoners program. These programs can be targeted to those communities and neighborhoods highlighted in this report that will be especially impacted by reentry and realignment.

---

[16] An intensive, family-based treatment approach for improving antisocial behavior of serious juvenile offenders.

In addition, **California needs better estimates about the numbers of children with incarcerated parents.** Given that much of the data is based on self-reported information with incarcerated parents and families having a disincentive to report this information, current estimates likely underestimate the actual number of children in need of services.

Programs also are needed that focus on caregivers for children of incarcerated parents, many of whom are the grandparents. The results of out focus group with caregivers underscored a range of practical needs, including respite care, knowledge about what resources are available to caregivers, and support and counseling services.

Finally, as highlighted in our focus group discussions, family reunification can be a very stressful process, because the individual returning from prison is grappling with such challenges as finding housing and employment and reuniting with children. These families are served by a number of different county agencies. **Programs are needed that support the family reunification process** and provide wraparound services that can address the multitude of needs of these families: mental health care and counseling and assistance with welfare, child welfare and child support, and housing and employment. Importantly, some of the recommendations listed above will help facilitate linkage to services for these families.

Final Thoughts

The changes described here that California is experiencing are also occurring in other states, as they, too, grapple with how to reduce corrections costs and the size of their prison populations. Ultimately, most individuals who are incarcerated will eventually return home to local communities. We began our study with the premise that much of the reentry population eventually will become part of the uninsured and medically indigent populations in counties. This is even more the case today.

In light of California's new Public Safety Realignment Plan and federal health care reform, California faces both substantial challenges and unprecedented opportunities to address the needs of this population by improving rehabilitative services at the local level and by improving access to health care for the reentry population (and other components of the criminal justice population) through Medi-Cal and other coverage expansions. Both will require counties to establish new partnerships with the various stakeholders that serve this population.

Lastly, private philanthropy can also play an important role in helping to address the uncertainty created by this unique confluence of public safety realignment at the state level and health care reform at the federal level. Such a role for California and national foundations includes supporting (1) local demonstration projects and collaboration among relevant stakeholders; (2) Medicaid enrollment strategies; (3) pilot projects to test innovative ideas; (4) efforts to increase the local capacity of local communities and organizations to provide reentry services; and (5) ongoing evaluations and research on the impact of realignment and health care reform on the reentry population.

APPENDIX A

Methodology

In this appendix, we summarize the methods used for the analytic results reported in Chapter Two. Please see Davis et al. (2009) for a more detailed description of the methodology summarized here.

Analysis of the Health Care Needs of the Reentry Population

To examine the health care needs of the reentry population, we conducted a state-level analysis using data from BJS 2004 Survey of Inmates in State and Federal Correctional Facilities sample based on all state prison inmates who resided in California. Although our focus is on understanding the socioeconomic characteristics, health care needs, and access to care of parolees, it is difficult to obtain detailed information on a large and representative sample of parolees nationally and in California. Thus, we used the self-reported data from the BJS survey as a proxy. In addition to national estimates, we constructed estimates for California (n = 1,757). All the results presented here are based only on responses among males incarcerated in state prisons.[1]

We conducted descriptive analyses of the inmate survey, reporting both lifetime and current health, mental health, and substance abuse problems. To estimate the reported prevalence of symptoms of substance abuse and dependence, we used the methodology developed

1 We excluded federal prisoners from our study.

by BJS (Mumola and Karberg, 2006) for the 2004 Survey of Inmates in State and Federal Correctional Facilities. Survey respondents were categorized as dependent on or abusing drugs or alcohol based on criteria in the *Diagnostic and Statistical Manual of Mental Disorders*, fourth edition (DSM-IV) (American Psychiatric Association, 2000).

In our analysis, we made the following comparisons and assessed the statistical significance of any differences found between (1) U.S. males and California males and (2) California males by race/ethnicity. We report statistically significant differences ($p \leq 0.05$) between U.S and California inmates and, for California only, between white and African-American inmates and between white and Latino inmates.

Analysis of Geographic Distribution and Concentration of Parolees in California and in the Four Focus Counties

To analyze where parolees go upon release, the study relied on geocoded corrections data for parolees released from California state prisons in 2005–2006 from the CDCR[2] and cluster analysis to examine the geographic distribution of parolees and identify concentrations of parolees across and within counties. To map where parolees go, we focused on the census tract location using the population-weighted centroid of each tract as the residential location.[3]

To create the parolee analytic file, we first combined data from two CDCR files. The first file (TERMGRUP) is essentially a log of all the times an individual enters or leaves prison for any reason. Using this file, we determined that 248,833 paroles occurred in 2005–2006. Some individuals were paroled more than once during this time period, so we selected only their first 2005–2006 parole, giving us 176,618

[2] Focusing on parolees captured the majority of individuals released from prison. We exclude from our sample those individuals unconditionally released from prison. In a typical year, approximately 97 percent of individuals released from California's prisons are parolees; only 3 percent are released unconditionally, having served their entire sentence.

[3] We chose not to use the Thomas Bros. map cell variable because 40 percent of the sample was missing this information.

parolees. The second file (TERMCASE) includes only records for new court commitments and returns to prison with a new sentence. Revocations of parole with no additional sentence, for example, would be included in the first file but not in the second file. The second file (TERMCASE) specifically includes information about the initial sentence, prior record, and demographic characteristics. By appending this information to that of the TERMGRUP file, we are able to analyze the demographic and other characteristics of the 2005–2006 parolees.

Of the total 176,618 cases in our file, 22 percent (n = 39,313) of cases did not have a valid Federal Information Processing Standard (FIPS) code. The FIPS county code is a five-digit code that uniquely identifies counties in the United States, with the first two digits representing the FIPS state code and the last three digits representing the county code within a state. In addition, we used the six-digit FIPS census tract code and used the concatenated FIPS codes to identify parolee location by state, county, and census tract. In this way, we were able to find census tract numbers for 137,305 parolees. To describe the characteristics of parolees, we used the entire sample of 176,618 parolees released in 2005 and 2006; however, all the maps in the Phase I report and those reproduced here are based on the subset of parolees (n = 137,305) for whom we had valid census tract data.

Besides mapping the location of parolees in the state by county and within counties by census tract, we also wanted to identify "clusters" or concentrations of parolees. To do so, we used the 2005–2006 parolee data to assign parolees to the population-weighted centroids of their census tracts. To determine the population-weighted centroid location of each tract, we used the geometric center point of each census block unit (equivalent to street blocks) nested within a census tract. On average, census tracts in California have eight blocks per tract. We then used the 2000 population and geometric center point coordinates of each census block to compute the weighted mean center location for the tract.

We used a Nearest Neighborhood Hierarchical (Nnh) cluster routine to group parolees into clusters based on spatial proximity.[4] In conducting the cluster analysis, we set the search radius at 50 percent, minimum cluster size at 30 (except for Kern County, where the minimum cluster size was set at 20), and at one standard deviation.[5] That is, we represented clusters on maps using one-standard-deviation ellipses of the population-weighted census tract center points. Our aim was to clearly delineate subcounty areas that include the largest proportion of the parolee data.

To name each of the clusters we identified with the Nnh routine, we used the nearest zip code area to a given cluster. We then overlaid this with the raw count of parolees by tract to get a better idea of where the highest density of parolees were in each zip code area to resolve ambiguous assignments or of where more than one cluster was closest to the same zip code area. This step was done to assign names to the clusters across California shown in Figures 2.1, 2.2, 2.3, 2.4, and 2.5 in Chapter Two.

Analysis of the Demographic Characteristics of Parolees and of the Socioeconomic Characteristics of the Areas to Which They Return

The CDCR data allowed us to summarize a limited set of characteristics of those individuals returning to communities in California. We used that data to look at the characteristics of the returning parolees for both the state and the four selected counties. Also, we were interested in understanding whether parolees tend to locate in areas that are similar to the characteristics of the parolees themselves (e.g., in terms of race/ethnicity) and whether they tend to locate in areas that are disadvantaged, as measured by high unemployment and high poverty rates.

---

[4] Specifically, we used the cluster analysis tools available in the freely available and widely used CrimestatIII software to create the Nnh clusters.

[5] For Alameda, Los Angeles, and San Diego counties, the minimum cluster size was set at 30. Because Kern County is less densely populated, we set the minimum cluster size at 20.

To do so, we relied on census data to describe the demographic and socioeconomic characteristics of census tracts in California, including race/ethnicity of the population, educational attainment, poverty rate, and degree of linguistic isolation of households. We used cluster analysis to aggregate the census tracts into seven clusters with similar characteristics. We then summarized the percentage of parolees that return to each of the seven cluster areas. The results are shown in Figure 2.6 and Table 2.4 in Chapter Two.

Analysis of the Health Care Safety Net in the Four Focus Counties

Below, we summarize our approach for identifying the composition of the health care, mental health care, and substance abuse treatment safety net in each of the four focus counties.

Data Sources

We tried to obtain data to characterize each of the three safety nets—health care, mental health care treatment, and substance abuse treatment—for the time period of interest to this study: 2005–2006. However, retrospective data were not always available, so we sometimes had to incorporate later data.

For the hospital and clinic data, we used data from the California Office of Statewide Health Planning and Development for 2005–2006. We augmented this information with a list of clinics and hospitals contracted with the Medically Indigent Services Program (MISP clinics and hospitals) for each study county. These were the current lists for the MISP facilities when we requested the information (in 2008), so there may have been some changes relative to 2005. But we felt it was important to include these providers in our assessment, even though we could not obtain retrospective data.

For the mental health care safety net, we used data on county mental health clinics and on MHSA providers (for the counties where this information was available). The MHSA program came into existence in November 2004, with counties varying in terms of how early they put these resources into place. So, we are likely representing the mental health safety net in our study time period and reflecting more recent changes. For the parole outpatient clinics (POCs), we believe our estimates are relatively stable over time because these clinics are co-located with parole offices in California.

For the substance abuse treatment safety net, we used data for county alcohol and drug treatment services and for Proposition 36 services. Proposition 36 was passed in 2001 and covers the study time period but has evolved over time. We use the current data on Proposition 36 providers in the study counties, which likely differ somewhat from what the picture of providers looked like in 2005–2006; but, overall, we believe it presents a reasonable picture of the distribution of providers during our study because the funding was similar between these two years. Finally, the Parolee Services Network (PSN) program has been in existence for a number of years, with the funding remaining level over time. We believe our estimates for the PSN program likely reflect this network in 2005–2006.

For our geographic analyses at the subcounty level, we focused on the availability and accessibility of safety-net resources for the reentry population. These resources include safety-net hospitals, primary care clinics, and mental health and substance abuse treatment providers. Because most of these facilities serve more than just the reentry population, our accessibility analyses took into account the potential demand for such services by considering the percentage of persons living in poverty. Further, because capacity likely varies across these safety-net providers, we incorporated data on facility capacity (when available) in our measure of accessibility (see below).

We examined the geographic distribution of health care facilities in each of the four counties using GIS to map the distribution of facilities relative to the concentration of parolees in each county. This enabled us to see where any potential holes or gaps in capacity exist relative to the parolee concentrations within a county.

Accessibility Measures

To understand the interaction between prisoner reentry and the safety nets beyond simple mapping, we generated quantitative measures of accessibility, which focuses on potential access. The term *accessibility* refers to the relative ease by which locations of activities, such as work, shopping, and health care, can be reached from a given location (BTS, 1997). Because we did not have access to data that could reveal actual access and utilization of health care services by parolees within California, we settled for a measure that measures accessibility from a single point in an area—in this case, census tracts.

To develop accessibility measures for hospitals and primary care clinics, we used total FTEs as our measure of capacity for facilities, computed the distance matrix from all census tracts in an area, and then used it to select all population-weighted centroids in the threshold travel time (ten minutes drive time) of each facility location. The resulting accessibility for a census tract can be viewed as the estimated average accessibility measure of all persons in the tract, and it incorporated all demands made on a facility from the surrounding area of that facility, not just the tract centroid-based buffer area of each tract.

Using these measures, we classified the accessibility scores for each census tract into four bins, or quartiles, that relate to levels of accessibility: lowest, mid-lowest, mid-highest, and highest. The quartile bins were constructed for census tracts in each county separately, not over all four counties. Thus, each classification scheme is based on the distribution of accessibility values for all census tracts in a single county, not on the full distribution in the state or across multiple counties.[6] However, one can still make comparisons across counties in terms of differences in relative levels of accessibility.

In mapping the health care facilities, we considered only what is available within a county's border. However, we recognize that some concentrations of parolees near a county's border may also be near facilities in neighboring counties. Therefore, in calculating the accessibility measure for hospitals, we included hospitals in neighboring counties. However, in calculating the accessibility measure for clinics, we could

---

[6] It is important to keep in mind that the size of the census tracts differ by county, with less-populated counties tending to have larger census tracts. Thus, it may appear, for example, that there may be large underserved areas within a county, as an artifact of differences in size of census tracts.

not include those in neighboring counties because of the challenges in collecting reliable data on these facilities. Therefore, our accessibility measure for clinics likely underestimates accessibility in some areas along the borders of our study counties.

In some instances, some hospitals and clinics were missing capacity data. To assess the effect of missing capacity data, we conducted a sensitivity analysis, examining whether the accessibility patterns within a county changed when using a simple count of facilities rather than capacity in calculating an alternate measure of capacity. The results of the sensitivity analyses are reported in Davis et al. (2009).

To develop accessibility measures for mental health and substance abuse treatment providers, similar to what was done for hospitals and primary care clinics, we computed the distance matrix from all census tracts within an area and then used it to select all population-weighted centroids within the threshold travel time (ten minutes drive time) of each health facility location. Because we did not have a measure of capacity for mental health and substance abuse treatment providers, we simply counted the facility as a single unit of supply. Thus, the ratio is interpreted as facilities per potential demand and represents the number of facilities per 10,000 population in a county.

APPENDIX B

Protocols

Below is presented the focus group protocols for the discussions with ex-offenders and family caregivers. Lastly, we also present the interview protocol for service providers.

Ex-Offender Focus Group Protocol

Focus Group Questions for Those Formerly Incarcerated—Phase 2: Public Health Implications of Prisoner Reentry

Introduction

Good morning/afternoon. Thank you for taking the time to meet with us to talk about your health care experiences and experiences in general upon returning to the community from prison or jail.

My name is {FOCUS GROUP FACILITATOR NAME} [give a brief background]. My colleague, [NAME], is a public health researcher from the RAND Corporation and will be assisting me today with our discussion.

For the past several years, we've been doing a study looking at what can be done to better meet the health care needs of those returning from prison.

Before we begin, Dr. [NAME] would like to review with you a few administrative tasks.

- Provide the focus group participants with the oral consent form and review it with them.
  - At the end of our discussion (which will go no longer than 90 minutes), we will give each of your $30 to thank you for your time and valuable input.
- Ask if it is okay to tape the focus group for note-taking purposes only—this information will be kept confidential (only members of the research team will review this information).
- Are there any questions before we start?

To begin our discussion, I'd like to go around the room and ask each of you to introduce yourself.

- Please introduce yourself (using a false name if you wish).
- How long have you been out of prison (or jail)?
- When was the last time you were in?
- Is this your first time being incarcerated or have you been in prison previously?
  - Are you currently on parole, probation or on non-revocable parole?

Release Planning

We'd like to begin with talking with you about any discharge planning and health services that you received before your release from prison. By health services we mean for any physical health, mental health, or substance abuse/ drug treatment needs you may have had.

- Let's talk a bit about the months leading up to your release from prison. Were you prepared at all by prison or a case manager or outside group for your release? If so, in what ways?
  - Probe: What types of classes, counseling, discharge planning did you have? Were these sponsored by the prison or by some other organization? (if other organization, probe about the name)

- Did you have any health care needs (specifically, physical health, alcohol/drug treatment or mental health treatment needs) in the months leading up to your release? How fully were they addressed before you were released?
  - If fully addressed, please describe how.
    - o If not well addressed or not at all, why not?

Resources Available and Health Care Experiences

We'd like to talk with you now about your experiences in returning back to the community with respect to your health care needs and what resources were available to you, any problems that arose, and where you typically go to get treated.

- If you had health problems after release from prison or jail, what were they?
  - Probes: Physical health, alcohol/drug treatment or mental health?
- Relative to other needs, how do your health care needs rank in importance?
  - Prompt with the same list as above: Employment, housing, family relationships, etc.
- How has your health affected, if at all, your ability to meet other needs such as finding employment, housing, reuniting with your family?
- What, if any, problems did you experience in terms of getting your health care needs met once out of prison? Describe the "typical" problems you've encountered.
  - Probes: Lack of health insurance or funds, lack of transportation, not knowing where to go to get help, location of the clinic or medical office was too far?
    - o Ask how many have health insurance (and how they got it).
- When you returned to the community, what or who helped you get access to health care or other services? If you could pinpoint

one person or organization that helped you the most, who/what would that be?
  - Probes: How did you find out about where to go to get services? Parole meeting? Local organization (e.g., community organization, church group)? Heard from other returnees? Heard from your family? Went to same clinic or setting where your family members get care?

- What role, if any, have faith-based organizations, churches, or religious leaders played in helping you re-enter the community? How have you gotten connected to them (if at all) and if so, what kind of assistance have they provided?
- What are some of the things that may have made it difficult for you to obtain health care?
  - Probes: e.g., lack of insurance, did not feel comfortable going to a doctor or clinic, long appointment wait times, difficult to understand the instructions given, not sure where to go for treatment, language barriers).
  - *Rank order the list that gets generated.*
- For those of you who have been in prison before, is it harder or easier this time around to get help for your health care needs? For your housing or employment needs?
  - If harder, why do you think it is harder (possible reasons for it).
  - If easier, why do you think it is easier (possible reasons for it).
- If health care coverage were made available to you just prior to your release from prison, would you have been more motivated to get seek treatment for your health problems upon release?
  - Probe to understand the reasons they say either yes or no.

Wrap-Up

Lastly, we'd like to ask for your thoughts and suggestions on what can be done to make it better for those returning back to communities.

- What advice would you give to others who are returning from prison or jail and have health problems?

- What are some possible ways to help to assist those returning from prison to access health care services? To access other services (e.g., employment, housing support)?
  - Brainstorm on priorities, possible solutions, and the role of the following organizations:
    - o Corrections or parole
    - o Health care providers

Family Focus Group Protocol

Focus Group Questions for Family Members/ Caregivers—Phase 2: Public Health Implications of Prisoner Reentry

Introduction

Good evening. Thank you for taking the time to meet with us to talk about your experiences as family members or caregivers of children with either a parent or a family member who incarcerated in the past 5 years.

My name is [RESEARCHER NAME AND BACKGROUND]. My colleague, [RESEARCHER NAME] will be assisting me with the discussion today and will also take notes.

For the past several years, we've been doing a study looking at what can be done to better meet the health care needs of those returning from prison. We are also interested in better understanding the needs of their family members, especially families with children.

Before we begin, I'd like to review with you a few administrative tasks.

- Provide the focus group participants with the oral consent form and review it with them.
  - At the end of our discussion (which will go no longer than 90 minutes), we will give each of you $40 to thank you for your time and valuable input.

- Ask if it is okay to tape the focus group for note-taking purposes only—this information will be kept confidential (only members of the research team will review this information).
- Are there any questions before we start?

To begin our discussion, I'd like to go around the room and ask each of you to introduce yourself.

- Please introduce yourself (using a false name if you wish) and say a little bit about your family and children.

Now I'd like each of you to tell us a little bit about how long you've lived in San Diego and how you became involved with the Project Live program.

Background Information

- Are you new to San Diego or have you been in this neighborhood for a while?
- Can you tell me how each of you became involved with the Project Live program?
  - How long has your child been going to O'Farrell Community School? How long have they been in this program (Project Live)? How did you find out about it?

Perceived Needs of Families and Children and Problems Encountered

I'd like to talk with you next about the needs of your family and children and what problems, if any, may have arisen and how you've tried to address with them.

- Can you tell me a little bit about the child/children's initial reaction to having a parent or family member being incarcerated? What were some of the initial concerns that the child expressed? Was this a new or familiar experience for the child?

  - Probes/examples: whether they'd be able to see or visit their parent or family member, whom they would live with, whether they'd be able to stay at the same school, what their friends would say?
- Does the child/children wish to keep in contact with their parent or family member?
  - If yes, have they been able to? In what ways?
  - Probes: visits, writing letters, telephone calls
  - If yes, how difficult is it to keep in contact?
- If no, why do you think they (or you) were not interested in keeping in contact?
- Have you felt that being in contact (or not in contact) has made a positive or negative difference for the child?
- Did your child/children's behavior change in a noticeable way leading up to or after the incarceration? If so, in what ways? If the family member has returned from prison, did the child's behavior change after the family member returned home?
  - Probes: became angry, sad, or withdrawn; started acting out, skipping school, or doing poorly in school
- What are the most difficult problems the child/children has struggled with? How are you addressing them or trying to address them?
  - Probes: sought counseling, talked with the teachers, talked with our church or pastor, with other family members
- What people or organizations have played a role in helping you address these problem(s)?
  - Probe: Project Live/O'Farrell Community School, case worker, counseling, teachers, pastor
  - How did these organizations help? What kind of services do they provide?
- What kinds of help do your child/children need, but they do not receive?
  - *Rank order the list that gets generated.*

- If you had to list a reason why they are not getting help with these needs, what would this reason be?
  - Probes: Lack of finances, lack of services, didn't know where to go?

Support Needs of Families/Caregivers and Resources Available

Let's talk now about what your personal support needs are, what resources, if any, have been helpful for your own needs, and whether you encountered any problems in getting help for these needs. We're interested in learning about your needs and resources available because we want to understand what programs or services might help caregivers like you.

- What were the most difficult issues you personally confronted in dealing with having a family member incarcerated?
  - Probes: Loss of financial support? How to meet basic needs? Bringing these children into your home or other change in family structure? How to pay for the support needs of the child? Whether child welfare would interfere? Concerns about whether child welfare department might get involved? Concerns about others finding out about the situation? Concerns about how (and whether) to keep in touch with the family member who was incarcerated?
- What type of help did you need most?
- What people or organizations have played a role in helping you address these issues?
  - Project Live (O'Farrell Community School)
  - Probe about other organizations: churches, social services, community organizations
- How did you find out about where to go to get services?
  - Probes: Local organization (e.g., the school, church, other community organizations)? Heard from the parole officer about services? Heard from your family or friends? Heard from the counseling or case worker?

- If you could pinpoint one person or organization that helped you the most when you began taking care of the child/children, who/what would that be?
  - How did you find this help?
  - Why did you find it so helpful?
- What, if any, problems did you experience in trying to get help? Describe the "typical" problems you've encountered.
  - Probes: Lack of funds, lack of transportation, not knowing where to go to get help, location of a service was too far?
- What kinds of help did your family need, but did not receive? Why not?
  - *Rank order the list that gets generated.*
  - Probes: Needed help getting counseling for themselves or the children? Needed financial help?

Wrap-Up

Lastly, we'd like to ask for some final words of advice and wisdom from you on programs or services that can better support family members/caregivers and children.

- What advice would you give to others who have a family member who is incarcerated or about to be incarcerated? Or who are caring for children of a family member who is incarcerated?
  - Specifically, what advice would you give those who are caring for the children of a family member who is incarcerated?
  - Or who has an incarcerated family member who is returning to the home?
- What would make it easier for family members or caregivers to have their needs met and get access to services?
- What do you think are the areas where needs are most often not getting met?
  - How could these needs best be addressed?
    - o Brainstorm on priorities, possible solutions, and the role of the following organizations: "What do you think of . . ." corrections or parole, health care providers, community at large

(probe for which orgs/people specifically—i.e., community organizations, FBOs, family, other).

New Caregivers

For those of you that are new caregivers—we'd like to ask you to stay for a few more minutes just to ask about what led up to child/children coming to live with you:

- For those of you who became new caregivers (e.g., foster parents or grandparents), was your child/children living with you at the time that their parent or a family member was incarcerated? Or did they come to live with you afterwards?
  - Probes: Who was the individual? Was this the first time they have been in prison or jail? For how long? Was this the first time the child has gone to an alternative caregiver?
  - At what point did the child begin living with you (e.g., time of arrest, when the individual was convicted and sent to prison)?
  - What was your relationship to the child and the incarcerated individual?
- Were you prepared to take this child into your home?
  - What factors were important in your decision to bring these children into your home? What concerns, if any, did you have?
  - How did this impact your own situation?
    - o Probes: in terms of finances, living situation, whether other members of their family were supportive or not
- Do you anticipate that your child/children will remain with you when their parent or family member returns from prison or jail?
- Do you anticipate that the parent or family member will also come to live with you?

Provider Interview Protocol

Provider/Policy Interview Questions—
Phase 2: Public Health Implications of Prisoner Reentry

Informed Consent

- Provide interviewee the approved oral consent form and review with them.
- Ask if okay to tape the interview for note-taking purposes only.

Overview of Interviewee's Responsibilities and Organization's Role

I'd like to begin by asking you to summarize your organization's purpose and mission.

- What population does your organization serve?
- What are your responsibilities?

Views Regarding Health Care Needs of Individuals Returning from Prison

- What proportion of your patients are ex-prisoners?
  - If you treat these individuals, how is it that they come under your care? (e.g., how do they find you? Do you conduct particular outreach to ex-prisoners? If so, why the focus on ex-prisoners?)
- What are the health issues you commonly see in this population?
  - In your view, what are the major health care needs of those returning from prison?
- Do the health care needs of those returning from prison differ, if at all, from the rest of the patient population you serve?
  - In what ways?
- In your view, what health care needs of ex-prisoners are most critical to address?

- What proportion of ex-prisoners (that your organization sees) do you estimate have mental health or substance abuse problems? Physical (acute or chronic) problems? Infectious diseases?

Services Provided to the Reentry Population

- What kinds of health care services does your organization provide, if any, to those returning from prison?
  - What kinds of other services does your organization provide?
    - o E.g., employment assistance, housing assistance, case management, referrals
  - What is the purpose of the social services that your organization provides to the formerly incarcerated; in conjunction with health care services?
- When an ex-prisoner needs treatment that you can't provide, whom do you refer them to?
  - Probe about specific names of service providers, including nonprofit community organizations.
- How would you characterize your community's service capacity to meet the physical, mental health, or drug treatment needs of returning prisoners?
  - What local treatment resources are available to provide services to this population?
  - What other resources are needed, if any?
- How have budget cuts by the city/county or by the State or Department of Corrections impacted (if at all) your organization's ability to provide services to this population? In what ways?
  - Impacted your community's treatment capacity?
  - What adjustments, if any, have you had to make as a result of budget cuts in terms of services, staffing, outreach activities, referral patterns?
- How has California's Non-Revocable Parole (NRP) policy impacted your organization, if at all?
  - How do you know if a patient is on NRP status?

- Is your agency tracking costs and services provided to NRP individuals?
- Are you receiving (or hope to receive) reimbursement or funding from the county or state to cover these costs?
- If there has been an increased in demand for your agency's services from the NRP population, has this impacted in any way your ability to provide care to regular clientele?
  - o E.g., has there been any effects on appointment waiting times? effects on quality of care?
- If there has been a decrease in demand for your agency's services from the NRP population, why do you think this is the case? What are your ideas for increasing use of your services by the NRP population?

Collaboration

- Do you collaborate or partner with any other organization(s) or service provider(s) to address the treatment needs of ex-prisoners?
  - If so, what other organizations?
  - Do you partner with non-treatment providers? E.g., community organizations that address housing, or employment needs? Faith-based organizations that address spiritual and social needs?
  - Is the collaboration formal or informal?
- What city/county agencies, community providers, and/or corrections/parole/ probation are involved in
  - Linking ex-prisoners to treatment services?
  - Providing services to this population?
  - With service delivery coordination?
  - In your view, who are the key organizations in your city/county focused on prisoner reentry?
  - Are there new (including nontraditional) stakeholders now involved in prisoner reentry?
    - o E.g., law enforcement, health department, etc.

- Is there a history of collaboration on prisoner reentry issues or is this a new area for your city/county?
  - What factors do you think have made it easy or challenging to collaborate on prisoner reentry issues?
    - To collaborate on addressing the health care needs of ex-prisoners?
  - In your view where are there opportunities to improve collaboration?

Access to Health Care Services for Individuals Returning from Prison

- In your opinion, what factors positively or negatively affect ex-prisoners' access to or use of health care services in your city or county? Mental health and drug treatment services?
  - Probes: number of providers willing to treat this population, lack of insurance, strained safety-net services, factors related to the ex-prisoners themselves (e.g., distrustful of health care providers, lack of knowledge of where low-cost care can be obtained, inability to get time off from work, etc.).
- What strategies has your organization or city/county developed or considered to improve access to services for individuals returning from prison?
  - Probes: e.g., established a medical home, established or ongoing reentry council, improved tracking data on service delivery, improved interagency coordination.
  - Is your organization or city/county receiving Second Chance Act funding? If so, for what purpose? Does your organization or city/county have any pilot or demonstration projects planned or underway?
- What challenges or issues has your organization encountered in providing services to this population?
  - Challenges having to do with staff training or familiarity with this population

- Challenges having to do with doctor-patient communication (language, trust, etc.)
- Challenges having to do with getting access to the clinic's services (including transportation)
- Challenges with adherence to medications or treatments
- Challenges with trust
- Challenges with lack of insurance
- [*Ask them to rank order the barriers they mention in terms of importance.*]

- Are these problems different or more challenging for particular subgroups of ex-prisoners? If so, in what ways?
  - Probes: e.g., dually diagnosed patients, those with infectious diseases, seriously mentally ill, female ex-prisoners, those with drug addiction, etc.
- What does your organization do to try and address these problem areas?
- What are some of the system or policy barriers to providing care to ex-prisoners?
  - E.g., parole needs to refer them to county services before we can see them; Medicaid doesn't cover this population; our county's policy is that they are to be seen only by certain clinics or county providers, etc.
  - What are your thoughts about how to remedy or address these barriers?
- What do you think should be done to address these barriers?
  - Probe with who specifically should be responsible for or involved in developing solutions (e.g., service providers, city/county government, community organizations, state government (corrections or parole), faith-based organizations, etc.).

Wrap-Up

- Overall, what do you see as the key challenges facing California in this area?

- What do you see as possible options for California to better meet the needs of ex-prisoners?
- Are there any topics that we have not addressed that you feel are important for us to consider?

References

Allard, Scott W., *Access to Social Services: The Changing Urban Geography of Poverty and Service Provision*, Washington, D.C.: Brookings Institution, Center on Urban and Metropolitan Policy, August 2004.

American Bar Association, Criminal Justice Section, "Report to the House of Delegates," August 2007.

American Psychiatric Association, *Diagnostic and Statistical Manual of Mental Disorders*, 4th ed., text rev., Washington, D.C., 2000.

Amity Foundation, "Amity California," no date. As of September 6, 2011: http://www.amityfdn.org/California/California%20Continued.php

Andersen, Ronald M., *Behavioral Model of Families' Use of Health Services*, Chicago: Center for Health Administration Studies, University of Chicago, Research Series No. 25, 1968.

Andersen, Ronald, and John F. Newman, "Societal and Individual Determinants of Medical Care Utilization in the United States," *Milbank Memorial Fund Quarterly*, Vol. 51, No. 1, 1973, pp. 95–124.

Bazelon Center for Mental Health Law, *LIFELINES: Linking to Federal Benefits for People Exiting Corrections*, Volumes 1, 2, and 3. Washington, D.C., 2009.

Betancourt, Joseph R., Alexander R. Green, J. Emilio Carrillo, and Elyse R. Park, "Cultural Competence and Health Care Disparities: Key Perspectives and Trends," *Health Affairs*, Vol. 24, No. 2, March/April 2005, pp. 499–505.

Binswanger, Ingrid A., Mark F. Stern, Richard A. Deyo, Patrick J. Heagerty, Allen Cheadle, Joann G. Elmore, and Thomas D. Koepsell, "Release from Prison: A High Risk of Death for Former Inmates," *New England Journal of Medicine*, Vol. 356, No. 2, January 11, 2007, pp. 157–165.

BJS—*see* Bureau of Justice Statistics.

Block, Kathleen J., and Margaret J. Potthast, "Girl Scouts Beyond Bars: Facilitating Child-Parent Contact in Correctional Settings," *Child Welfare*, Vol. 77, No. 5, September–October 1998.

BTS—*see* Bureau of Transportation Statistics.

Buck Jeffrey A., "The Looming Expansion and Transformation of Public Substance Abuse Treatment Under the Affordable Care Act," *Health Affairs*, Vol. 30, No. 8, 2011, pp. 1402–1410.

Bureau of Justice Statistics, *Survey of Inmates in State and Federal Correctional Facilities, 2004*, codebook, Ann Arbor, Mich.: Inter-University Consortium for Political and Social Research, no date-a.

———, "Survey of Inmates in State Correctional Facilities (SISCF)," no date-b. As of November 2, 2011:
http://bjs.ojp.usdoj.gov/index.cfm?ty=dcdetail&iid=275

Bureau of Transportation Statistics, U.S. Department of Transportation, *Transportation Statistics Annual Report 1997*, Washington, D.C., BTS97-S-01, 1997. As of May 21, 2009:
http://www.bts.gov/publications/transportation_statistics_annual_report/1997/

California Correctional Health Care Services, "Frequently Asked Questions," 2011. As of October 20, 2011:
http://www.cphcs.ca.gov/faq.aspx

California Department of Alcohol and Drug Programs, *At-A-Glance: Affordable Care Act Requirements for Substance Use Disorder Services*, Sacramento, Calif., February 2011. As of October 25, 2011:
http://www.adp.ca.gov/healthcare/pdf/HCR_Overview.pdf

California Department of Corrections and Rehabilitation, "Office of Substance Abuse Treatment Services," no date. As of October 10, 2011:
http://www.cdcr.ca.gov/DARS/index.html#CP

———, *Parolee Information Handbook*, no date. As of October 12, 2011:
http://www.cdcr.ca.gov/Parole/_pdf/ParoleeHandbook.pdf

———, "Low Income Health Program," 2007. As of September 19, 2011:
http://www.dhcs.ca.gov/provgovpart/Pages/lihp.aspx

———, *Historical Trends, 1987–2007*, Sacramento, Calif., 2008. As of October 20, 2011:
http://www.cdcr.ca.gov/Reports_Research/Offender_Information_Services_Branch/Annual/HIST2/HIST2d2007.pdf

———, "COMPAS Assessment Tool Launched—Evidence-Based Rehabilitation for Offender Success," April 15, 2009. As of October 12, 2011:
http://www.cdcr.ca.gov/Adult_Programs/docs/FS_COMPAS_Final_4-15-09.pdf

———, *California Prisoners and Parolees 2009: Summary Statistics on Adult Felon Prisoners and Parolees, Civil Narcotic Addicts and Outpatients and Other Populations*, Sacramento, Calif., 2010. As of October 26, 2011:
http://www.cdcr.ca.gov/Reports_Research/Offender_Information_Services_Branch/Annual/CalPris/CALPRISd2009.pdf

———, "Adult Programs Key Performance Indicators January 2010–December 2010: In Prison Substance Abuse Treatment Enrollment %," December 2010. As of September 6, 2011:
http://www.cdcr.ca.gov/DARS/docs/SAP-Enrollment-December-2010.pdf

———, "$150 Million Reduction Fiscal Year 2011/12: Program-Related Savings," 2011. As of September 19, 2011:
http://file.lacounty.gov/bc/q2_2011/cms1_161463.pdf

———, *Fall 2011 Adult Population Projections*, Sacramento, Calif., 2011. As of October 20, 2011:
http://www.cdcr.ca.gov/Reports_Research/Offender_Information_Services_Branch/Projections/F11pub.pdf

———, "Implementation of the Post Release Community Supervision Act of 2011," 2011. As of October 25, 2011:
http://www.cdcr.ca.gov/realignment/docs/PRCS-County.pdf

———, "Three-Judge Panel and California Inmate Population Reduction," May 23, 2011. As of October 17, 2011:
http://www.cdcr.ca.gov/News/docs/2011-05-23-Three-Judge-Panel-Background.pdf

———, "2011 Public Safety Realignment," September 15, 2011. As of October 17, 2011:
http://www.cdcr.ca.gov/realignment/docs/Realignment-Fact-Sheet.pdf

———, "Did You Know CDCR Continues to Work with Each County's Department of Mental Health to Provide Information for All Inmates on Post-Release Community Supervision?" September 29, 2011. As of October 20, 2011;
http://cdcrdidyouknow.blogspot.com/2011/09/did-you-know-cdcr-continues-to-work.html

———, "Post Release Community Supervision Release Planning for Mental Health," September 29, 2011. As of October 17, 2011:
http://www.cdcr.ca.gov/realignment/docs/PRCS-mental-health-info.pdf

———, "Public Safety Realignment," draft, October 13, 2011. As of October 20, 2011:
http://www.cdcr.ca.gov/realignment/docs/County-Handbook-10-13-11.pdf

California Department of Corrections and Rehabilitation, Division of Addiction and Recovery Services, *Annual Report*, June 2009. As of September 6, 2011:
http://www.cdcr.ca.gov/DARS/docs/Master%20AR%20FINAL101409.pdf

California Department of Corrections and Rehabilitation, Division of Correctional Health Services, "Release Planning Continuity of Mental Health and Medical Care," September 1, 2011.

California Health Care Foundation, *California Health Care Almanac—California's Health Care Safety Net: Facts and Figures*, Oakland, Calif., 2010. As of September 6, 2011:
http://www.chcf.org/~/media/MEDIA%20LIBRARY%20Files/PDF/C/PDF%20CAHealthCareSafetyNetFactsFigures.pdf

California Health Care Reform, home page, 2010a. As of October 17, 2011:
http://www.healthcare.ca.gov/

———, "Focusing on Prevention and Wellness," 2010b. As of October 17, 2011:
http://www.healthcare.ca.gov/Priorities/FocusingonPreventionandWellness.aspx

———, "Grants," 2010c. As of October 17, 2011:
http://www.healthcare.ca.gov/NewsInformation/Grants.aspx

California Kinship, homepage, no date. As of October 13, 2011:
http://www.edgewood.org/kssp/

California Prison Health Care Services, "What Is the Receivership?" fact sheet, July 2010. As of October 20, 2011:
http://www.cphcs.ca.gov/docs/resources/factsheet.pdf

California Rehabilitation Oversight Board, *Biannual Report*, Sacrameno, Calif., September 15, 2011. As of October 14, 2011:
http://www.oig.ca.gov/media/crob/reports/C-ROB%20Sept%2015%202011%20Draft%20Report%20%28Nov%207%20publish%20date%29.pdf

California State Auditor, *Department of Corrections: Though Improving, the Department Still Does Not Identify and Serve All Parolees Needing Outpatient Clinic Program Services, but Increased Caseloads Might Strain Clinic Resources*, Sacramento, Calif.: Bureau of State Audits, 2001-104, August 2001. As of October 10, 2011:
http://www.bsa.ca.gov/pdfs/reports/2001-104.pdf

Cammett, Ann, "Expanding Collateral Sanctions: The Hidden Costs of Aggressive Child Support Enforcement Against Incarcerated Parents," *Georgetown Journal on Poverty Law and Policy*, Vol. 13, No. 2, Summer 2006.

CDCR—*see* California Department of Corrections and Rehabilitation.

Center for Health Care Strategies, Inc., "Fact Sheet: Health Homes: Opportunities for Medicaid," March 2011.

Center for Mental Health Services National GAINS Center for Systemic Change for Justice-Involved People with Mental Illness, "Sensitizing Providers to the Effects of Incarceration on Treatment and Risk Management (SPECTRM)," February 2007. As of September 12, 2011:
http://www.gainscenter.samhsa.gov/pdfs/reentry/Spectrum.pdf

Centers for Disease Control and Prevention, "Colorectal Cancer Screening Guidelines," 2011. As of September 6, 2011:
http://www.cdc.gov/cancer/colorectal/basic_info/screening/guidelines.htm

Community Oriented Correctional Health Services, "About Us," 2011. As of October 17, 2011:
http://www.cochs.org/about

Conklin, Thomas, Thomas Lincoln, Rachel Wilson, and Kieran Curran, *A Public Health Manual for Correctional Health Care*, Hampden County Sheriff's Department and Massachusetts Public Health Association, October 2002. As of October 17, 2011:
http://www.mphaweb.org/documents/PHModelforCorrectionalHealth.pdf

Council of Community Clinics, "About Council of Community Clinics," 2009. As of September 6, 2011:
http://www.ccc-sd.org/about.aspx

Davidson, Pamela L., Ronald M. Andersen, Roberta Wyn, and E. Richard Brown, "A Framework for Evaluating Safety-Net and Other Community-Level Factors on Access for Low-Income Populations," *Inquiry*, Vol. 41, No. 1, Spring 2004, pp. 21–38.

Davies, Elizabeth, Diana Brazzell, Nancy LaVigne, and Tracey Shollenberger, *Understanding the Experiences and Needs of Children of Incarcerated Parents: Views from Mentors*, Washington, D.C.: Urban Institute, 2008.

Davis, Lois M., Nancy Nicosia, Adrian Overton, Lisa Miyashiro, Kathryn Pitkin Derose, Terry Fain, Susan Turner, Paul Steinberg, and Eugene Williams III, *Understanding the Public Health Implications of Prisoner Reentry in California: Phase I Report*, Santa Monica, Calif.: RAND Corporation, TR-687-TCE, 2009. As of September 6, 2011:
http://www.rand.org/pubs/technical_reports/TR687/

Davis, Lois M., and Sharon Pacchiana, "Health Profile of the State Prison Population and Returning Offenders: Public Health Challenges," *Journal of Correctional Health Care*, Vol. 10, No. 3, April 2004, pp. 303–331.

Derose, Kathryn Pitkin, Carole Roan Gresenz, and Jeanne S. Ringel, "Understanding Disparities in Health Care Access—and Reducing Them—Through a Focus on Public Health," *Health Affairs*, Vol. 30, No. 10, 2011, pp. 1844–1851.

Dorn, Stan, Sharon Silow-Carroll, Tanya Alteras, Heather Sacks, and Jack A. Meyer, *Medicaid and Other Public Programs for Low-Income Childless Adults: An Overview of Coverage in Eight States*, Menlo Park, Calif.: Henry J. Kaiser Family Foundation, Kaiser Commission on Medicaid and the Uninsured, 2004.

Farabee, David, Dave Bennett, David Garcia, Umme Warda, and Joy Yang, *Final Report on the Mental Health Services Continuum Program of the California Department of Corrections and Rehabilitation—Parole Division*, UCLA Integrated Substance Abuse Program, Neuropsychiatric Institute, June 30, 2006.

Farabee, David, Sheldon Zhang, Robert E. L. Roberts, and Joy Yang, *COMPAS Validation Study: Final Report*, Los Angeles, Calif.: Semel Institute for Neuroscience and Human Behavior, University of California, Los Angeles, August 15, 2010. As of October 12, 2011:
http://www.cdcr.ca.gov/Adult_Research_Branch/Research_Documents/COMPAS_Final_Report_08-11-10.pdf

Freudenberg, Nicholas, "Community Health Services for Returning Jail and Prison Inmates," *Journal of Correctional Health Care*, Vol. 10, No. 3, April 2004, pp. 369–397.

Gardiner, Christine Lynn, *From Inception to Implementation: How SACPA Has Affected the Case Processing and Sentencing of Drug Offenders in One California County*, doctoral dissertation, University of California, Irvine, July 2008.

Gelberg, Lillian, Ronald M. Andersen, and Barbara D. Leake, "The Behavioral Model for Vulnerable Populations: Application to Medical Care Use and Outcomes for Homeless People," *Health Services Research*, Vol. 34, No. 6, February 2000, pp. 1273–1302.

Girion, Lisa, and Mark Medina, "Hospitals Feel Ill Effects of Recession," *Los Angeles Times*, January 14, 2009.

Glaze, Lauren E., and Laura M. Maruschak, *Parents in Prison and Their Minor Children, 2008*, Washington, D.C.: U.S. Department of Justice, Bureau of Justice Statistics Special Report, NCJ 222984, August 2008.

Gonzales, Richard, "California's New Prison Policy Has Some Skeptics," NPR.org, September 29, 2011. As of October 17, 2011:
http://www.npr.org/2011/09/29/140901846/californias-new-prison-policy-has-some-skeptics

Goode, W. Wilson, Sr., and Thomas J. Smith, *Building from the Ground Up: Creating Effective Programs to Mentor Children of Prisoners—The Amachi Model*, Philadelphia, Pa.: Public/Private Ventures, 2005. As of October 13, 2011:
http://www.ppv.org/ppv/publications/assets/185_publication.pdf

Greenberg, Elizabeth, Eric Dunleavy, and Mark Kutner, *Literacy Behind Bars: Results from the 2003 National Assessment of Adult Literacy Prison Survey*, Washington, D.C.: National Center for Education Statistics, Institute of Education Sciences, May 2007. As of October 11, 2011:
http://nces.ed.gov/pubsearch/pubsinfo.asp?pubid=2007473

Hairston, Creasie F., "The Importance of Families in Prisoners' Community Reentry," *ICCA Journal on Community Corrections*, April 2002, pp. 11–14.

———, *Focus on Children with Incarcerated Parents: An Overview of the Research Literature*, Baltimore, Md.: Annie E. Casey Foundation, October 2007.

Hamblin, Allison, "Medicaid and Criminal Justice: The Need for Cross-System Collaboration Post Health Care Reform," Center for Health Care Strategies, Inc., November 2010. As of October 10, 2011:
http://www.chcs.org/publications3960/publications_show.htm?doc_id=1261195

Hammett, Theodore M., Patricia Harmon, and William Rhodes, "The Burden of Infectious Disease Among Inmates and Releasees from Correctional Facilities," in National Commission on Correctional Health Care, *The Health Status of Soon-to-Be-Released Inmates: A Report to Congress*, Vol. 2, Chicago, Ill., May 2002. As of September 9, 2011:
http://www.ncchc.org/pubs/pubs_stbr.vol2.html

Hayes, Joseph M., *California's Changing Prison Population*, San Francisco, Calif.: Public Policy Institute of California, July 2011. As of October 20, 2011:
http://www.ppic.org/main/publication_show.asp?i=702

Health Resources Service Administration, "Culture, Language & Health Literacy Resources: General," no date-a. As of October 10, 2011:
http://www.hrsa.gov/culturalcompetence/general.html

———, "Culture, Language and Health Literacy," no date-b. As of October 17, 2011:
http://www.hrsa.gov/culturalcompetence/index.html

Healthy Communities Incorporated, *Business Plan Executive Summary: 2009–2011 Growth Projections for Primary Care and Support Service Programs*, Oakland, Calif., 2008.

Healthy Oakland, Facebook page, no date. As of October 10, 2011:
http://www.facebook.com/pages/Healthy-Communities-Inc/117102093242?v=info

Heiser, Bill, and Junious Williams, *Reentry Health Care in Alameda County: Executive Summary—Initial Assessment and Recommendations of the Alameda County Reentry Health Task Force*, Oakland, Calif.: Urban Strategies Council, 2008.

Hiller, Matthew L., Matthew Webster, Egle Narevic, Michele Staton, Thomas F. Garrity, and Carl Leukefeld, "Prisoners with Substance Abuse and Mental Health Problems: Use of Health and Health Services," *American Journal of Drug and Alcohol Abuse*, Vol. 31, No. 1, 2005, pp. 1–20.

Hillestad, Richard, James Bigelow, Anthony Bower, Federico Girosi, Robin Meili, Richard Scoville, and Roger Taylor, "Can Electronic Medical Record Systems Transform Health Care? Potential Health Benefits, Savings, and Costs," *Health Affairs*, Vol. 24, No. 5, 2005, pp. 1103–1117.

Imai, Kent, *Analysis of Year 2009 Inmate Death Reviews—California Prison Health Care System*, California Prison Healthcare Receivership, September 2010. As of October 25, 2011:
http://www.cphcs.ca.gov/docs/resources/OTRES_DeathReviewAnalysisYear2009_20100907.pdf

Kahn, Carrie, "L.A. County Prepares to Take on State Prisoners," NPR.org, September 29, 2011. As of October 17, 2011:
http://www.npr.org/2011/09/29/140922171/l-a-county-prepares-to-take-on-state-prisoners

Kaiser Family Foundation, "Summary of the New Health Reform Law," 2011a. As of October 11, 2011:
http://www.kff.org/healthreform/upload/8061.pdf

———, "Community Health Centers: Opportunities and Challenges of Health Reform," 2011b. As of October 11, 2011:
http://www.kff.org/uninsured/upload/8098.pdf

Kelch, Deborah Reidy, *The Crucial Role of Counties in the Health of Californians: An Overview*, Oakland, Calif.: California Health Care Foundation, March 2011. As of October 11, 2011:
http://www.chcf.org/publications/2011/03/crucial-role-counties

Klein, Shirley R., Geannina S. Bartholomew, and Jeff Hibbert, "Inmate Family Functioning," *International Journal of Offender Therapy and Comparative Criminology*, Vol. 46, 2002, pp. 95–111.

LaVigne, Nancy G., Samuel J. Wolf, and Jesse Jannetta, *Voices of Experience: Focus Group Findings from the State of Rhode Island*, Washington, D.C.: Urban Institute, November 2004.

Loper, Ann Booker, and Elena Hontoria Tuerk, "Parenting Programs for Incarcerated Parents: Current Research and Future Directions," *Criminal Justice Policy Review*, Vol. 17, No. 4, December 2006, pp. 407–427.

Los Angeles County Department of Public Health, "Service Planning Areas," no date. As of September 6, 2011:
http://www.lapublichealth.org/spa/spawhat.htm

———, "Parolee Services Network Funding," memorandum from Jonathan E. Fielding, Director and Health Officer, to each Health Deputy, Los Angeles, Calif., May 26, 2011. As of September 7, 2011:
http://file.lacounty.gov/bc/q2_2011/cms1_161463.pdf

Los Angeles County Department of Public Health, Substance Abuse Prevention and Control, *Standards and Practices for the Operation of Participant Paid Fee Based Treatment Program Penal Code 1210*, Alhambra, Calif., October 1, 2011.

Los Angeles County Department of Public Social Services, "Guide to Free and Low-Cost Health Care Programs and Services: Outpatient Reduced-Cost Simplified Application (ORSA) Plan," 2011. As of September 6, 2011:
http://www.ladpss.org/dpss/health_care/orsa.cfm

Los Angeles County Probation Department, "Public Safety Realignment Act of 2011," fact sheet, September 2011. As of October 20, 2011:
http://probation.lacounty.gov/PDF/AB109_FACTSHEET.PDF

Los Angeles County Sheriff's Department, Correctional Services Division, Medical Services Bureau, "Overview," no date. As of October 17, 2011: http://la-sheriff.org/divisions/correctional/medical_srvs/ovrview.html

Mallik-Kane, Kamala, *Returning Home Illinois Policy Brief: Health and Prisoner Reentry*, Washington, D.C.: Urban Institute, 2005. As of October 11, 2011: www.urban.org/UploadedPDF/311214_health_prisoner_reentry.pdf

Mallik-Kane, Kamala, and Christy A. Visher, *Health and Prisoner Reentry: How Physical, Mental, and Substance Abuse Conditions Shape the Process of Reintegration*, Washington, D.C.: Urban Institute Justice Policy Center, February 2008. As of September 9, 2011:
http://www.urban.org/UploadedPDF/411617_health_prisoner_reentry.pdf

Mancuso, David, and Barbara E. M. Felver, *Health Care Reform, Medicaid Expansion and Access to Alcohol/Drug Treatment: Opportunities for Disability Prevention*, Olympia, Wash.: Washington State Department of Social and Health Services, Research and Data Analysis Division, RDA Report 4.84, October 2010. As of October 11, 2011:
http://publications.rda.dshs.wa.gov/1418/

Marlow, Elizabeth, Mary C. White, and Catherine A. Chesla, "Barriers and Facilitators: Parolees' Perceptions of Community Health Care," *Journal of Correctional Health Care*, Vol. 16, No. 1, January 2010, pp. 17–26.

McMurray, Harvey L., "High Risk Parolees in Transition from Institution to Community Life," *Journal of Offender Rehabilitation*, Vol. 19, Nos. 1–2, 1993, pp. 145–161.

McNichol, Elizabeth, Phil Oliff, and Nicholas Johnson, "States Continue to Feel Recession's Impact," Center on Budget and Policy Priorities, June 17, 2011. As of October 17, 2011:
http://www.cbpp.org/cms/index.cfm?fa=view&id=711

Mellow, Jeff, "Written Health Informational Needs," in Robert Greifinger, ed., *Public Health Behind Bars: From Prisons to Communities*, New York: Springer, 2007, pp. 265–279.

Miller, Keva, "The Impact of Parental Incarceration on Children: An Emerging Need for Effective Interventions," *Child and Adolescent Social Work Journal*, Vol. 23, No. 4, August 2006, pp. 472–486.

Mumola, Christopher, *Substance Abuse and Treatment, State and Federal Prisoners, 1997*, Washington, D.C.: Bureau of Justice Statistics, U.S. Department of Justice, 1999 (revised March 11, 2009). As of October 11, 2011:
http://bjs.ojp.usdoj.gov/content/pub/pdf/satsfp97.pdf

———, *Incarcerated Parents and Their Children*, Washington, D.C.: U.S. Department of Justice, Bureau of Justice Statistics, NCJ 182335, 2000.

Mumola, Christopher J., and Jennifer C. Karberg, *Drug Use and Dependence, State and Federal Prisoners, 2004*, Washington, D.C.: Bureau of Justice Statistics, U.S. Department of Justice, October 2006 (revised January 19, 2007). As of March 1, 2009:
http://bjs.ojp.usdoj.gov/index.cfm?ty=pbdetail&iid=778

Murray, Joseph, and David P. Farrington, "The Effects of Parental Imprisonment on Children," in M. Tonry, ed., *Crime and Justice: A Review of Research*, Chicago, Ill.: The University of Chicago, 2008, pp. 133–206.

Naser, Rebecca L., and Christy A. Visher, "Family Members' Experiences with Incarceration and Reentry," *Western Criminology Review*, Vol. 7, No. 2, 2006, pp. 20–31.

National Association of Counties, "Repeal the 'Inmate Exception' for Federal Health Benefits," Legislative Affairs Fact Sheet, February 2011.

National Center for Cultural Competence, *Sharing a Legacy of Caring: Partnerships Between Health Care and Faith-Based Organizations*, Washington D.C., 2001. As of October 17, 2011:
http://nccc.georgetown.edu/documents/faith.pdf

National Commission on Correctional Health Care, *The Health Status of Soon-to-Be-Released Inmates: A Report to Congress*, Vols. 1 and 2, Chicago, Ill., March 2002. As of September 8, 2011:
http://www.ncchc.org/pubs/pubs_stbr.html

National Institute of Corrections, "Thinking for a Change," no date. As of September 6, 2011:
http://nicic.gov/T4C

National Reentry Resource Center and U.S. Department of Justice Bureau of Justice Assistance, "Essential Elements of Reentry: Primary Care and the Transitions Clinic Approach," October 25, 2010. As of October 11, 2011:
http://www.nationalreentryresourcecenter.org/documents/0000/0783/Webinar_TC_final_ae_10.25.pdf

Nelson, Marta, and Jennifer Trone, *Why Planning for Release Matters*, New York: Vera Institute of Justice, 2000.

Newman, Anabel, *Prison Literacy: Implications for Program and Assessment Policy*, Philadelphia, Pa.: National Center for Adult Literacy, 1993.

Nickel, Jessica, Crystal Garland, and Leah Kane, *Children of Incarcerated Parents: An Action Plan for Federal Policymakers*, New York: Council of State Governments Justice Center, 2009.

Nieto, Marcus, *In Danger of Falling Through the Cracks: Children of Arrested Parents*, Sacramento, Calif.: California Research Bureau, CRB 02-009, April 2002.

Park, Annie, Nancy Watson, and Lark Galloway-Gilliam, *South Los Angeles Health Equity Scorecard*, Los Angeles, Calif.: Community Health Councils, December 2008.

Parke, Ross D., and K. Alison Clarke-Stewart, "The Effects of Parental Incarceration on Children: Perspectives, Promises, and Policies," in Jeremy Travis and Michelle Waul, eds., *Prisoners Once Removed: The Impact of Incarceration and Reentry on Children, Families, and Communities*, Baltimore. Md.: Urban Institute Press, 2003, pp. 189–232.

Pauly, Mark V., and Jose A. Pagan, "Spillovers and Vulnerability: The Case of Community Uninsurance," *Health Affairs*, Vol. 26, No. 5, September–October 2007, pp. 1304–1314.

Pearson, Jessica, "Building Debt While Doing Time: Child Support and Incarceration," *American Bar Association Judges' Journal*, Vol. 43, No. 1, Winter 2004.

Pebley, Anne R., and L. Rudkin, "Grandparents Caring for Grandchildren: What Do We Know?" *Journal of Family Issues*, Vol. 20, No. 2, 1999, pp. 218–242.

Pennsylvania Department of Corrections, *Annual Statistical Report, 2008*, Camp Hill, Pa., 2009.

Phillips, Susan D., Alaattin Erkanli, E. Jane Costello, and Adrian Angold, "Differences Among Children Whose Mothers Have Been in Contact with the Criminal Justice System," co-published simultaneously in *Women & Criminal Justice*, Vol. 17, No. 2/3, 2006, pp. 43–61; and James A. Swartz, Patrician O'Brien, and Arthur J. Lurigio, eds., *Drugs, Women, and Justice: Roles of the Criminal Justice System for Drug-Affected Women*, Abingdon, UK: Haworth Press Inc., 2006.

Phoenix House, homepage, no date. As of September 6, 2011: http://www.phoenixhouse.org/

Promising Practices Network, "Programs That Work: Big Brothers Big Sisters of America," November 2009. As of October 13, 2011: http://www.promisingpractices.net/program.asp?programid=125#programinfo

———, "Programs That Work: Multisystemic Therapy," March 2011. As of October 17, 2011: http://www.promisingpractices.net/program.asp?programid=81

Public Law 104-93, Personal Responsibility and Work Opportunity Reconciliation Act of 1996, August 22, 1996.

Public Law 105-89, Adoption and Safe Families Act of 1997, November 19, 1997.

Public Law 111-148, Patient Protection and Affordable Care Act, March 23, 2010.

Rossman, Shelli, "Services Integration: Strengthening Offenders and Families, While Promoting Community Health and Safety," Urban Institute, December 2001. As of October 12, 2011:
http://aspe.hhs.gov/hsp/prison2home02/Rossman.htm

Rotter, Merrill, Hunter L. McQuistion, Nahama Broner, and Michael Steinbacher, "Best Practices: The Impact of the 'Incarceration Culture' on Reentry for Adults with Mental Illness: A Training and Group Treatment Model," *Psychiatric Services*, Vol. 56, March 2005, pp. 265–267.

SAMHSA-HRSA Center for Integrated Health Solutions, "Integrated Care Models," no date. As of October 17, 2011:
http://www.centerforintegratedhealthsolutions.org/integrated-care-models

———, "Communities: Groups & Networks," 2011. As of October 17, 2011:
http://www.thenationalcouncil.org/cs/groups_networks

Simmons, Charlene W., *Children of Incarcerated Parents*, Sacramento, Calif.: California Research Bureau, CRB Note Vol. 7, No. 2, March 2000.

Smithgall, Cheryl, Sally Mason, Lisa Michels, Christina LiCalsi, and Robert Goerge, *Caring for Their Children's Children: Assessing the Mental Health Needs and Service Experiences of Grandparent Caregiver Families,* Chicago, Ill.: University of Chicago, Chapin Hall Center for Children, May 2006.

Somers, Stephen A., Allison Hamblin, James M. Verdier, and Vivian L. H. Byrd, *Covering Low-Income Childless Adults in Medicaid: Experiences from Selected States*, Hamilton, N.J.: Center for Health Care Strategies, Inc., August 2010. As of October 11, 2011:
http://www.chcs.org/usr_doc/Medicaid_Expansion_Brief.pdf

State Health Access Data Assistance Center (SHADAC), "When 133 Equals 138: FPL Calculations in the Affordable Care Act," 2011. As of October 25, 2011:
http://www.shadac.org/blog/when-133-equals-138-fpl-calculations-in-affordable-care-act

Steinhauser, Jennifer, "A City Where Hospitals Are as Ill as the Patients," *New York Times*, June 5, 2008.

Stoltze, Frank, "LA County Supervisors Worry About Prison Release Plan," Southern California Public Radio, August 24, 2011. As of September 6, 2011:
http://www.scpr.org/news/2011/08/24/28407/la-county-supervisors-worry-about-prison-release-p/

Substance Abuse and Mental Health Services Administration, "Health Homes and Individuals with Behavioral Health Issues—SAMHSA's Guidance Document—Affordable Care Act Health Home Provision," September 27, 2011.

Travis, Jeremy, Elizabeth Cincotta McBride, and Amy L. Solomon, *Families Left Behind: The Hidden Costs of Incarceration and Reentry*, policy brief, Washington, D.C.: Urban Institute Justice Policy Center, June 2005. As of September 6, 2011: http://www.urban.org/UploadedPDF/310882_families_left_behind.pdf

Travis, Jeremy, and Michelle Waul, eds., *Prisoners Once Removed: The Impact of Incarceration and Reentry on Children, Families, and Communities*, Baltimore, Md.: Urban Institute Press, 2003.

Tuttle, Rochelle, and Lucien Wulsin, Jr., *California's Safety Nets and the Need to Improve Local Collaboration in Care for the Uninsured: Counties, Clinics, Hospitals, and Local Health Plans*, Santa Monica, Calif.: Insure the Uninsured Program, October 2008.

Urban Institute, *The Public Health Dimensions of Prisoner Reentry: Addressing the Health Needs and Risks of Returning Prisoners and their Families, Meeting Summary*, National Reentry Roundtable Meeting, Los Angeles, Calif., December 11–12, 2002.

U.S. Census Bureau, "Interactive Population Map," 2010. As of October 26, 2011: http://2010.census.gov/2010census/popmap/

———, "State & County Quick Facts: Alameda County, California," 2011a. As of September 6, 2011:
http://quickfacts.census.gov/qfd/states/06/06001.html

———, "State & County Quick Facts: California," 2011b. As of September 6, 2011:
http://quickfacts.census.gov/qfd/states/06000.html

———, "State & County Quick Facts: Kern County, California," 2011c. As of September 6, 2011:
http://quickfacts.census.gov/qfd/states/06/06029.html

———, "State & County Quick Facts: Los Angeles County, California," 2011d. As of September 6, 2011:
http://quickfacts.census.gov/qfd/states/06/06037.html

———, "State & County Quick Facts: San Diego County, California," 2011e. As of September 6, 2011:
http://quickfacts.census.gov/qfd/states/06/06073.html

———, *Income, Poverty, and Health Insurance Coverage in the United States: 2010*, Washington, D.C., Current Population Reports: Consumer Income P60-239, September 2011f.

U.S. Department of Health and Human Services, "Disproportionate Share Hospital," no date. As of October 25, 2011:
http://www.hhs.gov/recovery/cms/dsh.html

U.S. Department of Veterans Affairs, "Health Care Re-Entry for Veterans Services and Resources," 2011. As of September 6, 2011:
http://www.va.gov/HOMELESS/Reentry.asp

Village of Promise Collective Mentoring Project, "Vision and Mission," no date. As of September 6, 2011:
http://sites.google.com/site/villageofpromise/our-mission

Visher, Christy, Nancy LaVigne, and Jeremy Travis, *Returning Home: Understanding the Challenges of Prisoner Reentry Maryland Pilot Study: Findings from Baltimore,* Washington, D.C.: Urban Institute, Washington, 2004.

Wakeman, Sarah E., Margaret E. McKinney, and Josiah D. Rich, "Filling the Gap: The Importance of Medicaid Continuity for Former Inmates," *Journal of General Internal Medicine*, Vol. 24, No. 7, 2009, pp. 860–862.

Waldrop, Deborah P., and Joseph A. Weber, "From Grandparent to Caregiver: The Stress and Satisfaction of Raising Grandchildren," in Francis Joseph Turner, ed., *Social Work Diagnosis in Contemporary Practice*, New York: Oxford University Press, 2005.

Watson, Donnie W., Winnie Tsai, Victoria S. Chu, Eugene Willliams III, Michele Mouttapa, Aliya Asghar, and Michael E. Shaw, "The Role of Faith-Based Organizations in Ex-Offender Reentry," *California Journal of Health Promotion*, Vol. 6. No. 2, 2008, pp. 25–35.

Wenzlow, Audra T., Henry T. Ireys, Bob Mann, Carol Irvin, and Judith L. Teich, "Effects of a Discharge Planning Program on Medicaid Coverage of State Prisoners with Serious Mental Illness," *Psychiatric Services*, Vol. 62, No. 1, 2011, pp. 73–78.

Western, Bruce, Jeffrey R. Kling, and David F. Weiman, *The Labor Market Consequences of Incarceration*, Princeton, N.J.: Princeton University Industrial Relations Section, Working Paper No. 450, January 2001.

Zack, Barry, "Community Health Services and Linkages Between Prison and Community," in *The Public Health Dimensions of Prisoner Reentry: Addressing the Health Needs and Risks of Returning Prisoners and Their Families*, meeting summary, National Reentry Roundtable Meeting, Los Angeles, Calif., December 11–12, 2002, pp. 10–12.